THE REVIEW *of* CONTEMPORARY FICTION NEW AUSTRALIAN FICTION

FALL 2007 | VOL. XXVII, NO. 3

EDITOR

JOHN O'BRIEN

MANAGING EDITOR

MARTIN RIKER

GUEST EDITOR

NICHOLAS BIRNS

ASSOCIATE EDITOR

IRVING MALIN

BOOK REVIEW EDITOR

AUDE JEANSON

PRODUCTION

DANIELLE DUTTON

PROOF READERS

JESSICA HENRICHS

MELISSA KENNEDY

BREANNE REINHARD

REVIEW OF CONTEMPORARY FICTION
Fall 2007
Vol. XXVII, No. 3

The *Review of Contemporary Fiction* is published three times each year
(January, June, September). Subscription prices are as follows:

Single volume (three issues):
Individuals: $17.00 U.S.; $22.60 Canada; $32.60 all other countries
Institutions: $26.00 U.S.; $31.60 Canada; $41.60 all other countries

ISSN: 0276-0045
ISBN: 978-1-56478-485-8

This issue is partially supported by a grant from the Illinois Arts Council, a state agency, and by
the University of Illinois, Urbana-Champaign

Indexed in *Humanities International Complete, International Bibliography of Periodical Literature, International Bibliography of Book Reviews, MLA Bibliography*, and *Book Review Index*.
Abstracted in *Abstracts of English Studies*.

The *Review of Contemporary Fiction* is also available on 16mm microfilm, 35mm microfilm, and
105mm microfiche from University Microfilms International, 300 North Zeeb Road, Ann Arbor,
MI 48106-1346.

Cover image: Australian Grass Tree

Address all correspondence to:
Review of Contemporary Fiction
University of Illinois
1805 S. Wright Street, MC-011
Champaign, IL 61820

www.dalkeyarchive.com

THE REVIEW OF CONTEMPORARY FICTION

BACK ISSUES AVAILABLE

Back issues are still available for the following numbers of the
Review of Contemporary Fiction ($8 each unless otherwise noted):

Douglas Woolf / Wallace Markfield
William Eastlake / Aidan Higgins
Camilo José Cela
Chandler Brossard
Samuel Beckett
Claude Ollier / Carlos Fuentes
Joseph McElroy
John Barth / David Markson
Donald Barthelme / Toby Olson
William H. Gass / Manuel Puig
Robert Walser
José Donoso / Jerome Charyn
William T. Vollmann / Susan Daitch /
  David Foster Wallace
Djuna Barnes
Angela Carter / Tadeusz Konwicki
Stanley Elkin / Alasdair Gray
Brigid Brophy / Robert Creeley /
  Osman Lins
Edmund White / Samuel R. Delany
Mario Vargas Llosa / Josef Škvorecký
Wilson Harris / Alan Burns
Raymond Queneau / Carole Maso
Richard Powers / Rikki Ducornet
Edward Sanders
Writers on Writing: The Best of The *Review of
  Contemporary Fiction*
Bradford Morrow
Jean Rhys / John Hawkes /
  Paul Bowles / Marguerite Young

Henry Green / James Kelman /
  Ariel Dorfman
Janice Galloway / Thomas Bernhard /
  Robert Steiner / Elizabeth Bowen
Gilbert Sorrentino / William Gaddis /
  Mary Caponegro / Margery Latimer
Italo Calvino / Ursule Molinaro /
  B. S. Johnson
Louis Zukofsky / Nicholas Mosley /
  Coleman Dowell
Casebook Study of Gilbert
  Sorrentino's *Imaginative Qualities of
  Actual Things*
Rick Moody / Ann Quin /
  Silas Flannery
Diane Williams / Aidan Higgins /
  Patricia Eakins
Douglas Glover / Blaise Cendrars /
  Severo Sarduy
Robert Creeley / Louis-Ferdinand Céline /
  Janet Frame
William H. Gass
Gert Jonke / Kazuo Ishiguro /
  Emily Holmes Coleman
William H. Gass / Robert Lowry /
  Ross Feld
Flann O'Brien / Guy Davenport /
  Aldous Huxley
Steven Millhauser
William Eastlake / Julieta Campos /
  Jane Bowles

NOVELIST AS CRITIC: Essays by Garrett, Barth, Sorrentino, Wallace, Ollier, Brooke-Rose, Creeley, Mathews, Kelly, Abbott, West, McCourt, McGonigle, and McCarthy

NEW FINNISH FICTION: Fiction by Eskelinen, Jäntti, Kontio, Krohn, Paltto, Sairanen, Selo, Siekkinen, Sund, and Valkeapää

NEW ITALIAN FICTION: Interviews and fiction by Malerba, Tabucchi, Zanotto, Ferrucci, Busi, Corti, Rasy, Cherchi, Balduino, Ceresa, Capriolo, Carrera, Valesio, and Gramigna

GROVE PRESS NUMBER: Contributions by Allen, Beckett, Corso, Ferlinghetti, Jordan, McClure, Rechy, Rosset, Selby, Sorrentino, and others

NEW DANISH FICTION: Fiction by Brøgger, Høeg, Andersen, Grøndahl, Holst, Jensen, Thorup, Michael, Sibast, Ryum, Lynggaard, Grønfeldt, Willumsen, and Holm

NEW LATVIAN FICTION: Fiction by Ikstena, Bankovskis, Berelis, Kolmanis, Neiburga, Ziedonis, and others

THE FUTURE OF FICTION: Essays by Birkerts, Caponegro, Franzen, Galloway, Maso, Morrow, Vollmann, White, and others ($15)

NEW JAPANESE FICTION: Interviews and fiction by Ohara, Shimada, Shono, Takahashi, Tsutsui, McCaffery, Gregory, Kotani, Tatsumi, Koshikawa, and others

NEW CUBAN FICTION: Fiction by Ponte, Mejides, Aguilar, Bahr, Curbelo, Plasencia, Serova, and others

DALKEY ARCHIVE ANNUAL 1: Fiction by Markfield, Szewc, Eastlake, Higgins, Jonke, and others

SPECIAL FICTION ISSUE: JUAN EMAR: Fiction and illustrations by Juan Emar, translated by Daniel Borzutzky

Individuals receive a 10% discount on orders of one issue and a
20% discount on orders of two or more issues. To place an order,
use the form on the last page of this issue.

CONTENTS

THE REVIEW *of* CONTEMPORARY FICTION

INTRODUCTION

Australian fiction has been widely published in the United States. But, with some exceptions, it has been published under a commercial aegis. The marketing rationale for Australian literature has, in fact, particularly emphasized Australian literature's old-fashioned narrative appeal, its ability to provide the vivid stories deemed absent in more technically advanced but less narratively meaty British and American fiction. The Bolaños, Houellebecqs, and Murakamis, who, as foreign authors, have managed to both sell well and provoke thoughtful critical reaction in the U.S. and U.K., have not had their Australian equivalents.

Even when it led to misunderstandings of such undeniably innovative writers such as Patrick White, Thea Astley, or Peter Carey, this distorted commercial view has predominated. Earlier Aussie yarn-spinners such as Joseph Furphy (1843-1912) who wrote in a decidedly "Shandean" vein have not been afforded access to a metropolitan readership.

The fiction collected in this special issue of *RCF* forms a very different constellation. The writers included here are consciously experimental, in style, approach, and subject matter. They represent Australian literature as world literature, rather than as a peripheral branch of English-language writing. They write less to epitomize a national temperament than a sensibility. They ask about the dreams, premises, and questions of Australian culture rather than trying to prepackage it in a consumerist mode. They are unafraid of either humor or pathos, and they don't restrict themselves simply to "important" subjects. Though not obtrusively wearing postmodernist labels, they all partake in a risk-taking and non-objective aesthetic that puts them in the company of the international corps of writers featured in, and championed by, *RCF.* They all, in their different modes, contend, as Tom Flood puts it in *The Little Gap in Talk,* that "characters are not people." They are aware of fiction as a process of reelection, not a transparent registering of the given. And, as Gerald Murnane's story shows, they do not overly romanticize the imagination, which is strange enough on its own without needing to be gilded with the flowery rhetoric of self-loving art.

Australia is a large and heterogeneous country, and these writers cannot be grouped into one school or tendency. As A. L. McCann's story makes clear, the gap between Melbourne and Sydney can seem as wide as that between Sydney and New York. But they all display the liveliness and invention at play in Australian literature in a way that has simply not been represented in American publishing so far. Let's hope some American publishers read these stories and sit up and take notice.

Gerald Murnane is an obdurately original writer of fiction, who works within the idiosyncratic geography of mind and memory. He is the only living Australian writer comparable to, in both achievement and slant of mind, Proust, Borges, or Calvino, though possessing a keen and gentle insight all his own. Yet Murnane also (before his 1995 retirement) excelled as a teacher of writing, and, as we see the excerpt from *Barley Patch* presented here, none of his students have ever contemplated giving up the craft. Two of Murnane's former students, Tim Richards and Christopher Cyrill, have developed distinctive and high-spirited styles that are exuberantly on display in their contributions. Richards may be described as pioneering a zany fictional sociology, while Cyrill uses fiction to register the unrecognized, surreal rituals that surround us.

Michael Wilding's vigorous, irreverent prose evokes, with a scalding empathy entirely his own, the rush of social and cultural experimentation that overtook Sydney in the 1970s. In the next generation, Christos Tsiolkas evokes a dark sense of wreckage and cultural clash in contemporary Melbourne. Tsiolkas has challenged cultural pieties in a bracing way, all the while producing prose of great suppleness and skill. Carmel Bird's sense of the wounds of memory makes her psychological vision distinctive. Bird's focus on the repressiveness of institutional authority combines with a bravura style and a welcome willingness to let the reader make up their own mind to conjure an unusual mixture of playfulness and plangency. Brenda Walker, who has been acclaimed for her historical fiction, shifts to a contemporary setting with her contribution to this volume. Walker continues her metaphorical imaging of interpersonal relationships in mysterious yet pellucidly fresh prose. Delia

Falconer possesses a talent for haunting analysis that is unmatched among contemporary writers. Falconer has read widely in international fiction, ranging from Sebald to Tanizaki in her significant influences, and her vision has a cosmopolitan reach.

Falconer's contribution also has the added value of alluding to Kenneth Slessor (1901-1971), Australia's great modern poet, virtually unknown abroad. Bestselling in Australia, Falconer's work has been published in the U.S. but so far has hovered beneath the radar of the cultural opinion-makers. Tom Flood's contribution shows a daring and gifted writer stretching the possibilities of prose fiction to the maximum and giving us a glimpse of a vast fictional universe. Flood is bringing Australian fiction to a place where it might take ten or twenty years for most other writers to catch up. Like Wilding and Walker, A. L. McCann is a respected academic as well as a creative writer. His fiction has explored the fetishes and cultural contradictions of colonialism and terrorism, and in his contribution here he turns to the contradictions of the contemporary literary life, especially among "ex-Generation X writers" (likely to be a burgeoning category). Somebody who has stretched boundaries in several genres is Tom Shapcott, known as a poet and as a novelist, and his haunting contribution to this volume displays his aptitude for evoking extreme mental states amid exactingly rendered settings. Greg Bogaerts, from working-class Newcastle, and Ouyang Yu, originally from China, hammer on the doors of the Australian literary establishment; Bogaerts and Ouyang also share a responsiveness to situations which is far from merely naturalistic. Ouyang, like Shapcott, is better known as a poet. Many of the best-known Australian novelists, Rodney Hall, Roger McDonald, and David Malouf among them, started out as poets; among other benefits, their familiarity with twentieth-century world poetry has kept their fiction in touch with international standards.

And it is this contact with international standards that, paradoxically, the international conglomerates who dominate Australian publishing have dismally failed to do; they are content to churn out would-be commercial blockbusters. It has been left to small, independent publishers to fill the gap, and none has done this with more flair and cogency than Ivor Indyk and his Giramondo Press. Giramondo has taken up writers such as Murnane and Brian Castro whose much-admired work is as yet ignored by the commercial consensus. Giramondo's latest feat is its publication of Alexis Wright's *Carpentaria,* winner of the 2007 Miles Franklin Award, Australia's most prestigious prize. This ambitious and moving book is, in the company of Kim Scott's *Benang* (2000), the most notable novel produced so far in the twenty-first century by an indigenous Australian. This is only one of many promising recent developments that challenge our received image of Australian writing as the preserve of rip-roaring, realistic historical fiction, and opens up Australian writing to the world. The selections in this issue, analogously, aspire to open up an international readership to Australian writing.

—Nicholas Birns, 2007

CARMEL BIRD

Carmel Bird was born in Tasmania in 1940, on Mary Shelley's birthday, and now lives in Victoria. In the sixties she spent time in Europe and the United States, and in 1990 she was a visiting writer at Rollins College in Winter Park, Florida. She has been a visiting speaker at a number of universities in Spain, and frequently speaks at universities in Australia and at writers' festivals.

Bird is the author of eight novels and four collections of short fiction. Her most recent novel is *Cape Grimm*. Most of her books have been shortlisted for major Australian prizes. She has edited several anthologies, including *The Penguin Century of Australian Stories* and *The Stolen Children*, a collection of the oral histories of Australian indigenous people who were forcibly removed from their families. She has written a radio play, *In My Father's House*, inspired by the life of Mathinna, an indigenous girl who was informally adopted by the Governor of Van Diemen Land in the 1840s. She has also written three books for writers, the most recent being *Writing The Story of Your Life*, and she is a popular lecturer on the art of writing fiction and memoir.

Bird has always been interested in seeing her work in media other than print. When her novel *Red Shoes* was published in 1998 it was accompanied by an interactive CD-ROM, shots from which are available on www.carmelbird. com. A short film inspired by Carmel's story "A Telephone Call For Genevieve Snow," directed by Peter Long, won the Silver Lion Award at the Venice Film Festival in 2000. The Tasmanian ballet company "Tasdance" has interpreted many of Carmel's narratives in dance, and in 2003 they performed a full-length work *Fair Game*, inspired by one of her stories. She is the fiction editor of *Meanjin*, the literary journal of Melbourne University.

Her Voice Was Full of Money and They Were Careless People

The Lisieux Convent. Not situated, as you might expect, in rural France, but in Leafland, a comfortable, affluent suburb of Melbourne, Australia. Such suburbs are often described as leafy and this one certainly was lined with lovely European trees as well as rows of flowering gums all of which mysteriously did not suffer badly from the drought that gripped the country in 2007. Yes, the country was in the grip of drought. Rainbow lorikeets chattered, flittered, and darted from the blossoms of the gums that bloomed forever in a kind of long long hot forever and ever. Summer, autumn, winter, the drought-affected gum trees sent out honeyed fluffy pink and creamy white puffs all across the leafy lanes. The aroma of the honey! Never had there been so many lorikeets living for so long among the flowers and insects of Leafland. They were luminously bright birds, all the colors of the rainbow in splashes and splats and stripes, if you looked at them up close. Some of the sisters at Lisieux were French, and the school was renowned for its success in teaching languages and music.

Olga Bongiorno was five when she went to school at Lisieux. She was educated there for the following twelve years, a dozen years from 1952 to 1964. She was from the beginning one of those girls whose broad linen collar was always starched white, perfect as a seagull. In 1965 Olga went to the university, and then she went to the teachers college, and then she returned to Lisieux where she taught French and English until she retired at the age of sixty. She herself would say if you asked her that she walked in the valley of the shadow and that she feared no evil. This grandiose biblical conversation-stopper concealed the death of a fiancé in a motorcycle accident when Olga was twenty-five. It wasn't as if Olga was a nun exactly, but it wasn't as if she wasn't one either, if you can follow that. She did one world trip with her sister and they went to London and Paris and Rome and also Loreto where Olga was keen to visit the Holy House. She was interested in miracles. But Olga truly was happiest in her role as senior mistress of French and English at Lisieux, and she was mildly famous and widely celebrated among the families whose lives she touched through her years of teaching. What Olga did after retirement isn't relevant to this story. For our purposes she is the Beloved Miss Bongiorno, sometimes known as Old Olga da Polga, named for the character of a guinea pig in a children's picture book. The guinea pig was a teller of tall tales, very tall tales, wild exaggerations. Nothing could be further from the character of Olga Bongiorno who resembled rather the aunt in a poem by Hilaire Belloc, an aunt who from her earliest youth had kept a strict regard for truth. Olga was a woman of high moral principles and a virtuous Catholic morality. What she saw and what she heard in and around her classroom were frequently matters of severe distress to her. She worried so about her girls, and was known to be, as a result of her anxieties, a devoted lighter of votive candles in the chapel of the Little Flower.

Some of these things I tell you for the purposes only of clarification and orna-mentation, since my focus is in fact on the year of the drought, the year 2007, and on Olga and her class of final year English students. I should add at this point that Loyola, the brother school, was situated just three leafy lanes away as the tram runs. Now that Loyola has entered the picture, things are becoming more promising, and you can begin to see where they are moving.

In Olga's English class, in the year of the drought, Marina Delaney was known to be sleeping with Caroline Herbert's boyfriend. The other girls in the group rallied behind and around Caro, and they turned on Marina in a pack. To the Loyola boy in the case (one Teddy Buchan) there attached, it appeared, no blame whatsoever for Marina's misdemeanors. Sometimes in the classroom it seemed to Olga that all nineteen cells of their hive vibrated and lit up in unison, as the news of the progress of the Marina-Teddy Affair traveled in thrilling beelines across the desks, down the leafy lanes, over tennis courts and football ovals, round and round the garden like a teddy bear.

Caroline wept. Marina wept. Juliette, Tiffany, Marie-Claire, Ching Ye, and Veronica sighed and frowned and gurgled. Trinity and Pieta squirmed. Wanda the Giggler giggled.

So it was not always possible, as you might appreciate, to teach the girls very much. Not that Olga had ever really understood, in all her years of teaching English and French, quite how the process of teaching really worked. Somehow her students ended up as literate, fluent, engaged, informed young women, but the chemistry or the physics or the metaphysics of the thing remained a mystery. All Olga knew at this point was that the Buchan boy was a terrible nuisance to her, that he was getting in the way of everything. He was the son of Buchan the leather-furnishing millionaire, and Olga knew his grandmother, Violet Fish, who had had her front teeth knocked out at the Lisieux/Good Counsel hockey final in 1961. But that was really just another irrelevant little factoid. No, Olga couldn't get very much into the heads of her girls who were a flurry and sizzle of pink and gray dresses with the same huge white detachable collars as Olga used to wear. Some of theirs resembled hers in seagull-snowy starch, but most did not. Olga must proceed, and so the day arrived when the curriculum, like a tram on a track, brought them all to chapter one of *The Great Gatsby* by F. Scott Fitzgerald.

And still the beelines hummed in the zipped or unzipped side pockets of the pink and gray dresses. If you half closed your eyes those dresses resembled a shimmering, spreading splat of young and healthy brain tissue. Would Teddy ever go back to poor darling Caro? Would that slut Marina ever give him up? You can of course guess what happens here: on the tram Teddy Buchan meets a cute blonde mega-slut from New Hudson High, a tart in a short black skirt and tiny satin thong, and before you can say honey pot he drops Marina (serves her right), forgets all about Caroline (brave but inconsolable), and moves on.

Now, girls, the plot turns on a hit-and-run accident. The sleepy sun slants across the honey-colored desks, stopping to glitter on the tiny diamond in the ear of Ginny King. Some cells glow and hum as the beelines are kept open. Marie-Claire has worked out the name of the New Hudson bitch. What, Patricia, is the correct procedure in the case of a driver who knocks down a pedestrian?

All the pencils in Patricia's pencil case rattle across the timber top of her desk and sail down onto the carpet as Patricia suddenly sits up at the sound of her name. Her eyes are as blank as her mind. She doesn't know anything about the correct procedure. Anybody? Wanda? What is this procedure Old Olga da Polga is going on about? Eighteen pairs of eyes look vacantly at Olga. Wanda is silent since she has had a big night and is asleep, sitting upright in the corner. The correct procedure? You must stop, render assistance, call for help.

This is news to the owners of the thirty-six eyes who are all on the brink of getting a license to drive a motor vehicle. What? Why? Oh really?

Stop, render assistance, call for help.

Myrtle Wilson was killed instantly, and the driver of the big yellow car, the death car, the car belonging to the Great Gatsby himself, put her foot down and drove swiftly on. To this information Olga's students register no surprise. So Daisy was driving the car and she killed Myrtle and left the scene at high speed. So Myrtle had it coming. She was sleeping with Daisy's husband and she was only a slut anyhow. Daisy is Gatsby's girlfriend and longtime love, and she's as lovely as an ice white blossom floating on a silver pool and her voice is full of money. Wanda the Sleepy Giggler hears none of this. She is thought to be the richest girl in the school. Her father owns a city in the Middle East. Her mother is one of the Chicago van Cleefs. You might wonder what brings Wanda to Olga's classroom in the middle of leafy Leafland in the middle of the warmest autumn since time began. Well, for one thing one of her grandmothers went to Lisieux in San Antonio, Texas, and for another it was a matter of the miracle of modern marketing. Leafland Lisieux had come a long long way in cyberspace since Olga was a child in a great white collar. Wanda will in any case be finished at a school in Switzerland where there are princesses of all descriptions and of every stripe, and where her down-under bloom will carry an exotic cache all its own. Wanda Lust they will call her, and they will wave a butter knife in her face gleefully crying "this is a knife!" But that is all in the future and does not concern us here.

They were careless people. Olga tells them to write that down. They disappeared into their money. Learn that quote. A few pens quietly scrawl the short quotations onto paper. A number of silent laptops register the words as well. It rather nicely, really, disappeared into their money. Pieta was editing her photos and had no time for quotations; Marina was composing an email to Teddy Buchan who was never going to reply.

Well, you can see how things were, and I am not exaggerating in the manner of the guinea pig in the story. If anything I am being restrained and conservative and playing things down in the interests of believability. But you can sense how this story is making its own beeline towards a sharp and gleaming and hot dry night in early summer when these girls have all closed their books and jettisoned their collars and have graduated from school with honors and accolades and laurel wreaths and stacks of valedictory books and higher school certificates and not a few glossy new cars. Pieta backed her lovely little Mazda into the muddy gurgle of the Merri Creek, and it is truly a miracle that she got out of it alive. Pieta is a survivor. Wanda is now on holiday in Florida with an aunt, so she is out of the picture.

Who, you wonder, is driving the death car in our story? Who is this speeding down steep Kennedy Hill Drive at three in the morning after a party to celebrate Teddy Buchan's eighteenth? It's Veronica Vale, deluxe dux of Lisieux, in her sleek green minty Volkswagen. And who should come tottering barefoot and intoxicated from behind a leafy elm where a watchful owl lives? Look, it's Trinity Maxwell in a glittering slivery silvery slithery slice of a wisp of Armani silk and sequin which she bought on eBay. Through drooping yellow fringes of sunny yellow hair, with large gray eyes that almost focus, Trinity sees Veronica coming and she calls and waves, thinking in what you might describe as a split second that Veronica will stop and give her a lift back to Leafland. But Veronica is on the beeline of her cell, talking to Caro who is passing out in Teddy Buchan's mother's suite, and is about to get back in the pool with Teddy if he ever stops horsing around in the deep end with Charlie Beluga and a bottle of very expensive bourbon.

So a teenager is killed on Kennedy Hill at three minutes past three, and the dogs in the vicinity howl as the sirens worry and wail their way to the accident, the fatality, the tragedy, the waste.

Choose Your Own Conclusion:

The driver put her foot down and disappeared into her money.

She stopped. She rendered assistance. She called for help. Yes, she called for help.

GREG BOGAERTS

Greg Bogaerts was born on May 26, 1954, in Newcastle, a manufacturing city north of Sydney in New South Wales. He attended school in Newcastle then received his Bachelor of Arts at Newcastle University. He later studied law correspondence and taught full time. He practiced fitfully as a solicitor, eventually returning to driving cabs. This all finally led him to begin writing at the age of forty, and he has since published one novel and more than 250 short stories in anthologies, journals, and newspapers in Australia and North America. At the moment he is completing the third in a trilogy of comical novels set in Newcastle. Bogaerts exemplifies the vigor of Australian writing outside major literary cliques; he makes regional and working-class writing international.

From *Every Shilling a Prisoner*

The cooee whistle cracked through the dawn like a baton slammed into a body. Echoes rang over the Hunter River and were lost in the masts of mangroves growing thick upon the river's black mud edges. Darkness paused above the restless pulse of water, the flow of fresh water from the inland opposed by the bunting push of the salt water of the open ocean. Silently, figures arose among the river reeds; men clambered out of the mangroves and from under scrubby brush cover. Silently, they came together and stood, their faces shadowed, the features undefined as though every one of them was a mystery.

Dawn came and some of them blinked when they turned to look at the man next to them. It was as if they were strangers to each other and would not be able to explain if they'd been asked what they were doing there. The ranks of men shuffled uneasily, some murmurs broke the instruction for silence, but then another man came striding down the rise. The strange stiff jitter of limbs contradicted the determination of his gait; the men became silent again and fell into lines.

He stood in front of them and looked at them, his glare as fierce as cold fire, as merciless as one of the lathes in one of the steelworks' sheds downriver, spinning steel, shaving feathers of metal, making something hard and shiny but lifeless. Some of the men quailed before that stare and wondered, again, why they were there, how they'd been cajoled into this. But most of them looked at their leader and embraced his merciless fire. They remembered the trenches, the wire and smoking metal, the howl of flying shells, the rattle of machine-guns, and the thrill returned, the prospect of indulging in some of that chaos and slaughter again.

The sun broke the ocean horizon, a storm of yellow light setting the men alight. Then the flames fell away as the sun rose into the air, leaving the men steel solid, smelted from ore, seemingly indestructible.

Their leader smiled, placed his hands on his hips, his uniform creasing only slightly. It still fitted him as snugly as it did at Gallipoli; its cut and color were repeated on some of the men, his look of pride replicated on many faces. Raising his hand, he waited, inspecting each man, looking for any sign of weakness, but there was no sign his training of them had been in vain.

With deliberation, the leader lowered his arm, and some men later swore they heard his shoulder joint creak, the gravel of bone rot grinding like a machine needing oil. The men moved forward briskly; there was to be no charge. Over the small sandy swells of the riverbank they strode towards the Mayfield West shantytown where most of the families were still asleep behind whitewashed hessian, scraps of wood and iron.

On a knoll of land above the river, halfway between the marching men and the canvas town, a young girl sat making daisy chains, listening to the strumming hum of the river moving eternally. A glint of metal from an ex-soldier's medal embedded itself in the girl's eyes. She blinked away the blindness and saw the men coming up the rise towards her; she sprang to her feet and ran towards the shantytown where she lived.

Swifter than the wind breaking away over the river, the girl ran, blonde hair streaming back, her face a mask of terror, eyes green gemstones flashing. Behind her the measured tramp of the men pursued her.

The young girl, Vera, sped across the paddocks, grass and lucern lush; she swathed a trail in the mass of green twitching back and forth like the estuary tide. She stopped, knowing she should get back as quickly as possible to warn the others, but she had to look behind her, to see the men coming after her.

They were just at the edge of the paddock and she watched them spreading like dark stains across the land. She could hear grass stalks, lucern leaves being broken under leather boots, polished business shoes, gumboots.

Then she was running, knowing the men behind her hated her and her kind even more than the residents of Mayfield did. She breasted the next hill; the camp was in sight. In the middle of the dwellings, next to the one unconnected tap, shone the length of steel stolen by some of the camp men, one night, from the steelworks.

Vera sprinted for the steel. Dashing through the makeshift dwellings, she took up a chisel and hammered it into the girder. It pealed like the warped and cracked bell of some mysterious and alien church, founded there upon the bank of the Hunter in 1932.

The clamorous clanging brought forth men, women, and children from their beds and Vera tried to treat the perilous situation with the gravity it deserved. But Bluey James, half an erection pushing against the material of his long underwear, and Vera's mother, Helen, papers curled in her hair, and Henry Redman, unshaved and bleary-eyed from last night's port wine, and Jim Jenkins, once a prosperous tailor with five shops, now with a face quilted with the lines and lumps of sleep, and Rosa Cock's big breasts slipping from her nightgown, all made it difficult for Vera to be serious.

Sudden tears welled up in her eyes; they were all so broken down, made weary with the hand-to-mouth existence they led day to day. They looked at her, waiting to hear why she'd summoned them, but their lost beauty, their destroyed handsomeness, transfixed her. The caved-in toothless mouths, the cracked, barely lipsticked lips, the hangdog expressions perpetually creasing almost every face, the rank smell of sweat coming from rarely bathed bodies. But she heard the sound of marching.

"They're coming, the soldiers with that man, just on the other side of the rise," said Vera.

"Quick boys, get the clubs. Ladies, children, get inside and don't come out until we tell you," said Redman, the leader of the camp.

The men scurried to a hut and Redman handed out the scrap wood nullas. The women and children hid in tents and shacks huddled down close to the earth floors, listening intently as the tramping of leather came closer.

"Courage now boys. I know what they did to us last time, but this place is all we've got and if we run from 'em we'll never find another place to live in Newcastle," said Redman.

The men drew close, pulled back shoulders, braced themselves, and over the rise came the New Guards, determination etched in foreheads, mouths straight lines of distaste for the shantytown people. Only when they were feet from the camp men did the ex-soldiers, the well-to-do businessmen of Newcastle, and some farmers and grazers from further up the Valley, charge, wielding batons.

The two groups met in the camp clearing. Redman smashed one fat businessman in the face and he went down with barely a whimper. But four other New Guards were upon Redman because they knew he was the leader, the strongest man there, and if they could down him, or make him turn tail, the day would virtually be won.

Redman, the worse for wear from rough wine and years neglecting his health, felt punches in his belly but willed himself not to fall. Quickly he came back, felling two assailants with his club, opening a long wound over one's eyes, tearing open the other's cheek. They screamed and staggered away. The sight and sound of their panic and pain set the other two attackers back on their heels, their indecision lasting long enough for Redman to hammer them both with his hands made hard from long years coaxing molten steel from the hearth of a steelworks furnace. Before management got wind of Redman's militant unionism and sacked him.

Redman waded into the fray taking on two or three of the New Guards at a time while the other camp men battled on. Bluey James went down, two New Guardsmen kicking him in the head, breaking his collarbone before Redman grabbed the two by the scruffs of their necks, hammering their heads together. The sound of skulls breaking made men, in the midst of the pitched battle, sick to their stomachs, but they fought on.

Both sides felt there was too much at stake. The New Guard leader stood to one side, a sardonic grin on his face as he rubbed his clean-shaven chin and observed the battle like some sort of god bemused with his creation and quite prepared to let that creation destroy itself if it so desired. He watched Redman, but whereas many of the New Guard ranks were cowed by Redman's fierce fighting, the leader was not intimidated in the least.

The New Guard leader walked backwards a few paces when the fighting came close to him. It was as though he had no real interest in it, as if he did not share the determination of his men to drive the unemployed from Newcastle forever.

Only when one of his men fell right at his shoes, when one of the camp men hit him with a club, did the leader step in. His arm shot out, his hand gripped the camp man's neck and slowly, with relish, the *Fascist* leader lifted the man from the ground and held him in the air until his eyes goggled, blood trickling from his mouth. With a flick of his wrist, the leader broke the man's neck and threw him into the middle of the battle.

The murder stopped the fighting; men on both sides looked at the corpse, and the vertebra bones protruding from its broken neck made some vomit. Enraged, Redman lunged out of the melee and went for the leader, who turned, almost nonchalantly, to meet the attack, but New Guardsmen flung themselves upon the camp leader before he could reach his target. Redman was surrounded, his men losing, many lying bleeding and broken on the earth.

The shantytown men fell back towards the camp perimeter; it was only a matter of time before one of them turned and ran, and then the panic would spread and others would follow suit. Then the words came from the New Guard leader, the words that turned the battle tide.

"Get stuck in now boys. The women are waiting for you. They're yours for the taking and there's some nice young girls there too that need to be blooded."

Fury flamed in Redman, heat charging from his body like a fever passed to his men; they redoubled their efforts, flailing the New Guards with wood and knucklebone. Timothy Jackson, mild, but with three young daughters, was a man possessed. He lost his club when he embedded the nail on the end in the skull of one invader. Timothy went after another and had him in a head lock;

Timothy bent his head down to the captive's face and bit his ear off, spat it in the dirt but held the man hard as he howled and shat himself.

Arthur Riley was blood-pressured and old, but the vision of New Guards corrupting his granddaughters made a much younger man of him. Holding onto a man's neck, Arthur sank two fingers into the eye sockets gouging out both eyes that fell and lay in the dirt. The scream of pain was unearthly, and it unnerved his comrades and one of them turned and ran. But the Guard leader reached out, caught him, and administered several sharp smacks across the man's face jolting it from side to side. He was thrown back into the battle, fear of his leader far greater than the wounds he might suffer from his enemies.

The fighting shifted beyond the camp. Men fought at the edge of the mangroves, the rising tide lapping at feet and ankles. Small crabs nibbled at the toes of barefooted camp men and they cursed this extra nuisance, lifting legs, shaking, flick-flicking their feet trying to dislodge the animals. Some of the camp battlers laughed, but it was no laughing matter. Although the battle seemed to be turning in their favor, the fact that they were barefoot made it painfully clear to many of the shantytown men just how perilous it was feeding themselves and their families, let alone having to engage in battle with men who came from the same city. Men they knew, some they'd grown up with.

Miles Brown, up to his knees in saltwater, blocked the blow of Greg Smith, the kid he'd sat next to at the Carrington Primary School. The kid he used to knock around with, skimming stones across the harbor water. Sometimes Miles and Greg had sat on the edge of the Carrington mud flats with an old bike wheel baited with smelly steak lowered into the water waiting for a crab to go for the meat and find itself enmeshed amongst the spokes.

They threw punches, and their past friendship seemed to bring out a seething anger born of the contempt of knowing each other. Miles resented Greg's shiny shoes and his business suit. Greg hated the sight of Miles with his ragged, patched trousers and shirt, his bare feet.

Amongst the gnarled roots of mangroves Mike Peters, one of the camp men, came face to face with Macka Wright, his old sergeant from the Western Front during the Great War. Eyeball to eyeball they stood, poker faced, breathing heavily, waiting. Mike threw a haymaker and Macka ducked and punched the man in the stomach. Mike reeled; stunned, winded, gasping for air, but the sergeant was upon him hammering blows, gritting his teeth as he punished one of his old tropps. As far as Macka was concerned, Mike should have kept himself in order and joined the ranks of the ex-soldiers who met at the post office in town each morning, drilled, marched, and kept themselves aloof from the other unemployed.

Two brothers, Steve and Roger Heart, found themselves battling each other in the mangrove mud. Steve didn't want to hurt Roger even if he was a tenttown dweller—a lesser life form the New Guardsmen said should be exterminated or moved on, out of sight, out of mind.

But Steve became aware of the New Guard leader's eyes on him and Steve knew the man could tell that he was going easy on Roger. All the New Guardsmen said that the leader seemed to be able to see through flesh and bone into the hearts and souls of men to fathom their weaknesses and use those weaknesses against them.

Steve redoubled his efforts and Roger was soon reduced to a mass of cuts and bruises, both eyes closed, spitting teeth, staggering through water up to his waist, finally slumping between the branches of a mangrove tree.

The tide rose higher but both sides fought on. With the bulge of water came fish, bream and flathead, whiting and small mullet swimming amongst combatants' legs, caressing bare flesh with scale and tail flicks, nosing the men with their cold fishy noses, tickling them like lovers. It was as if the fish, unable to understand this mayhem, were trying to distract the men, to dissuade them from doing each other harm.

Rising out of mangrove mudcaves, turtles swam upon the water surface snapping at insects and small mullet, silver bullets spitting through the air. The turtles swam among the combatants looking with ancient wrinkle-lidded eyes that had seen black men standing in the river shallows once upon a time. Men with one leg crooked, the foot placed on the side of one knee of the straight leg half-buried in river silt, an arm raised, unmoving until a fish swam past, the spear flying and the prong finding the sleek flank of the fish.

Pelicans came flying in diminishing circles, landing on the water with a pedaling of pink feet. The big white and black birds folded their wings, swam among the fighting men and dipped their long beaks and baggy throats scooping up fish, letting them slide into capacious gullets and honk-honking their French horn pleasure.

The unemployed and the New Guards kept on throwing punches and wielding clubs but they were tired, some exhausted, many down on hands and knees, their faces close to the rising water. Some of the men from both sides looked around and saw and felt the fish, felt the bump of a turtle and realized they might drown.

By some sort of tacit agreement hostilities ceased, men waded out of the water, but then they went at it again with a renewed vigor. It was as though the water had baptized them and made them new and ready for a stoush. They seemed unaware of their sore heads, closed eyes, bleeding lacerations, and the fatigue in their joints—as much from the hard living in a tent city as from battle blows.

The camp men were still winning, but the New Guards obeyed their leader's silent expectation that they should fight to the bitter end. Redman and some of his men wondered what would break the stalemate.

Vera had been ordered to stay inside, but being told what to do rubbed her the wrong way, and besides, she wanted to see the New Guards up close, the people who hated her so much they would come sometimes under cover of darkness to beat her family. Vera Drummond, twelve years old and stroppy as a butcher's dog, loved her father to distraction, so when she saw him being belted by two of the strangers it was too much to bear and she screamed blue murder and sprinted from the humpy.

Hurling herself upon one of the men she clawed his face, leaving long bloody lines in his cheeks; the man yelled with pain and dropped away from Merv Drummond. But Vera kept at him, flailing him with her fists. Merv would have stopped his daughter, but he was too busy parrying the blows of the other man and trying to find an opening for his deadly right hook.

The bleeding man managed a backhander that caught Vera square in the middle of her face and dropped her on her arse; she sat, stunned, and although she tried not to cry the stinging pain in her face brought tears that rolled down her already-swelling cheeks. And it brought Helen Drummond from the house in a tearing rage.

Helen found a dropped club and she battered black and blue the man who'd hit Vera. Behind her, the faces of women peeked from humpies, tents and make-do houses and the word spread as to what had happened to Vera. Women swarmed into the opening.

No quarter was given as mothers, sisters and grandmothers backed up their men folk. Such savage loyalty from women of all ages was too much for some of the New Guards and they ran, and there were too many this time for their leader to stop them. He let them go, didn't look in their direction but watched the final stages of the battle petering out.

Redman, who'd hammered his final opponent, looked around to take on the man, but he'd vanished like mist above the river water burned off at sunrise. Redman shook his head, puzzled because it was only a matter of seconds since he'd seen the leader from the corner of his eye. The surroundings of the camp were open; no vegetation to hide in, but the Guard leader wasn't to be found.

CHRISTOPHER CYRILL

Christopher Cyrill was born in 1970, of immigrant Indian parents, and studied at Christian Brothers College East St. Kilda, Victoria and then at Deakin University in Melbourne. At Deakin he came under the guidance of the poet Judith Rodriguez and the novelist Gerald Murnane—both of whom remain friends and influences. His first novel *The Ganges and Its Tributaries* was published by Mcphee Gribble/Penguin Books in 1993. The novel went on to be shortlisted for many Australian awards. Critic Andrew Reimer described it as a "breakthrough, an incredible flowing lyric from a talented young man." Cyrill's second novel was published by Allen & Unwin in 1998. Its title—*Hymns for The Drowning*—was borrowed from the work of the Indian saint-poet Nammalvar. One of Cyrill's most respected contemporaries, the novelist James Bradley, wrote in *The Australian:* "His prose is remarkably controlled, poetic in pitch and rhythm, without the self-conscious verbosity that is too often mistaken for the same . . . Calvino is present, even—perhaps unavoidably—Proust." Cyrill has taught creative writing for over ten years at various universities, and also works as a reviewer and freelance editor. In 2002 he was appointed—and remains—fiction editor of the prestigious Australian literary magazine *Heat.* He is also the current fiction editor of Giramondo Publishing Company, publisher of Gerald Murnane, Brian Castro, and Alexis Wright. "Match Day" is an extract from his novel in progress, *Crown & Anchor,* which is itself one of a trilogy, each novel in the series being comprised of three intersecting novellas. In 1995 Cyrill met the poet Melissa Curran. They currently have three children and live in Sydney.

Match Day

In the fairy tale of Cinderella . . . versions containing the gathering of the bones are documented in China, Vietnam, India, Russia, Bulgaria, Cyprus . . . So immense and varied a distribution precludes the possibility that the presence of this theme in the fable's plot is the result of a casual graft. A further hypothesis is permissible: namely, that the version which includes the resurrection of the killed animal is the more complete one.

—*Ecstasies*, Carlo Ginzburg

2) Though the wedding took place at St Obadiah's on Easter Sunday, Amos's daughter said she expected no miracle. The previous Friday seemed inappropriate, even for an atheist like Amos, and Saturday nights were busy. "Cars, killings, alcohol," the hospital chaplain whispered to me before the ceremony. "Last night even . . ." he said, waving one hand past his ear. Nor did any of my family seem consoled by our old saying, "Friday's woe is Sunday's blessing, as Friday's fall is Sunday's rising." Amos was dead by the Tuesday following the wedding—I can't remember the exact time. The cancer that had begun in his throat had "leaked into his bowels"—his daughter's expression.

In my mind I saw it uncoiling. But what had begun with reassurances from Dr. Salmon—"simple, simple treatment . . ."—and ended with Amos's death, did not in the end kill him. His heart stopped beating. Isn't that how all the dead die, or is it lack of oxygen to the brain? I don't remember, if I ever knew. His heart stopped beating. In my mind, I saw a veined wall collapsing.

3) No one around his bed that Sunday had become morbid on hearing the initial diagnosis—simple, simple treatment—three months ago. He smoked, he drank "like an actor, my parents said. His bride-to-be, my aunt Carmel, rarely complained of his habits. She said he could drink and smoke as long as it was always only half a bottle of scotch or eight beers a night, Hunter's Chicken every Wednesday, Fruit World on Monday—"like dogs, all men have habits . . . all love is compromising . . . and thank the Star of the Sea he doesn't gamble." Amos had survived a war and I guess the five of us who accepted the wedding invitations—thirty-five declined—presumed that he smoked and drank because he had survived a war. Amos doesn't talk about the war, we said to one another and when introducing him to strangers. It stopped them—us— asking about his five missing fingers—three from the left, two from the right, shot off at the knuckles—or the scars across his forehead. At the wedding my family lined up on one side of his bed, as if awaiting communion. His daughter stood on the other side, beside my aunt, who was holding a cushion pinned with Amos's medals—one star-shaped, the other a cross, engraved with "the thirty-ninth." The hospital chaplain read the traditional vows, and though Amos found it painful to talk, neither groom nor bride paused or mumbled over "in sickness and in health." My aunt kissed Amos on his palms—leaving an arc of red lipstick—and asked the chaplain to administer the last rites. My aunt and I must have looked into Amos' eyes simultaneously—he looked crestfallen—for she clicked her fingers three times and smiled and claimed that her kiss could kill him. My family and the nurse and Veronica laughed.

27) The running man would have been more supportive of Veronica's desire to become a dramaturge, more empathetic to her want of a child, more willing to discuss her wants. The running man prayed, he helped people when the need

arose—the mother and her pram on the steep incline near the scoreboard, the old woman scared by unleashed Dalmatians, the schoolgirl struck on the thigh by a falling palm leaf—"It's stinging, it stings . . ." Each day the running man resolved to do what I couldn't: looking for full-time work, cooking as if Veronica still lived with him, writing to the war memorial offering them Amos's pamphlets and medals. In the shower after a run I resolved to tell the groundsman to "Fuck off and leave me alone . . ." and the next day the running man would talk to him—". . . good price for something so rare . . . talk to your union . . . better get that checked out . . ."

28:1) "I got two cinnanin rose's, ya'ave to buy them in pairs, the boss won't buy them to ya' otherwise. I took 'em home in a box and came in the front door and 'ooked for the dog but he wasn't about. He was behind me and I never seen him. I had to buy two more birds because a' my birds died 'ast week 'cos I was sick and so I couldn't feed them and the wife hates birds. 'et 'em die, she said straight to my face, think of that, 'etting a thing just die 'cos ya' say ya'ergic to feathers. So I put the birds down on the ground in the box and went to open the back door. I see the femay fy past me and the may'n the dog's mouth. Behind me a' the time. Fifty do'ars, think of that. Each. Hey? Get another pair, one dead, one gone. Think of that. That' be the new names, 'dead' and 'gone.'"

12:1) "You told her that the spleen needed to be cauterized regularly to ensure against samoxosis or Santa's complex or something," the host said, as thousands of Australian flags waved behind her. "Diana thought you were hilarious . . . just think, you could have had her that night. You might as well have, but who am I to talk? A son and no father . . . anyway, both our birds have flown. Good luck Simon."

15) Veronica had a small face and wore her red hair in a bob on the night I first met her. After we moved in together she grew her hair—let it out— down past her waist. Men in passing cars began to beep their horns at her. I had imagined we would meet again, had rehearsed my lines, but not even in daydreams did I see us reunited in St. Kilda. She was only a few meters

away from me, holding her black hair back with one hand and pressing numbers at an ATM with the other. In a moment she will turn to face me, I thought. She will ask after my health and then the health of Amos—fine, fine, I will say, still drinking, still riding. My parents too, well, well. Further, I convinced myself for a moment that if she had not left me or even if we were to reunite that day, Amos would not have died, my parents would come back to life—stupid, stupid—he died before she left, how could a lover bring all the dead back? I returned to the flat I inherited on Dove St., wanting to know her bank balance, wanting never to see her again. We had met after an Ashbury Trouveres opening night but last week, when I saw her—perhaps it wasn't her, I have allowed for that possibility—I felt that this event had never occurred, that what I was remembering was the production—make-believe, fiction, theatre—and that I had led another life, elsewhere and with someone else. Perhaps the actress who played Veronica wore a red wig and she had not left me, the season had only ended or perhaps I had entered as audience and exited as cast.

7) Amos said he loved my aunt because she was the color of gingerbread and in spite of her "pitchfork tongue." He had a plaque made naming the Dandenongs' home "The Gingerbread House" and turned his study into a sewing room. Amos had, to use my parents' expressions, "risen higher than high up at Fynmark's . . . taken a fair package . . . put his money into property . . ." and he bought the flat on Dove St. in St. Kilda for my aunt, who insisted that she was "a girl of city tastes"—and besides, she hated spiders and horses. The horse stank, she said. She hated seeing it shit. I spent many nights with them at the Dandenongs' property, sometimes returning Carmel to him after one of their monthly separations—"who can live with all his bad habits?"—or staying to help him with odd-jobs—mowing the acre or fixing the acre fence, handing Amos his customized pliers, pushing a wheelbarrow to wherever Amos pointed. He always insisted on paying me and he paid better than I worked—sixty, seventy, eighty an hour. I once had a three-week affair with his daughter—Katherine? no, Karen—which Amos ignored. My sense was that he thought us unworthy of each other. The time of the affair I was helping him

build a separate toilet for my aunt, who said it was inappropriate for fiancées to share the same seat—wrong color, she would say, waving her ring finger in his face.

23) I presume the fairy tale was read to me as a child by one of my parents—both died, along with my aunt Carmel, in a car accident, a year this Saturday—or else I have re-imagined it or corrupted another story with memory, or else it is the remains of a dream that I have spliced onto another half-forgotten story. Whichever way the story entered my mind I remember it as beginning, "One hundred years ago, in a valley covered with lavender, between two villages, there lived a girl with raven hair . . ." The author then wrote of how the young girl had taken on the milking and trapping for her ailing parents—who were "ill in the stomach . . ." The girl's name was Alice or Alicia or Avril, and when she was not wiping the foreheads of her parents or making them soup and bread or attending the well, she spent her days wandering in the lavender fields. She became known amongst the neighbors who shared the well as the "lavender nursemaid" and many of their sons imagined what dowry or tribute or escapade would persuade her to marry them. I cannot remember the middle of this story or even if there is a middle—I remember it as a series of conclusive vignettes—but I do remember an illustration from whatever book my parents read to me from or whatever dream the story has its genesis in: a wolf is stalking Alice near the well. The well itself resembled a small, strawberry-colored apartment block. The wolf looked like a fat German Shepherd. There is later an illustration—in the real or dreamt book—of a whiskered hunter, who also looks like a fat German Shepherd. The hunter will later marry the "lavender nursemaid"—perhaps her name was April. The story had two climaxes—April throws the wolf over her shoulder into the well where it treads water for three days. The neighbors save a disconsolate April from drowning herself. In the denouement, the neighbors forgive April and April forgives the neighbors. Somewhere in the story there is a talking crow.

20) I began running at the end of March, as the soccer goals were being reconstructed and the practice wickets began to descend into the overall

verdancy of the oval, though even by the middle of May the ghost of the center pitch was still visible beneath the green veneer of the center circle—a palimpsest, I thought. In May the groundsman drew four white lanes around the oval and marked them at one, two, three, and four hundred meters—the chalk circles were still faintly visible in cricket season—writing "relay change" at intervals with spray paint. I saw the groundsman on occasion, wearing his green council uniform with A.M.C. written on his back. When the ground was sodden he put up a small "Closed" sign on the oval's fence and no one trespassed, even when his Toyota Stanza wasn't parked beneath the scoreboard. On days when I ran he seemed to tolerate my presence—that's what I felt, possibly he did not notice me at all. I have allowed for that. I had heard from the dogman—a Japanese man who walked his five dogs every morning—that the groundsman, although deaf and mute, was in line to curate the S.C.G . . . , ". . . if he gets in the good book . . ." From a distance, the groundsman irritated me for no reason I could name.

22) Emberton Park enclosed the oval within its four walls. The park itself included a children's playground, a lawn bowls field, four tennis courts—one always fallow—a pavilion, two toilet blocks, a basketball hoop and a Georgian home that housed the historical archives of Ashbury and a resident artist each year. Between the oval and the walls were grassy embankments and concrete embankments and green bins dispensing black plastic bags—the dispenser was printed with a cartoon dog that resembled a wolf from a fairy tale I remembered—and on the grass embankments, palm trees, elms, and jacarandas stood in clusters of three. Six sixty-foot-tall light towers stood over the oval and had become the battlegrounds of magpies and cockatoos— not for nesting it seemed, but for roosting. The cockatoos lived in the palm trees—they seemed to stand vigil over me when I ran. From a distance they looked like wine bottles. Magpies roosted in the elms. Parakeets flew in each morning. The lights from the light towers filled the one-way streets flanking the park, lighting nests in trees, reflecting off the eyes and elastic skin of bats and the numbers on the backs of the soccer players—I could see a quarter of the oval from my balcony—as the young men ran laps counter clockwise,

three abreast. Though the pavilion seats were smattered with bird shit and infested with bird lice, homeless men and women—eight, ten, sometimes twelve—slept on them each night, and on training nights the light towers illuminated their faces—their skin became iridescent, their heads haloed—as they tipped bottles to their lips. On the back of the pavilion a mosaic of the bird life, with missing tesserae, showed one eye of a cockatoo, the wing of a parakeet, and the outlines of all the original birds. The pavilion burnt down recently—I read in the Melbourne papers.

36) The crow made a sound at first like a zipper being undone and then a second sound, a rasping, as if it were trying to expel the pain. It then seemed to say a word—"new" or "no" or "now." It felt like scratching my fingernails across my face—hearing that word. The crow moved its left wing to its beak—the marble had struck the top of its head—and then it lay down and died and out of the corner of my eye I saw a man running towards us.

5) We ate with our fingers and licked our fingers and wiped our fingers on hospital towels. My fiancée—Veronica—squirted three tamari "fish" onto her sushi while my mother unwrapped the rice from the seaweed and we made little piles of chicken bones on the three green oval plastic platters my mother had brought the food in on. A leftover platter of food was taken away by the nurse—"Who said we were finished?" my mother complained on the drive home. My aunt stayed bedside with the remainder of the gin and lemonade.

12) At the party the mirror ball woman seemed to laugh or smile at any absurdity I invented to convince her of my surgical qualifications. I learned later, years later, when I ran into the host on an Anzac Day march, that the mirror ball woman was a nurse and thought I knew this and thought my knowing was the joke. She told the host that I was the funniest guy she had met in "donkey's years."

21) Draw the inner, balk the halfback, lob the goalie—tic-toc-tic. "Create space, options," the coach of Victoria said to me when I was seventeen. "Go

thru' them like a bloody fire. Ya'n the team to create space, son." I could run at defenders, when I was a teenager, run and dribble and pass them. I heard it then—tic-toc-tic—felt it in my left wrist, my right palm—heard it, felt it. On my first day of running, I set up water bottles in a straight line and aligned cricket balls to act as makeshift goalposts. I began an old practice drill that required me to dribble between the bottles before shooting between the balls—a drill done one thousand, two thousand times before. I tripped twice, stood on the moving ball twice, kicked over the bottles three times. Watch the seam, be the ball, listen for the music—I heard the coach—make the game spread her legs. Tic-toc-tic. The ball went one way and I went the other. I felt like apologizing—to whom, the birds?

30) —where to live, what to work at, whether to sell the Kipling, whether, everyday, everyday to try to find Veronica, to apologize three times, three ways? The running man waved, as he ran, to the groundsman, to the dogman who had replaced his euthanized fox terrier with an Afghan, to the Falun Gong women and even to the leather-girl, who never waved back. The running man confessed, as he ran. The running man confessed—to whom, the birds?—that he had coveted the Kipling since he first heard of Amos's ill-health, that he masturbated over the leather-girl twice a day, "wasting your seed . . ." my father once said, when he caught me as a teenager in the living room. I missed the taste of Veronica's cunt, the riding crop between her legs, her face pushed against the pillow. The running man imagined the leather-girl in similar postures, similar positions, her hair stuck to her sweaty back, her tongue at the corner of her mouth. By the fourth lap—each day, every day—the running man felt a weight in his lungs, as if a pendulum had lost its anchor and dropped, dropped. His sight began to blur. He pushed on—for a match day that would never come. The magpies swooped at schoolchildren, the cockatoos closed wings and seemed to keep vigil over the entire park. And the parakeets and crows and wattle birds conducted their strange arrangements and alliances, their strange formations that established pecking order, partner, territory—all their unseen order defined or decided in flight

or in the abandonment of flight. Six, seven, eight—I'd take six thousand—for the Kipling. Enough to get home to St. Kilda, or a bedsit in Ashbury. Enough to get through until I inherited something else. How to make it all fit? The drip, drip into his calves, the tight hamstring. Hail Mary . . . pray for us. Five, six, seven. Pray for him. The rough shapes of India and Sri Lanka and Algeria rising out of the darkening earth of the practice wickets and the center pitch being flattened under the groundsman's hammer—Scotland emerging from the bowler's footmarks at the creaseline. Eight. Fall on your knees. Put your arms across your chest. Ten. Twenty. Thirty. Don't hold your breath, breathe.

25) I ran past the dogman, the deadman and the groundsman. I had awoken late so I knew that the leather-girl—she ran in leather pants and a leather jacket, wearing headphones—would have completed her five laps. The Falun Gong women, who had assumed a pose, in unison, that resembled a stork holding up the world, would be gone by my second lap. The groundsman was nearing his break, the dogman rounding the oval for the last time. As I ran I remembered a photo I had seen in my year-nine biology text. The photo showed a muscular man swimming through green water and it was captioned with the phrase "One hamburger provides enough energy to swim the English Channel." Although I had no real evidence that the swimmer was swimming the English Channel, I decided I had eaten enough hamburgers in my life not to ever have to eat again. I fasted. I fasted for three days. I drank water because I presumed the muscular man must have drunk water but I did not eat until my father put a plate of chicken and rice in front of me and stood behind me holding his slipper, threatening to hit me on the back of the neck unless I finished the plate. I showed him the photo—". . . and I work overtime to send you to that rubbishing school . . ."—and I ate then and the night after and the night after that, calculating the distances I crossed with each mouthful of rice and potato and ghee.

17) Eight days after the funeral, after drinking the last of Amos's Glenfiddich—six bottles in eight days, wedding gifts from those who chose not to attend—I

rang my aunt. I can't remember what time it was but she answered the phone immediately and the phone was in the "Louvre," not by her bed. Still, she began by saying "Huh, who?" so I presume she had been dozing.

17:1) "What is it son?" she said, coughing, then drinking something.
"The Kipling," I said.
"Now? We must talk tonight? Oh, he never said anything to me about it."
"But he told me, he told me he wanted me to have it. He read it to me . . . surely, my word . . ."

17:2) Amos had willed me *Kim* because he believed it was the book he read to me as a child. The book I remember him reading to me was *The Jungle Book,* I'm sure of it. But I wanted *Kim*. It was a first edition.

6) I had eaten a toasted sandwich the night of his death and as my aunt talked—which parlour? would I take her to Fruit World next Monday? why not cremation, wasn't it unnatural to just rot, rot, rot to the bone?—I kept touching the burnt roof of my mouth with my tongue, touching the blistered skin. When the phone rang I knew Amos was dead. I picked up the phone and heard my aunt say that Amos had died. I replied, "Did he?" Still, years later, whenever I remember the call, I touch the roof of my mouth and my stomach starts to throb—why didn't she call his daughter first, or my mother, who would then have called me? Why not let the phone ring three times and hang up? I would have understood. I was ready for him to die the previous Friday, all the previous Fridays of the month before. What was she asking me to say or do, why shouldn't I have replied with "Did he?" as if he had just bought a car, won two hundred dollars at bingo, rejected a lucrative job.

10:2) "Think of it, I was twenty-one and just married," Amos said, before putting the bowl to his mouth. "My boys averted their eyes but the creek kept bringing the faces of our wives, or at least the idea of our wives, before us. Look away, try to look away . . . the creek was covered in them, like they were stepping stones."

18) Six hundred and fifty thousand for the "Gingerbread House," plus the money he had set aside for the funeral and the lawyer of which five thousand still remained. Plus twenty-five thousand of savings, money in his day-to-day account—Carmel inherited half of all that, his daughter the other half. Further, his daughter inherited all except three of his books—signed first editions of Narayan, Tagore, Kipling—which she sold for one thousand, though Amos estimated they were worth ten. My aunt had talked of the money as if it were money she won at the trots or bingo, as if she had won the daily double, touching her temple at the daughter's stupidity. The three books were "in his house, in a box." The Kipling—eight thousand, he estimated—had belonged to his father and was never to be sold, which was why he wanted me to have it. The inscription read, "To Alicia, with fond regards and memories."

16) Over the two weeks that the production ran, Veronica would arrive at my apartment at about ten. I'd pour her a drink, a cocktail of my own invention—lychee juice and vodka with a mandarin slice, ginger beer and gin with crushed ice and lime—and she would tell me about Tyrone's prostate problems and "that Mary bitch," who expected a plate be brought to her each night—"I work best on a full stomach." Jaimie kept offering her Feldenkrais massages and Edmund's new boyfriend kept hitting him, just never in the face—"And Simon I don't feel like drinking so much, after seeing the play each night." After she talked we fucked. Sometimes we fucked on the balcony, sometimes on the couch. She liked me to come on her breasts. She brought home a stage prop one night, a green riding crop that had hung behind the front door of the Edwards' home.

39:1) "Simon, it's me, sorry, but understand . . . and I am not leaving my number. I thought I was pregnant when I left you, yes yours, and well, you know, I wasn't. Silly mistake hey? Silly. It's just, just a waste, all that time of us."

31) The resident artist began running, as did the old Falun Gong women, as did the dogman, the deadman, Veronica, and the various practitioners of Tai

Chi—old men who were strangers in my waking life yet recognizable within the dream. I ran before them with the leather-girl—"Tangled Up In Blue" faint from her headphones. And on the third lap the running man began to lead us all—my shoulders ached, my calves felt as if sandbags were attached to them—and the running man lengthened his stride and the old Tai Chi men passed me as did the dogman and his pack and the deadman and the leather-girl looked back at me from a quarter lap in front and put up her middle finger. The dream only ended when I collapsed and a fox terrier sat on my chest, its right paw held up in a Black Power salute.

26) I grew bored and irritated listening to how the groundsman's mortgage prohibited children, hearing about the new antique clock he had purchased on eBay, about all the territory he was responsible for, the owners who would let their dogs onto the oval. I was there to run. I have never understood why people talked so much, why he talked so much, why talk? What did it matter if I knew something he wanted to tell me—the price of antique clocks, the possible lawn bowls job in Burnsville—what difference would it make to the price of the clock or the outcome of the interview? Why did he think I wanted to know that he had assembled a family tree without birth dates? His clocks and his family and his land, fuck them. I set aside ninety minutes for my routine and many days he took ten, twenty of those minutes. I tried to walk away from him as he talked or to begin a lap as he approached. On occasions he would jog beside me, our footprints running roughly parallel in the sandy soil. At other times he would stand in my way and expect me to stop.

39) The phone rang while I was shaving. I left it to the machine. I recognized Veronica's voice more by its pace than its pitch or lilt. Don't tell me, don't tell me, I thought. It was the first call she had made, a month—a month—after she left. A month. I put a hot towel over my face—just leave the message, leave the message. In my mind I began a bingo card where all the possibilities of what she was about to reveal—money owed, things left behind or left unsaid, CDs, books—replaced numbers. The card was half-filled by the time she hung up.

Her news could wait until I had shaved and after I shaved, I thought, my life will be different.

11) On a Thursday night, a month after Amos's death, my fiancée—I called her that though I had never proposed—said she would leave me. We had returned to our apartment after a dinner party where I was seated next to a woman who had darker skin than mine and who wore mirror ball earrings. During the party, which was catered, the host brought the game Battleship out and whilst cocktails—Cosmopolitans, Black Russians—were served by waiters in green aprons, we each took turns guessing the whereabouts of our enemies' ships and blowing them out of the water. I looked at the mirror-ball woman often—I never asked her name and all the women referred to her as "girlfriend." I whispered into her ear that I was a doctor—she asked, and Billy Bragg was on at full volume—and she grinned and shook my hand. Her breasts swayed in her silver top. She licked her teeth. Her tongue moved to the corner of her mouth when she smiled. I heard Veronica say "K8."

35) If I read the brand names on the guns I saw I cannot now recall them. The names that occur to me now—Winchester, Colt—could easily have been learned from the Sunday afternoon Westerns I watched with my father when I was a few years younger than on the day my friends and I purchased the slingshot. I remember the names of the knives though—Finch, Oberon, McDuff—"A Cut Above." They were displayed in a cabinet of the same size as the cabinet my mother kept her porcelain doll collection in. Her dolls had names too—Barbara, Penelope, Antonia—and she talked to them, sometimes assuming a Cockney accent when addressing Barbara. The knives were displayed on paper that was printed with a picture of a naked woman. The woman's body was repeated over and over again. She had blonde hair that circled beneath the rim of a German World War Two helmet and wore an open barmaid's skirt that revealed a rough diamond of black pubic hair. Many of the posters up around the shop showed armed women in crop tops or bikinis or lingerie and some of the knife-handles had silhouettes of large-

breasted women upon them whereas the butts of rifles and shotguns were embossed with the heads of steer, stags, and American Indian chiefs.

33) Amos named his horse Ashes—". . . ashes for the rain . . ." He said it was a quote from a Bob Dylan song that I would not have heard of. Ashes was white with black fetlocks. Veins the width of my middle finger popped up on his rump and torso when he galloped. He scared me, especially when he was asleep, for the horse's cock was seemingly always erect when he slept and some nights, when I slept beside Amos's daughter, my cock would thicken thinking of Ashes. I would awake imagining Ashes standing at the top of the bed or of Amos's daughter on her knees beneath him—a pose she never assumed for me. Both father and daughter rode him, sprinkled their palms with sugar—his long blue tongue sickened me—and filled his nosebag with homemade muesli. I asked Amos to tie him up whenever I worked on the acre alone but Amos refused because the horse would pull and kick at the sight of crows and black cockatoos—". . . like elephants and mice, crazy bloody animal, not scared of anything else except black birds . . ."

9) The sun shone through the wooden blinds of the kitchen and streaked the stumps on Amos's left hand pink. The severed fingers looked like tiny, uncircumcised penises. I put a bowl of scotch in front of him. His right hand shook. A vein in his forearm rose, as if awaiting a needle.

9:1) "Forgiveness only occurs to me when I'm drinking. I've seen things when I've been under, recurring faces, been in other men's bodies, was even a woman once. Just drugs and dreams, I know. But let me introduce you to my angel, my nonsense. In the cupboard under the sink in the rice cooker are some papers."

34) One Sunday, when I was thirteen, I killed a crow. Two of my friends and I had pooled the money we had stolen from cars left unlocked in our various apartment garages. We didn't consider ourselves thieves—we didn't take their cars. On Saturday mornings we played hockey, on Saturday afternoons we'd go

to the movies, on Saturday nights we looked for unlocked cars. Some Saturdays we'd come home with runners or watches or porn—once a tape-recorder—but every Saturday we'd find money. Often we found loose change in the glove box or ashtray but on good nights there'd be a handbag or wallet—we only took the money—which meant fives and tens and twenties and this meant junk food and pinball and more movies. We were saving for a pocketknife—a black and silver knife with a flick spring—the custody of which would be shared according to a weekly schedule. That Sunday we rode our bikes for forty minutes to Blazington where I knew there was an ammunitions shop on Esperance Street because my father had bought bullets from it the previous duck season.

34:1) "Your father around, boys?" a man in a green shirt asked as we entered.
"We're not brothers," I said. "We're just the same color."
"We have money," one of my friends said.
"So've I," the man said and grinned; above his head a pair of antlers cradled a shotgun.
"You've come for a knife, I can't sell you a knife boys."
"Can we still look around?" I asked.
"Ten," he said, putting up both hands with outstretched fingers.

13) Veronica flicked the switch and the bulb fused. As we stood in the dark landing and I fingered the grooves of my keys—I had the absurd feeling that lightning would strike me if I put the wrong key in the door—I could hear a woman practicing scales beneath us. She had a deep, off-key voice. The door opened.

19) I took the phone over to the window and looked down into the street. I saw a group of boys running, throwing something—stones, marbles—at parked cars and pulling down antennae. I tapped the phone against the window and then remembered my aunt and stifled my shout.

19:1) "Kids," I said into the mouthpiece. "Just kids on the street."

"Criminals, criminals, all these children. Always looking at your handbag. Drugs. These bastard Abos."

"No, just bored kids, probably neighbors' kids . . . just kids . . . the book, aunty?"

"And their fathers, drunks, drug addicts, in jail . . . no one to screw their ears . . ."

"Aunty . . ."

"He never told me Simon, son. You can have it . . . no need to talk to discuss it . . . what is there to talk of? You're like our son. Don't get all hot and buggered. Even the solicitor Tom Brown and Sons said that I should give you the book, goodwill, he said."

"I'll come by tomorrow."

"Simon, from Sydney? Are you healthy in the mind? In the stomach? Do you know where you are?"

"Tomorrow," I said and hung up.

32) The entrance walls looked as if someone had taken them apart, brick by brick. Bricks were arranged in a rough circle. Other bricks were piled in towers of seven. The groundsman held a plumbline over one edge of the wall. Another man in the same uniform was on his knees with a measuring tape. Six black birds I could not name flew above me in a rough K-formation. The groundsman waved. I looked away, looked ahead at my goals. Stay low, move fast, I said to myself. And I sprinted towards the ball. Low, lower. I took the ball on the stubbynose, fixed my eyes on the revolving seam. I dribbled, veered left, came back inside imaginary defenders, cut away and had space—tic-toc-tic.

14) In the morning the dresser drawers were piled in a rough pyramid on the bed. Her wardrobe was empty except for one green shoe. One of the wardrobe doors had fallen off its hinges. A teabag lay in the sink and Special K clogged the sinkhole and burnt toast stood in the toaster. The rest of the apartment seemed awry, as if she had looked for something in a hurry before leaving

for work—jewelry, CDs, a book—though most of what she owned she had left behind. Everything seemed there, just not the way I was used to. Perhaps she was running late and couldn't find her keys. Perhaps she will call soon and call me a prick and ask what "three acts" I intend to apologize with—"three acts." Once she saw me kissing another woman's hand—it was a joke—and she said that I would have to "perform three tasks to gain forgiveness . . . like a knight." The first time she wanted a pendant, a massage and outdoor sex. The next time it was the theatre, a watch, a facial. I waited for her call the day she left, planning, planning.

28) The next day I set the alarm for four A.M. I wanted one morning when I would not encounter the groundsman, his chat, chat. I dressed and jogged through thick mist in the direction of the oval—from my street I could not see the Georgian house or the tennis courts but faint above the mist I could see Orion. I jumped the fence. The pavilion was invisible from where I stood—less than one hundred meters away. It seemed as if the spheres of the sky had dropped one level. It seemed as if Emberton Park had been covered over by white sheets, awaiting removal. Figures moved on the ground. One of the figures moved at the pace of a jogging man, but something else moved, faster, in the middle of the oval. I heard a whistle. The thing slowed down and turned. Then another creature—greyhounds, I guessed—began an arcing run and obeyed the whistle and returned and then a third or fourth or the same dogs twice in the same quarter oval sprint—black, fast, two or four. I jumped back over the fence. The stairs to the pavilion emerged, looking like a nasty grin. At the top of the stairs was a transparent cup full of brown, broken glass. The house appeared and Orion disappeared. I waited, waited—no more whistles. The groundsman's Stanza pulled in through the fallen walls of the park's entrance gates—a car accident, the groundsman later said, ". . . o'der than me . . . the wa's I mean, bys the ways, my birds are dead and gone."

29) By the sixth month I could run ten laps without stopping. Ten laps—two hundred sit-ups—ten hockey drills—faster, faster. I added the revolutions as I

ran so that I began to equate Friday with sixty, Saturday with seventy, Sunday with ten. I counted, counted—sit-ups, dog-walkers, the number of birds within flocks. When the running man was not praying I was counting and occasionally a passerby or another runner would look up at me as I passed, perhaps wondering what insult or message I had meant by eighty-four—steps between one light pole and another—six, six, four—cockatoos perched on the light towers—five—dogs on a leash.

8) When I first heard of Amos's diagnosis I took a bottle of scotch over to the Dove St. apartment. We sat in the kitchen because the lights of the living room were always dimmed to protect the fabric of the sofa—an "antique," my aunt called it, assuring me that one day it would be mine—and the clock with the Christ face was never wound—"it spoils the springs"—but ticked between nine past six and ten past six. It was maddening, maddening—Christ's cheekbone forever being struck. Amos called the living room "the Louvre." In the apartment below a woman was singing an aria. I did not know it was an aria until Amos named it as such.

13:1) "Do we have to do this now?" I asked in the dark.
  "Why wait till the morning?"
  "Tell me what I did wrong?"
  "Did you want to fuck her?"

10) I put the bowl of the rice cooker on the table before him and opened it and when I saw that it was full of envelopes I searched for and found and handed him a pair of tongs. With the tongs he pulled a sheaf of papers from one of the envelopes and laid them before me. I unfolded three sheets. They were the size of fliers or pamphlets left in mailboxes advertising cleaning services or menus for Chinese restaurants. Each sheet was covered with illustrations—cartoon figures. On the first pamphlet—burnt at each of its four corners—a tall man with an Australian flag poking from his hat is buggering a small black man who looks like a golliwog. The second pamphlet—covered with dark spots— showed a man who resembled Errol Flynn re-buttoning his cufflinks while in

the background a semi-naked woman lay with arms outspread on a bed. She had money in her bra—ten, twenty American dollars—and the pamphlet was headlined "Aussie men your wives miss you." The third pamphlet showed a woman at a desk in the act of writing. A thought-bubble emerges from her ear: "Dear John, please come home, don't fight for the Yaks," and before I spoke Amos said "Yanks," and on the reverse side a man with both legs missing and a cross through his heart is holding a letter inscribed "Dear John."

10:1) "We were carrying a young boy who'd lost a leg the same day I lost my fingers, the day before, three miles west of Buna-Gona. Carrying him—I wasn't doing the carrying mind you, giving orders, a regular Chester Nimitz—on a stretcher woven out of vines. We were crossing a creek and those pamphlets starting falling on us. I almost burnt them at once. Don't ask me why I didn't. I saw these things coming down like confetti and thought, they're telling us we won—fuckin', fuckin' stupid. We had half a bag of rice between us and we all knew we were carrying a corpse—he had a blue feel, a death-cold feel. And then these things, they hurt my feelings. In a war mind, after I've garroted men. See that little darkie—no offence mind—that little sambo with his arse up in the air, that's who I see even when I go under: my angel. The radiologist says don't move, don't move a muscle and straightaway I feel my missing fingers tapping, all the rest of me still, my fingers going like on a typewriter. I then start to doze. Of all that I could recall . . . children's heads used as footballs, all the raping I've seen, all the waste of it . . . I won't put it all in your head . . . aren't all these memories meant to haunt you? I am not haunted by any of it, like it wasn't me. I've had some bad dreams, bad nights of dreams, but I've gone on. Shouldn't I be sorry for that? But he returns every night, every night in my dreams, the black boy, black cartoon boy. He does things, helps out, finishes the wallpapering, sows and waters the lawn, regular spare set of hands. But this is what he says, each dream before he leaves—"I forgive you for what you did today"—as if I'd buggered him or not paid him or god knows—beat him?—what did I do to him? Crazy darkie."

24) The wolf—from my memory of the illustration—leapt at April's left

shoulder. My sense of the story when I was a child, as it is now, is that rather than tossing the wolf over her shoulder—which may have meant looking it in the eye—April ducked. The writer wrote a long sentence describing the wolf's caterwauling descent and the scrabbling of its claws against the well walls—"the story does not end there . . . the wolf lived for three days"—magically treading water. While it lived the lavender withdrew into the earth and the villagers stayed away from the well—some say the wolf begged them in a human voice for help—and when the wolf eventually drowned the water became thick and fetid. Potatoes popped from the earth, wheat blew away—I see the wheat in my mind, swirling as if in a cyclone. April's neighbors accused her of betraying the wolf—she had promised her hand or the bodies of her parents or her first child. "Surely, we thought . . ."—the narrator for the first time introduced himself into the society of the story—"the wolf was more man than animal . . . how he swims, how he talks . . ." and had been charmed as all the village men had been charmed by April's raven hair and selfless nature. Perhaps this was, after all, a dream, certainly I have never heard the story again. "A promise not kept will sour the season." Even I began to doubt April's virtue then—the illustration on the next page showed her with her blouse unbuttoned to her sternum—her breasts were hidden—lying with her arms outspread beneath an elm.

38) I declined to travel in either of the limousines. The crematorium was within walking distance. Family and other people I only dimly recognized shook my hand and left. I found it difficult to believe, standing alone in St. Leonard's, St. Kilda—twenty years ago I was confirmed there—that the Christ above the altar did not terrify me more than the bas-relief of the Fifth Station of the Cross. The crucified Christ—nails through wrists, not palms—had an expression of lamentable pain, as if he had anticipated atrocity and then felt that atrocity upon his own body. As a child attending St. Leonard's I remember the parish priest instructing the congregation to contemplate the wounds of Christ whilst singing the hymns or taking communion—"imagine the thorns in your forehead, the deadly thirst, imagine the heaviness of your own flesh

pulling down, down, down . . ." Perhaps I looked away from the thick nails that cut through the bound feet, the blood hanging like stalactites from the wrists, the awful face. Perhaps I looked toward the Fifth Station—where Christ was bowed but to my mind unbroken—and saw myself in the predicament of my namesake, bearing a heavy cross for a worthier man. Certainly I did imagine that my namesake could have been mistaken for the condemned man and this imagining woke me some nights—or woke me in church—breathless. However, what now puzzles me is that in the years of living with Veronica, hearing our names said one after the other by a third party—"Simon and Veronica are having an engagement party . . . Simon and Veronica, are you free on the eighth? . . . don't ask Simon about Veronica . . ."—and after seeing our names printed together on wedding invitations, rental leases, phone bills, I at no stage recalled the Sixth Station, where Veronica removes her veil and Christ puts it to his face.

4) Amos could not swallow anything for the last eight days of his life and talking pained him, but on a Magna Doodle supplied by the hospital he had written out the food he wanted at the bedside reception—sushi, Singapore noodles, teriyaki chicken wings. He then pulled a lever and the writing disappeared. When he did talk he sounded like a rasping bird. He pronounced one word then held his breath before the next word—"forsaking . . . all . . . others." The nurses ate with us, as did the two other men in the ward. My family drank vodka mixed in a lemonade bottle. Amos's daughter did not drink. The nurses delayed Amos's needles—one vial read ephedinen or episinnen, I can't remember—and though neither my aunt nor my fiancée nor my mother cried, one of the nurses did, as she replaced a drip filled with a liquid the same color as the vodka mix. Amos's daughter handed the nurse a breast pad. She wiped her eyes. My aunt was drunk and I sensed Amos wanted to be and so I took a flask of scotch from the inside pocket of my coat and swung it three times beneath his nose and put an unlit cigarette in his mouth and only removed it when his saliva caused the tube of tobacco to collapse. Doctor Salmon limped into the room as the chaplain walked out. The doctor then smiled and limped

away. Another nurse came in, smelling of smoke. One of the men, who had been poured a drink from the lemonade bottle, asked if he could kiss the bride and my aunt agreed, though I thought I saw disagreement in Amos's eyes. My aunt, in the end, kissed both of the men and both men died on Monday.

Addendum:

i) I waited one night until the light towers went out. For the first few weeks I ran in the late afternoon and never saw the groundsman. The dogman told me that he worked in two shifts, early morning and late evening. He couldn't explain to me why, or, rather, he tried to explain but I couldn't understand him. I had something to say to the groundsman—maybe that I appreciated the state of the ground, that I thought the summer pitches looked like they held plenty of runs, that the graffiti on the sightboards was criminal, criminal. I was not sure. I felt anger towards him as well for no reason I could name. Cars pulled out of the main entrance and sped past me along Eagle St., "gangsta rap"—". . . the bitch goes down, the bitch goes down . . ."—coming out of open windows. Young men, I thought, younger than me. I entered the grounds through one of the disused turnstiles. I heard, but could not see, people in the pavilion. The groundsman was sowing the mouth of the goals, on the far end of the oval. His green council uniform reflected the lamplight. A magpie sang. A cockatoo squawked. A bottle broke in the pavilion. The groundsman did not look up. Why not do this in the morning, I thought, why not let the ground tend itself overnight. 8 P.M. 6 A.M. What difference did it make? Only the drunks would know. Then I saw his shining uniform running toward me—he was not fast. His arms were waving above his shoulders, a sound—"whoah," "go," "ho"— coming from his direction. He seemed to be waving and screaming at me. Cockatoos alighted before him and then turned in the air and landed behind him.

"'Uckin birds," the groundsman said, dropping seed from his pockets.

ii) The pitches, from east to west, were numbered in spray paint behind the batting crease—one, four, five, two, three. He said he raised each one according to the team playing, the date of the fixture and the instructions from the coach. He said they never wanted greentops against Randwick-Petersham but Manly was another story—". . . green and wet, green and b'oody wet . . ."

"Oberon and bu'i, Bradman 'oved bu'i, fair to batsman and bow'er. I prefer oberon, cheaper, grass come up quick."

iii) The memory of my father walking in late one night, still wearing his balaclava, returns to me whenever I feel a coarseness within my fingers—the seam of a hockey ball, string, the unraveling braid of Veronica's riding crop. He holds in his right hand a Hessian bag, heavy and bloody at its bottom. Yet, in these last months it is the running man who now drags the Hessian bag up the stairs—he looks inside though I did not, at the oily, broken neck, the oily, blood-smeared emerald feathers. He makes a finger puppet out of the head. When the duck is laid before him the running man rolls rice and meat around in his mouth before swallowing. The running man has never tasted meat—rubbed with cumin and coriander, salt and pepper—as sweet as this before. I could not and still cannot bear the taste of duck—this disgusted my father, who could eat a whole duck and six parathas in one sitting. In memory, the running man—he is a man, not a boy—sits with him, fingering the excised bullets sitting in a bowl in the middle of the table, making quick circles so there is a scraping against the porcelain. Amos and Carmel and my mother have eaten—my father likes to eat with the running man alone. I felt as if I had become the running man's imaginary friend, perhaps even his son. And I remember a question I never thought to ask my father or perhaps I did and my father never answered: whose dogs did he use? To retrieve the ducks—whose dogs?

iv) I had no reason to believe the man I called the deadman was in any way sick, nor do I doubt that he is still alive and shopping in Ashbury mall, walking around the oval or borrowing crime novels from Ashbury library—I moved back to the flat I inherited in Dove St. three years ago. The deadman was tall and slim for middle age and perhaps of Russian origin. He ran more laps than I ever could, though he took to walking them within a month of my first seeing him. Perhaps it was this change that made me think of him as dying, or, because he had started growing a beard—stupid, stupid. He lived in the nearby strawberry-colored block of flats whose plaque read "Gondwanaland"—other neighbors had christened their house or apartments "Emoh Ruo," "Ice Castle," "Mermaid Avenue." I saw him often around Ashbury. I never greeted him. He did not look sick. He had no family as far as I could glean from what he purchased from Coles—bananas, oven dinners, lightbulbs. I never saw him smoke and never did I see him with the drunks in the pavilion or the old men sitting over 6 A.M. schooners at "The Fox's Teeth." No reason for me to presume that he would be dead soon. No reason for my nose to start bleeding when I saw him talking to the groundsman. However, in my mind I saw him walking, running, eating in death's skin—death's skin was vermillion. I dreamt about giving him mouth to mouth, about wrapping him in linen and carrying his liver in a bowl. Even in my waking hours I felt—stupid, stupid—that I would die, if our skin touched, as if his death could be made to be mine.

DELIA FALCONER

Delia Falconer was born in Sydney in 1966. In 1992, she won the *Independent*'s Young Writer of the Year Award, and in 1994 she was awarded first prize in the Island Essay Competition and the HQ/Joop! Short Story Competition. She currently lives in Sydney where she teaches at the University of Technology, one of Australia's most innovative and consciously postmodern universities. Her first novel, *The Service of Clouds* (1997), was a bestseller in Australia. Set in the craggy, rustic Blue Mountains resort area west of Sydney, and spanning the end of the nineteenth century and the beginning of the twentieth, it is written in incantatory yet sinewy prose that depicts a world on the verge of a massive change in mentality. Falconer, who has a Ph.D. and is a noted critic, has also written influential essays on the practice of fiction, and engaged in a memorable debate with novelist and critic Malcolm Knox on whether historical fiction shrinks from the challenges of contemporary life. Falconer, who has set both her published novels in the past, argues that re-examining history can be a way of challenging contemporary pieties and carving out a counter-cultural role for fiction. In her second novel, *The Lost Language of Soldiers* (2006), she exemplifies this position. Falconer has said, "all my writing is in some way or other about the way technologies define our lives: whether these technologies are cinema, or photography (the subject of my first novel), or ancient aqueducts." For Falconer, historical awareness is, in the deepest sense, part of an environmental awareness, a sensitivity to our surroundings and our awareness of the forces that practice upon us. The story included here takes its inspiration from Kenneth Slessor, Australia's major poet of the modern period and the consummate conjuror of Sydney urban life.

The Intimacy of the Table

But here I am in Sydney
                At the age of sixty-one
With the clock at a quarter to bedtime
                And my homework still not done.
—Kenneth Slessor

I was twenty when I met the great poet. It seemed to me then that I would always live in a long and narrow flat in a street between two steeples, that there would always be a bright arm of the harbor glimpsed sidelong through the eye's corner as I read in trams or trains. All that year I wore a shabby cream suit with a crimson handkerchief folded at the breast and a hip flask in one pocket. This day I had a nervous quiver at the corner of my mouth, my hair was brilliantined and combed. Is it possible that I also clutched a sheaf of my own poems in a buckram folio, marked with the date and place of their composition, in the hope that he might notice them? I admit I did. It was late on a summer afternoon when I climbed the steps to the Journalists' Club at the back of Central Station. The bar was dark; the sun still squeezed in transverse cracks of heat through the edges of the blinds, and the air was close and thick, as if it had been strained through dirty corduroy.

I saw him immediately, at a table in the furthest corner, the thin neck and browless eyes I recognized from photographs, that broad and wizened head, the blue bow tie. There was a claret and a paper and a jug of water on the table. He wore a double-breasted suit, fastidiously buttoned. He made notes as he read the paper with a crabbed hand in a tiny notebook. From where I stood at the bay, ten feet away, I could hear the sharp, swift indentations of the pencil.

I wonder now exactly what I expected from him. I still imagined then that each writer knew himself as part of a brotherhood of authors, that the rules were sensible and clear, that one great writer would always recognize another. I had come across his famous poem for the first time in my school reader where it had been placed, miraculously, among the work of well-known, foreign poets; and I could still recite it. I knew that he had rarely published another poem since.

At last he put away his heavy spectacles and came up to the bar.

"Which do you think is quickest transport up to the University, the train or bus?" he asked the barman. "I believe I'm to deliver a paper there at the English Department in an hour."

"No you're not," I said.

He turned. His glare was quick and blank, the appalled expression of the recognized and put-upon which to my shame I feel sometimes flash across my own face if some reader taps me on the shoulder while I am standing at a festival with my literary friends, or if I meet a student in the street. His mouth was the same grim line which I saw on the faces of my father's friends, and I also recognized something of their brittleness, which, with some fear, I considered a symptom of the office life, as if the atmosphere of heavy ashtrays and high-backed leather chairs had permanently pressed itself upon them.

"It's next week. You can take my word for it." I fished the crumpled flyer from my folio with shaking hands. I could not stop talking. "It's true. I study there. Believe me, if there was a change of date I'd know about it."

He nodded as he read, then shook my hand and thanked me. His palm was hard and surprisingly bony, for he was not a small man. He had the formal kindness I was later to associate with men who spent long periods of time alone, the outback reserve of country gentlemen or mining engineers.

"I've been dying to read your next collection," I said.

"Not dying, I hope." His eyes had lost a little of their flint. "I'm sure there are better things to die for."

We moved to the table he had just abandoned. "Do you drink claret?" I nodded although I did not. "Good," he said, as he waved the barman over. "Rituals are the great comfort of growing older. It is important to remember that eating and drinking are also a kind of life. I knew a man once, a barrister, whose great pleasure in life was to go to the Lawyers' Club in Bridge Street— do you know it?—they served up English boarding school food at tuck shop prices, quite dreadful preparations: tapioca, sago, trifle with the stale hint of confiscated cake about it. The rest of us would amuse ourselves by making up new names for the dishes: Matron's Surprise, willow sausage, flannel soup. My friend was a rather wealthy man, but I have never seen him happier than when he ate their thrippenny tart and custard."

I could only nod, faced with the scrupulous mechanics of his conversation. The club began to fill. Occasionally, one of the men, with the lines of his hat still imprinted around his forehead, would loom and greet him loudly. He responded quietly and introduced me to them as his "friend." Yet I could sense his eyes move across the backs lined up at the bar and felt that he would soon dismiss me, before I could show him my poems about flying foxes and Moreton Bay figs, or ask him why he did not write.

He asked me where young people "went" these days. I said I did not know; that I was fairly solitary "by choice" because I was "too busy writing;" that I did go to the "usual" Greek cafeterias in Castlereagh Street and that I went sometimes with my friend Robert who was a student politician to the branch meetings to which he was so frequently invited. He had no particular political calling, but had calculated that by these means we could save ourselves the price of around three meals a week. He had chosen the Liberal Country party because the women tended to be richer and the catering of a higher standard.

The disadvantage was that we had often to travel up and down the north shore train line. We traveled to Willoughby only if the necessity was very great, for this required a bus, and the hostess at this particular branch served without fail mayonnaise on a lettuce leaf balanced precariously on a piece of toast.

He had a charming way of laughing. He chuckled gently with his hands placed across his belly, bending back slightly, as if he took pleasure in gauging its vibrations.

I seized my chance. I told him where I lived, next to the deaf hospital in a pink federation villa that had been divided into bedsits; about the bathroom with its view of the railway tracks and the long ferny garden, the toilet pressed at an ungainly angle in the corner, the cantankerous water heater which I lit before each shower. I had been talked into minding a friend's axolotl which hung suspended in its green tank on the washstand and regarded my ablutions with the single lugubrious eye that remained in its possession.

"Is there a Salvation Army trombonist?" he asked. "And an old lady with two sycophantic Pomeranians and an addiction to Epsom salts?"

There were no musicians, I said, but there was a thin American cartoonist who went out each Saturday evening and who, if he returned alone, played Mario Lanza on the gramophone and sang until the early morning. And once, I said, disturbed by his music which drifted unimpeded through my always-open windows, I had looked out of the bathroom at the grounds behind the deaf hospital and observed in the moonlight a game of naked rugby played in perfect silence.

The claret bottle was empty. "Let's go to Holderigger's," he said.

The evening was diffuse and golden. Above us, the golfer on top of Sharpie's Golf House began, endlessly, to guide his bouncing neon chip shot along its illuminated path towards the nineteenth hole.

He was not as robust, I noticed with surprise, as he had appeared inside the club. Once he paused at the window of a shoe store and dabbed with his handkerchief at a thick vein in his forehead. He walked slowly, and did not talk much. He hummed instead from time to time.

At last, off a lane at the center of the city, we entered a chilly portico of sandstone and stepped down through a set of double doors into a restaurant.

I could smell the starch of the tablecloths, the sweet and desiccated scent of breadsticks. The mirrors were deep and edged with brass, the walls paneled with some dark unshining wood which still held the thrill of polish. The maitre d' greeted him by name.

"And how is Madame Holderigger?" he asked the waiter.

"She's very well, sir. Her grandson graduated this afternoon, in engineering, so she won't be coming in this evening."

"That's splendid news. Please convey my congratulations."

He sat, without glancing backward, in the heavy armchair as the waiter pushed it in and draped the napkin across his lap. I hesitated when the waiter gestured; I perched on my chair's edge, then readjusted it myself.

"I have known Madame Holderigger," he said, when the waiter left us, "for almost forty years. She is a Swiss, originally. She must be nearly ninety. You will no doubt have seen her at some event. She wears her hair scraped up into a tiny lacquered topknot like a cocktail onion. Many years ago she used to run some private clubs—when I was a young journalist she still had a reputation for sly-grogging."

Although I smiled I had begun to panic. I had imagined, when he first suggested it, that Holderigger's was another bar. I realized now that I didn't have enough money for this sober restaurant. I began to say that I should be on my way once we had shared our drinks, that I was not particularly hungry.

If I had another appointment, he said, he understood, but asked if he might first show me something. He reached into the inside pocket of his jacket, opened a leather billfold on the table, and produced an uncashed check for five pounds. It was a royalty, he said, for his last collection, published twenty years before. One should regard writing simply as a pleasant hobby, he said. In this way, any reward would come as a surprise, rather than one's due. It was his great pleasure, when those checks turned up, to buy dinner for his friends.

Our meal arrived which he had "taken the liberty" to order. I had never tasted oysters on the half-shell, or seen a salad tossed at the table or a fillet steak girdled tightly by a piece of bacon. We drank a bottle of red wine. I remember that he spoke—as he forked and cut methodically with his dry white hands—of the board of the *Bulletin* and its effect on various journalists unknown to me, which I could only, dumbly, nod at; of other restaurants where I had not yet been; of his cadet days covering pet shows and sewing fairs and go-kart races where young boys with cunning faces lashed fox terriers and pugs like Mawson's huskies.

As the food came he pointed out the rituals of the service, the way the waiters wheeled out another table and placed it by our own, the way they plated out the vegetables from a serving platter. In this way the labor of the kitchen remained invisible but the hospitality of the cook was performed before us, recreating what he referred to as the "intimacy of the table." He also made me observe the salmon-colored tablecloths and napkins which created, with the brass and wood, the atmosphere of a cruising liner. The pale green menus that the waiters carried worked like a contrasting thread which relieved and lifted up the orange, he said, wound by their constant movements through the room.

Towards the end of the meal he ordered another bottle of the claret. I had been drinking cautiously but I still felt flushed. My eyes were vague and heavy, but he sat upright, a posture I have come to think of since as the mark of a truly dedicated drinker: movement conserved, the body held in a state of relaxed anticipation. He seemed, if anything, to have become more pale and grave.

I do recall that a younger waiter about my own age arrived and dug clumsily with his corkscrew at the cork. The poet flinched and snatched the bottle from his hands. He opened it himself with a single turn and twist, and poured out two full glasses.

At last he asked me who I liked to "read." I had been reading the minor poets for the last few months, I said, but I remained rather fond of Larkin. I found his use of para-rhyme quite daring. I stopped. There was the hint of a smile on his thin lips. Yet I sensed, in the way he looked about for the waiter and winced when he saw no one, the chill edge of some distilled, exquisite anger.

Poetry should be the least interesting of topics to a young man my age, he said. What about the great Germanic verb in our English language? Did I find myself at present in a domestic situation?

I looked down, and blushed. No, I said, at last. Of course, I added quickly, there had been "encounters." I hoped the term was vague enough. He waved down the maitre d' and gestured for the bill.

It was deep blue night outside. The air of the laneway was still and damp. He hunched over a cigarette and I noticed he swayed a little as he lit it. Five girls and several young men passed us, laughing, on the street that led uphill to the Gardens, and he watched them. I thought I could smell the tank stream which ran for blocks beneath our feet.

In the end, he said at last, as if he spoke to no one, he recommended women highly. Women, with their tight little jackets and impossible perfumes, he continued, had always infuriated him more than they had pleased him. But they were indispensable for poets.

He turned and looked at me intently. "They understand faith, you see. They are the great interceders."

I stared at him. I was not sure if he expected me to laugh.

He straightened and seemed suddenly quite sober. He began to walk, stiffly, ahead of me, in the direction of the Cross. I should not take him seriously, he said. Seriousness was the affliction of old men. Here was a limerick I might enjoy instead:

> There was once a girl, called Priscilla
> Whose pubes were of perfect chinchilla.
> Each day she would trim
> The hairs of her quim
> And use them each night as a pill-ah.

He smiled tightly. His was a rather pedestrian para-rhyme, he feared, compared with Larkin's.

I followed because he seemed to like my company, or at least he did not mind it. Now and again, he would point out some place he remembered or pause to share a joke. He showed me the boarding house where Virgil the hunchbacked artist had invited pretty girls and sketched them for Smith's *Weekly*. And I seem to remember, although I have been unable to recognize the street again, that he took me through a breach in a wall behind a block of flats where there was a mossy grotto, its steps and niches carved into the cliff.

It was all that remained of one of the colony's first gardens and the optimism of that time, he said.

His building was a white mansion, divided into quarters. The carpets in the vestibule were gray. I had glimpsed a small chandelier behind one window. There were dwarf maples in the garden. Inside I exclaimed at the view. The harbor, lit by a full moon, filled the window of the lounge room. The water had the febrile glow of cine-film, I added. He appeared with two glasses from the kitchen and searched the drawer for coasters. He said he was glad I liked it.

The flat was dustless. I could see a music room with books of librettos piled up on the floor, his study beyond it which also faced towards the harbor. I noticed gradually the smell of thinning carpet and dark suits.

He poured two whiskies and added water with a silver teaspoon from a jug. No ice, he said, not ever. And one teaspoon only. The water released the flavor of the scotch. He had also brought out a platter of Stilton and some water crackers. "Some of life's small compensations." He placed them in front of the sofa where I sat. He settled in his armchair.

I had placed my folio on the floor and it sat between us. His eyes closed each time he sipped the scotch. I decided at last to ask if he would look at them. I took a breath to speak.

"When I was a cadet journalist, about your age," he began quite suddenly, "I was approached to write a small pamphlet on Australian vineyards. In Victoria I discovered that I despised everything about the countryside—the low skies filled with imperturbable gray clouds, the mournful cattle, the tattered yellow paddocks—but the wines were pleasantly surprising. On my last day there I met a German who made ice wines. The wine he brought out for me to try was miraculous: clear and sharp, and infinitely sad, as if cursed with an awareness of its own chill depths.

"He brought up three more bottles from the cellar and we walked across the yard towards his house. I had come to expect a cautious wife, a prolific flock of children, but the house was empty and quite bare, with the exception of a piano and a clock. There were a variety of corks lined up along the piano lid and there were grafted grape vines, their roots bound up in handkerchiefs, between us on the table.

"Each winter, he told me, he waited for the perfect temperature to pick his grapes. For a fortnight he would set thermometers among the vines and sit a vigil, singing songs to the mice to keep himself awake. The grapes had to be picked, with the ice still on them, at precisely minus four degrees. By the second bottle he had become quite sentimental, and with the third he began to stop every few minutes and look about the room. I remember that he said he thought he was probably the greatest aristocrat upon this earth. For he could not bear, even for a second, the thought of any uncomplicated pleasure."

A distant foghorn sounded on the harbor.

"I have thought of him quite often since."

I went to speak again but he seemed to have withdrawn himself from the room and into his armchair by some elusive alteration of his posture. I put my empty glass down. He did not offer me another. When I reached for my folio he jumped up to see me out.

At the door he shook my hand and said he hoped that we would meet again although I knew that he did not. He brushed aside my thanks for dinner. He said he hoped I had not found it boring. I said sincerely I had not.

"A young man who wanted to be a poet once asked for my advice," he said. "I told him. Invest in fine stationery. Be open to all social occasions. Always be shaved by a barber."

I expected him to smile but his face appeared remote and blank again. He closed the door behind me.

Random laughter drifted down from the high white cupolas and minarets of the Del Rio apartments next door. The smell of gardenias mingled with the weed and mussels of the sea wall. I flattered myself, as I stood for a moment between the dwarf maples, that he stood at the darkened window, watching. Then I began to walk towards my narrow rooms.

---

*Author's Note: The headquote is the last stanza of Kenneth Slessor's last published poem which begins "I wish I were at Orange . . . ," written for class 5A at Orange in April 1962. It appears in Geoffrey Dutton's *Kenneth Slessor: A Biography* (Melbourne: Penguin, 1991), page 11.

TOM FLOOD

Tom Flood was born in 1955 in Sydney. He grew up in South Perth in Western Australia, graduated from the University of Western Australia, and is currently pursuing a Doctor of Creative Arts Degree at the University of Technology, Sydney. He is the son of noted novelist, playwright, and memoirist Dorothy Hewett (1923-2002). His first novel *Oceana Fine* (1989), made a clean sweep of the major Australian prizes, winning *The Australian*/Vogel Award in 1988, along with the Melbourne Premier's Award and the Miles Franklin Award in 1990. Since then, he has worked as an editor, musician, and songwriter. He is also currently working on a number of children's stories and picture books with illustrator and artist Zoë Fletcher. The novels *Septimus Grout* and *Kande & Bonco* are major works in progress. *The Little Gap in Talk,* the project from which the excerpt below appears, is itself from *Septimus Grout,* a vast, over-arching, and polyphonic project that will incorporate the already-published *Oceana Fine.* Flood's gift for capturing colloquial idioms is matched only by his adeptness at splaying them into multilayered, patchwork, interactive compositions. At once intrigued by the inherent limitations of narrative forms and fascinated by the many permutations of their possibilities, Flood surely has thought through what "tabulation" means more than any other Australian writer of his generation. Flood has published sparingly since his first novel appeared, but this glimpse from his long-brewing project should whet the reader's appetite for what is to come.

From *The Little Gap in Talk*

Here am I, in line, talking about myself again. Who am I talking to? No one in particular. One on one is not something I can say I've experienced. Although now, with you and me, well . . . Have you ever thought that someone may be inventing you? Or me? If you pinch yourself, you feel a corresponding pain. Is that actual, that pain? And whose pain is it after all? Is the line my own? And these others? Am I being manipulated to test the sentence I endure—to leave the line? To leave the line is to give up hope. The line comforts me, sustains me. I have my place. This is my sentence, isn't it? The book is what makes me doubt. Doubt, once allowed in, is everything; like belief; like faith. A book like that, a character could really find their place with that book. I can feel your eyes on me. You expect things from me. I might blush but I don't know. It's not in my character. Oh, I am a character. Or, at least, a complex mix of character traits. I suspect my personal development might need some work. I have doubts. I don't know. It's really all I can be sure of right now. Not very convincing, I know. Can anything be built on a belief in doubt? If someone invented you, then you do have Purpose as that invention—so the line. But what is the line? And if it has Purpose, then why do I feel like it might not be my Purpose? Perhaps it's yours. I do feel I might not be meeting your expectations. Like I wonder about a past when all you look to is a future—and if you can see it, you can catch it.

There's something to sicken a stolen glance. Brush a button and anything concealed will come flying random to the remote. An epidemic of sight is what it is. Nothing must remain unseen. Perhaps the will that invented you is sought, surveyed, scanned by another. Perhaps that's what can be built on doubt, a system of corresponding invention. If I pinch myself, do you correspond to that pain? If you blink does my world disappear? Your eyes—and it's true, I do desire your glances—seem to contain two forms of life, like the subject and its hidden implications. The usual surfaces, yes, but there's a sea-life moving deep in the iris of your eyes as if you want to communicate in this way, communicate through optic fluids. Like you once dreamed of a world where words were both heard and seen and it was like the liquid of your eyes was heavy and you could give voice to every stone and shadow and see a word for every sound you heard. Words might be the opposite of children, you know, always dearest when they're heard but never seen. Sometimes they sleep and dream, and tell each other stories about what they dreamed—when they're awake? I'm sorry. Now I'm inventing things. All this is just talk. You're probably wondering where the dots connect because everything connects in the end, or only seems to, or seems to only because it does. So I was wondering—because I don't seem to connect, really connect, that is, even with you—if I am really a character in this line. You know the way—and I know that . . . a word is like a face—the way with real characters, the way they sort of float on their words. Characters are unrealized possibilities. Each of them has a Purpose. It's that Purpose—the end towards which my own eye bends—which attracts me most. Beyond that end begins the secret I ask about. You see.

Lo to you an late in comin Septimus Grout what some as call Septic an betters Sep second drainer an ex-mariner Side Pass The Hark Set down here due to what I said before Girt bein a paper an me a thikkin an people bein what they are Just so Id as soon be on queer street as not Charlie Mange as never ate a fish in his life reckons at queer streets always been his address Charlie keeps the Sidepass once to gangin ont Tubes two fingers missin provin it Dug Pipers Heaven himself when he had a light for some girl till she to dousin him reckoned at she wasn for it

And Girt Girt is Girt just so never sayed no more or less Met me once good as not met me twice all theres to it Theres her way to say how we come about In the Artesians it was Me to workin the Marine an she to seein whats about Just a girl an took fear at a fish an I to tellin her whats about As good as not just so but memory come to us both Next I see late in comin Girt in the Broadway grown an some to say come down I to say come to the know How are the fishes I to say Whos to pullin the line she to say Give me a sound to make somethin of Got a light there an then did I but couldn reckon any such in Girt for the wantin This head was clamped just like a Book First light first light touch a star an catch as might

Thats somethin Theres Girt to say in that first meetin whats a star An I to say somethin you shouldn have the know of Doan be queer Girt to say so I to tell her of the light that comes shinin an dancin out of nowhere An whos to makin it she to say An I to say theres much to that an maybe no more than old talk of the Mariners Those that say its Willow the Wish wholl be to catchin the light in your eyes an steal it away so you must foller But whats to foller in that talk is dark song an savage in deed better the late in comin Well Girts not to likin I stop short here an I to reckon at this so I to tell her the talk I hold to The stars are the light of the Fish caught by we the Mariners left to search for their lost scale through all the dark Artesian

Here I could be to tellin you some story Story of the Fish Whoppers just so When Fish swim high then shit will fly Thats as they say But Girt is to sayin fill in the hole which is what Im set down here about

To start theres that about characters Characters are not people I to gettin you you to say a sandbaggin no matter Maybe as I reckon at bein a ferret but save a rock job til first camp This is the chalk Characters live on top just so Reckon thats as how theyre to squeezin us rift an seam hot fissures in the Artesians Heres the hole Characters are a shape somebody got the know of stuck in pens Bent eyes is what they got An sentences

If I'm not real and I'm not really a character—no description, no name, nowhere but this line—and what I'm after, counter to your expectation, is before, then I beg to extend your good grace. I'm painfully aware we've only just met. Come back with me. I'll be your counter-character for today. No need to push. These characters, they're going the other way. Don't worry, I'll invent something we can depend on. In a line there's always someone before you, someone who comes after you.

The character behind me—an unsavory type, worn-out hat, coat cut well but offensive with tobacco and alcohol, notes crumpled in the pocket, talk peppered with money troubles—I must have invented . . . him. He begins to be recognizable as I speak, to take shape and voice. I've half a mind to make him a writer . . . small things amuse half-minds. He mutters to himself, snatches of verse, elaborate imprecations, raw remembrance. Now he turns on me, perhaps aware of his determination, a dark gaze, at once hostile and open to promise. As if he may be a stranger he has met at some desolate crossing. He begins.

A looker-on, they say, sees most of the game.[a] Once I was as proud as a dog with a tin tail. I could knock out a line for a daily as well as most and write better than any man might expect. And where's it got me? Crow low and roost high is my advice.[1] These days the new chums that come out, they think they're hard done by; they blew their thousand pounds in Melbourne or Sydney, and they don't make any more nowadays, for the Roarin' Days have been dead these thirty years. I wish I'd had a thousand pounds to start on!

I am back from up the country, very sorry that I went
On the runs to the west of the Dingo Scrub
There was drought and ruin and death.

Burnt a lot of fancy verses all right—oh, I was a mug! Pity the Southern writer who, for beer and johnnycake, must sell their entire heritage, the bread and the wine of years of sweat and blood; for, mark me, that's the stuff, and not printers' ink, that crosses the lines and makes a reader turn and turn the page; for when it comes to buying and selling, the guns in the city'll be already turned and on the whipping side before you've even rigged up your Ward and Paines.

From The Banjo to Barmy Harry,
From The Bloke to Boake and back,
I work the rhyme for reason,
Though the reason's not you, Jack.

Where was I? That's right, why's it I keep scratchin' when they've shown me the boot from here to Wellington? Well, it's not for the look on the likes of that lady casts a cold eye over Sappho Smith's letters. Just once before this grand first decade of "The New Age" gets too far gone for hell or heaven (I'm as likely as any man to throw a seven before forty), I'd like to serve one of those shicers from the City of Smells who lays on the jam, but as I'm not in a position to go where there's influence without the demons jerries to me, the strong of it is once I had to write or burst and all that came of it was country crumbs, now I scribble what I can in the sincere hope that all editors, publishers, critics and their hangers-on, those paper giants with their circles and spheres of influence, will put their considerable fund of reputation into the publication and promotion of this doodling and consequently be gone a million and never guess the game. If this veriest wreck in the drink-fiend's clutch could just see his way clear of their palaces of graft and infamy, where sport is God and fat-fed narrow workers, well-paid billet loafers, moral cowards and shirkers talk of nothing but the races or the strike,[b] why then, he'd join the last crusaders work on the bastard Teuton-Turk[f] and clear a path to perfect nationhood, joy in 'is 'eart, an' wild dreams in 'is brain,[4] a hero's death, that alone would clean a man's dirty slate and leave the bill wiped out![b]

Knowin is believin take it as thikkin or paperkin no matter the Divider hold us all What some as calls Ymir and some Goliath most to sayin Fin just so Fin the Divider as lay down to restin to dreamin long as that lamprey no matter

Take a shell Whats to come unheard from its mouth to whisperin across a wall you to near hear where breaths end to be Reckon at the little gap in talk that pass among us all to unlisten good as not All to tearful fall from what we are so here we to be just so well gone to lee mouth the moment the hole talk and talk to tellin A gianter I immortal prawn a dredge scavenger just so foragin no sense stupid as a thikkin abovedecks interferin to be at orders of minitude unheard infiltratin no feel for map none needed commandin the far capillaries of whatevers to tidin in a soul like blood

Touch it them tiny shells one a sphere next to fillin in an in again Them markin stones whose ever mystic purpose are at requirin this makin lime changed for iron oxide magnet exact such metal lode some as say to calibratin our own linear emplacement that gianter engine an a body to surroundin that an ylemic history unfoldin without all unknown to we as are within Ceptin the tremors a complete unsensed worl our own to holdin as a child a womb that wait for summons

In the rusted ending last light to bein just that far from no light at all over where the tongues near to stilled where the ears unspin a little less solid each turn I to driftin an toward my own absence uncontrolled to any end or purpose with rules fatal to knowin Where all as are dust dust to be no more Faith none to be I could get the know of that even to respectin it yet here not much more ceptin faith full an fervent Harmonies such as strange louden on approach Even the currents of the earth are with them An I to treadin water backgrounded spirit level to that perilous flux roarin all ebb an flow little more an that to come but once spillin cross a worl all levigation an elutriation particlar in a current planetold that soundin the bein charge me with such to be flung among elodea among nettlesome weed a course set an fed poly porus the black earth the chestnut soil elvan to eluvium measure me chainman Chaldaic chalazae of chakra sevenfold

Downriver I spin widenin out of dankness into the singin fleets of keels penned upon the tide the river arumble boom an rail serpentined an chicaned the great water punctuated by scents of earthwork insea for miles down to the Bite beyond Care a worl that never was the killin mound waitin someplace pale an shiftin the flanks of aqueous creatures seethin slithery as stargrazers an shouts of keelmen bell somewhere closer alarm on their invisible rounds ship to ship iron seekin iron an then just so out of the sea fret a strange jibber jabber talk unheard but vowels as such unmistakable

hylem an hyte wood it matter halem an hate wud it hole an hote hele an hete ulam an ute ilem an ite wheresal Bite over yaw near to jaw sing the light the lute to sight

An avoweled as they be forward they come through din an drubbin loudenin still though may it be I that come to them as a dream a worl so sharp with light that the Fish be to none at all just a lack an all be to eyein so much as talk to lose its sound An they each to raisin their arm as in that dream I times be to havin where light smooth as pearl to be an every knowin thing an more hails so silently crowdin roun to more than an eye be to bearin as if be to holdin the worl an all to touch completed in your hans an every smooth an rough every soft an hard every warm an cool right there be to feel an talkin at in ways short an strange

An just so the light is to takin it as if it never were down my time none to be an all is to fallin

1 Steelman
4 Ginger Meggs

a Banjo Paterson
b Henry Lawson
f Christopher Brennan

A. L. MCCANN

Andrew McCann was born in Adelaide in 1966, but grew up in Melbourne, the city that supplies the setting and the presiding obsession for his writing. He began publishing fiction as A. L. McCann in 2002 with *The White Body of Evening* (HarperCollins), which was set in late-nineteenth-century Melbourne and has been described as a "Gothic-historical melodrama" that recreates a frustrated Bohemian milieu at odds with emerging forms of Australian national identity. His second novel, *Subtopia* (Vulgar Press, 2005), developed this tension in a more contemporary setting: Melbourne's south-eastern suburbs in the 1970s and 80s. Both novels range between Australia and the German-speaking cities (Vienna and Berlin, respectively) that represent cultural and political capital for their protagonists. McCann uses this geography to explore the relationship between national and cosmopolitan identifications, and to interrogate aspects of Australian culture from positions exterior to it. His fiction is frequently self-conscious in its use and referencing of other literary texts, a feature that reflects his academic background. He completed a Ph.D. in English literature at Cornell University in 1996, and has since taught British and Australian literature at the University of Queensland, the University of Melbourne, and currently Dartmouth College. In 2004 he published the first ever monograph on the nineteenth-century Australian novelist Marcus Clarke—*Marcus Clarke's Bohemia: Literature and Modernity in Colonial Melbourne* (Melbourne University Publishing). In 2006 he was awarded a new work grant in fiction from the Australia Council's Literature Board. The story "Mid-List" is an extract from a novel in progress, tentatively titled *The Terrorist System of Novel Writing*.

Mid-List

From zis shithole, he told me, you must go.
—Peter Carey, *Theft*

When I published my second novel, the commissioning editor, Sophie Cousins, came down from Sydney for the launch and gave me a bouquet of flowers. She was good like that, Sophie. Fifty-something. Loose black hair streaked with gray. Bright lipstick. Puffy skin around the eyes and mouth. A white shirt with a Nehru collar. She had no real family of her own and because that fact was widely known, people concluded that she treated her writers with a warmth stored up for the children she never had.

Six months later my novel had come and gone. A couple of reviews, negligible sales, and a flood of store returns, the numbers mounting with each passing day like the death toll in some sickening third-world catastrophe. "Sometimes it just takes something slight," Sophie reassured me over the phone, a sinking sound in her voice. "Something slight, and everything starts ticking over."

I squinted at the bitumen. The petrol burn-off shimmered like a mirage across the Doncaster Freeway. I imagined Tim Winton whimsically leaping over a rock pool, or gazing out over the surf in thoughtful, existential repose. The car felt like a furnace. As my foot hit the pedal I had a premonition of someone dropping a brick onto the windshield from one of the overpasses: exploding glass, high-speed impact, fatal head injuries.

E-mail from Penny Murakami, publicity and marketing: "Hey there Tommy. Please don't forget about the reading. The Lower Plenty Bookend. It's likely to be intimate. But all to the good. Cheers, Penny."

That was how I met Roger Siefert. We were both what the critics call, with a wink and a nod, mid-list authors, which explains why we would have bothered to drag ourselves out to the edge of the city in the hope of selling a few books. I was living in South Melbourne at the time. With the stalled traffic on Kings Way, it took ninety minutes to drive across the city and then out along the freeway. I pictured Penny Murakami e-mailing away in her office, looking out over some sun-drenched patch of North Sydney, the geography of Melbourne and its outlying areas a trivial irrelevance.

Roger was already there when I arrived. Peering through the shelves, past copies of Ricky Ponting's *A Captain's Diary*—Punter, hands on hips, baggy green, posing against the gray void of uncertainty that turns captains of the Australian cricket team into philosopher-kings—I got a glimpse of a largish guy perched uncomfortably on a stool nestled into the young-adult section. An audience of four or five locals—lonely, aging people—sat in front of him like well-drilled school children.

"Hi. You must be Thomas," a matronly woman said from behind the counter.

"Hi," I said, sounding deliberately dead.

"I'm Joyce," she said. "Joyce Hartley. We are just about to kick off." She put a glass of red wine into my hand. "No need to read if you don't want to," she continued, lowering her voice as she tilted her head towards the audience. "I think they'd just like to chat a bit."

She guided me past a special display stand that held a stack of my own books. *The Block: a Comedy.* Embossed lettering over a sepia-tinged vision of Collins Street circa 1890. Alongside it was Roger's book, which I hadn't read and didn't intend to. *Creaturely Travels*. A blurred cityscape. Somewhere in Asia I thought, judging by the profusion of neon and the sense of crowding.

"Your novel is wonderful," Joyce said to me. "Not a word out of place."

She made the introductions, said something about supporting young writers, and then, with an open palm and a step into the wings, handed over the reins.

Roger read a few pages. He looked like the sort of guy who could be a nasty drunk. Handsome, balding, a bit grizzled. His face was starting to thicken with age. He spoke posh, grammar-school English (long "a"s and a bit of a lisp), but under it you could hear disdain, cynicism, a hint of aggression. His reading was about a backpacker who gets lost in Bangkok and meets a young Thai woman who is studying agriculture. That was as much as I gleaned. I did my bit and after that members of the audience asked us stale, politely self-serving questions.

"Thomas, it is funny," an elderly woman said with a sort of singsong lilt in her voice, unconvincingly tailored to communicate inquisitiveness, "I thought your book was related to that television program about home renovation."

"Oh," I smiled.

"But you see, then I remembered. When I was a girl my granddad used to talk about doing the Block with his girl. That was my nana, of course."

"Now, was that deliberate?" a leathery old man asked. Retired high-school principal, I thought. "To call it 'The Block,' I mean. Get people thinking about a tie-in with the television show. Boost the sales."

The bloke looked at me with a mild kind of distaste.

"No no," I said, "I thought everyone would have known that it's a historical novel." Sell it, I told myself. Sell the fucking thing. "A historical novel full of crime and period erotica," I added. "And it touches on many places you'd recognize from your own experiences of the city."

"Is it true that Melbourne used to be called Bearbrass?" the woman asked. "I think I read that somewhere."

"Now tell me," another, slightly younger woman said, patting her neighbor gently on the knee in order to shut her up and move the conversation along.

"I want to know because I write a little bit myself. How would you go about getting a novel published these days?"

Roger gritted his teeth. "It helps if you know someone," he muttered morosely.

"They all write," Joyce said with a faint, but affectionate cringe. "Any advice on getting published would be greatly appreciated."

At that point we were both eager to leave. When things finally wound up Roger bounced to his feet and made as if he were shaking dust off his clothes.

As we headed out I congratulated him on his novel.

"Have you read it?" he asked.

"No, actually I haven't," I said. We both smiled.

"No worries," he said. We shook hands and said good-bye with the weary camaraderie that had become second nature to most of the writers I knew back then.

A few months later I was at a book launch in the bar of the Trades Hall Council building on Lygon Street. The place was buzzing. Minor poets, freelance critics, independent publishers, small-time luminaries, student activists, and the odd coterie of creative writers from the university. A union official introduced a book of poems with militant, working-class themes. He said that he was never much of a reader, but that these were poems that spoke to him. I slouched down the back, well away from the stage, and sucked away at a stubby of VB, conscious of the attractiveness of the girl behind the bar. The guy beside me had unbuttoned his shirt halfway down his chest and was carrying on about making it into *Meanjin* before he'd turned twenty-one.

"Don't care for militant poetry," he said under his breath. "Don't care for the mannered stuff either. I could tell you horror stories about poets who steal their best lines from American soaps. And what's this?" He traced out an elaborate arabesque with his hand, wrist rotating, fingers fluttering. "A question mark? Fuck that."

After the reading I went to have a smoke on the veranda and there was Roger Siefert hunching over towards the railing, rolling a cigarette.

"I got your book the other day," I said. "Haven't had time to read it yet. How's it going?"

He shrugged. "A good review in Sydney. Almost nothing in Melbourne. What about you?"

"Nothing much. Falling between the cracks I guess."

"That's just the way it goes these days. There are a lot of ex-Generation X writers out there."

Our conversation limped along in this vein. We sat on the veranda smoking, drinking the subsidized beer, talking about the sorry state of literary publishing, and passing the odd comment about the cute, creative-writing students—black fishnets and Blundstones—that embraced the abandoned, slightly lumpen atmosphere of these launches.

"You know," he said. "It just goes to show you what a piss-weak place it is. And it's our moment in time too."

As the crowd thinned we both made our way down onto the street. Again we shook hands.

"Why don't you come over sometime?" I said to him.

"Sure," he said. I jotted down my address on a page of the notebook I carried in my coat pocket, tore it out and gave it to him. "Come next Saturday," I said. "Ian Dalton and his partner are coming."

"How do you know him?" Roger asked blankly.

Ian was a critic at a leading broadsheet, an old school friend, and the main reason my books had had any press at all.

"Let's go over the road and get another drink," Roger said, letting the question slide.

I'd had enough really, but he insisted, so we walked over to the John Curtin Hotel, a pub I hadn't been to since my student days. The place had been gutted and renovated beyond recognition. In fact the atmosphere was so dismal we only lasted one round and then stumbled back towards the city. By then I was drunk enough not to care where we went. We ended up in a bar a few blocks away, somewhere between Lygon and Swanston, and the conversation continued in a way that started to annoy me. Roger worked himself into a temper about his book and the lack of attention it had received. At one point he strutted out something ridiculous about translating his own novel into French, a la Beckett, and finding an alternative publisher in Paris, a la Burroughs and Nabokov. He seemed to expect me to play along. When I didn't he got kind of edgy. I guess I could have kept pace with him. But I was tired, booze-addled, not up for much of anything. We ended up sharing a taxi back over the river. At one point, swerving around the arts center, we were talking incoherently about Japanese cars, and even then there was the hint of an argument.

"Pull over here," Roger said to the driver, fed up.

He fumbled some notes towards the front of the cab and motioned for me to get out. We were a block or so off Kings Way, in a semi-industrial neighborhood near the Maori Chief Hotel. And in all honesty that's where I thought we were going until Roger staggered up the steps of a single-story, redbrick terrace. A buzzer went off as he pushed open the door.

"Did you read that shit about Elliot Perlman interviewing a prostitute for his novel?" he said, looking over his shoulder as he held the door for me. "Paid her by the hour."

"What are you on about?" I said.

We were in a small, overheated waiting room. Worn carpet, a velveteen couch and a red lampshade. An old woman lumbered through a beaded curtain. She said something that I couldn't quite make out. It sounded like "'allo boss." Then a girl appeared at her elbow. Leather skirt, high heels and a tight black top that left one shoulder exposed. "Okay?" the old woman asked. Roger nodded and followed her down a narrow passageway. The old woman said something else unintelligible and more girls came out. Thailand, Burma, Vietnam. Slums and shantytowns. I stood there, tremulous, as they materialized, one after the other, like images in a disjointed flicker book, each posing for a second before retreating through the curtain.

"No more," the woman said, dismissing me. I walked back onto the street in a stupor. A pink neon heart and an ATM sign glowed in the window behind sharp metal rails. On the other side of the street there was a beaten-up SUV with a guy asleep in the front seat, shielding his eyes from the street light with his arm. I walked the rest of the way home, about twenty minutes, conscious of trying to outpace the moist, filmy atmosphere of the place.

The next Saturday, Sara and I prepared dinner for Ian and his partner, a journo who covered the courts. Another friend of mine, a sculptor who specialized in obscure sexual allegories made out of wood and wire, was there as well. It was part of the folly of my life back then that I had taken on the burden of entertaining in this way. It didn't come naturally, but I was publishing books, and somehow it made sense that I would preside over erudite dinner parties. I really had no expectation that Roger would show up. We were already seated and eating when a knock on the door told me that I'd misjudged.

"I thought you'd blown us off," I said, without much conviction. I pulled up an extra chair and quickly set another place.

The conversation resumed. We were talking, predictably I suppose, about such-and-such's new book and how it had been pushed by the publisher, and Roger, to his credit, picked up the thread quite effortlessly. He was perfectly pleasant, until somehow, according to the undulations of the conversation, he cottoned on to the fact that Ian seemed to have no idea who he was, no idea, I mean, that he was an author who had written a novel. Here we go, I said to myself.

"Well, I never imagined finding myself face to face with a genuine arbiter of taste," he said finally, self-conscious in his pomposity, fishing for a prompt. Ian looked a bit stunned. "I've written the odd book in my time," Roger continued. "Though not the sort of thing that anyone would notice, not like Thomas here, who has made a much better fist of it. But you don't do it for the dough. More important to fill the cup of experience."

It occurred to me that he was going to mention the brothel. He was trying to maneuver the conversation until he had an opening. For a second his eyes rested on mine. Then he winked at me, making no effort to conceal the gesture.

"I'd be happy to have a look at your book," Ian said.

"Thanks," Roger said. "Much appreciated."

After that the evening fizzled. It was as if the clock had struck midnight, guttering candles and spoiling food. Roger stayed until the wine was gone. After he left Ian confided that he had already read *Creaturely Travels* and found it offensive, which naturally enough piqued my curiosity.

Of course I'd lied when I told Roger that I'd already bought the thing. In fact it was quite hard to find. In the end I had to order it, and the book arrived with the front cover bent back. It wasn't exactly a love story, as I had imagined, but a sort of abject, pornographic descent. I'm not sure "offensive" is the right word. I guess it depends on what you're used to reading.

About a year later Roger managed to publish another book. I hadn't seen him since the dinner party. And this time he did get reviewed in Melbourne, a terrible review that dwelt upon the obscene nature of the subject matter and the depravity of a narrator who descends into a squalid underworld in the conviction that it represents the only freedom left to him. Misogyny, inanity, ambition gone rotten. It was hard to imagine a more mortifying write up. Usually you could expect that kind of press to sell the book, but this was calibrated to sink the thing in one go. "Tedious piss-a-bed writing," it said. "Artless mental masturbation." It occurred to me that Roger might have to kill himself, if only to lend his own story the dignity of a truly miserable end.

My own work was progressing slowly. My second book had vanished as thoroughly as my first. Correspondence with Sophie Cousins had slowed to a trickle and then dropped off altogether. To tell the truth I had grown tired of the self-deprecating nature of the whole thing. My time was drying up as well. Sara and I were diligently saving for a house, but the market was next to impossible. My weekends were spent driving to inspections and auctions in increasingly remote suburbs, and having tedious conversations with bullish real estate agents, men who dressed like undertakers and spoke as if they were chewing gravel. One for your portfolio. Café society. All the space of the 1950s in a suburban classic.

It was in the grip of this malaise that I bumped into Roger again. I was crossing Flinders Lane going towards Degraves Street, a part of the city in which the last embers of literary ambition could still glow in the ambience of huddled shopfronts and flagstones. Roger was coming out of a café, a newspaper under his arm. He looked at me. I waved, but he seemed to be staring past me, or through me. Then he turned on his heel, looked at his watch, and moved quickly in the opposite direction. The narrow street was crowded, and passage through it was obstructed by scaffolding at its far end. For a second I thought about following him, but I stopped on the pavement, and soon lost sight of him in the congestion.

A moment later, there he was again, bobbing buoyantly out of the throng, his eyes firmly fixed on me.

"Thomas," he said, thrusting out his hand. "I thought it was you."

He dragged me into Degraves Café, as if we were old friends, and insisted on buying me a coffee. We sat at the window and stared out onto the narrow street.

"Screw the coffee," he said. "It's nearly dark, let's get a drink."

So we had a couple of vodkas each, then a smoke on the pavement, and finally walked a block or two to a Vietnamese joint on Swanston Street, where we ended up wallowing in spilt beer and fish sauce. Roger's news was that he had finished translating his first novel into French and was heading to Europe in the hope of finding a publisher. He said he was fed up with the puritanical, middlebrow world of Australian publishing. He dished dirt on virtually everyone. "Oh Brisbane. Oh Baudelaire," he said at one point, a vague sort of disgust in his voice. "Oh Melbourne. Oh Mirbeau." The hint of a smile crept over his face. Improbably, I knew exactly what he was talking about. What were the chances? It was like having poison poured into my ear. Places and people, real and imagined. Phantoms making their way across hemispheres and centuries.

"Publish a book here, and no one gives a rat's arse," Roger said. "We're beggars in the world republic of letters. Excreta. It's like the third fucking world."

When he asked me how my next novel was coming along, I tensed up. The summary I gave sounded trite, and by the time I had finished the whole thing was in tatters.

Roger looked amused, and already seemed to radiate the smirking superiority of the metropole, confident that I would never be able to follow him over the threshold.

I could feel something hardening in me, or something going dead. I had the ugly sensation of looking at myself from the street. Fluorescent lighting and chipped Formica. A stolid, thirty-something body hunching over the ruins of a meal and the threads of a faltering conversation.

We parted outside the restaurant. The street had a dry, flinty ambience. Crowds of city stragglers. Neon and plastic. Detritus crushed into the pavement like fragments of fossilized life. Roger seemed suddenly distracted. We shook hands—we always shook hands—and he hurried away as if the world were full of people he'd rather be talking to. I pushed off towards the river, springs wound tight. Half an hour later I was wandering the streets off Kings Way. Glowing cupids and cash machines. Caverns of cadaverous, bloodstained light. A Thai girl in a diaphanous blue dress. A shitty little room with sagging acoustic tiles, mouthwash and lubricant on the nightstand.

After that the city started to drive me mad. It was as if I had closed my eyes and opened them again to find that every mundane detail was tinged with shame, secrecy, and an intangible sense of dread. Nothing was quite itself. Everything had the strange illegibility of a hieroglyph: cars backed-up in the hot morning sun, schoolgirls talking into mobile phones, Sudanese kids wandering out of the housing commission flats, shadows stretching over blistered bitumen, ripples of light in the water.

I never saw Roger again, though I heard by happenstance that the bastard was living in the rue des Abbesses, which struck me as improbable. And apparently he'd written something online that had been printed out and passed around during the riots that broke out after two North African kids were killed fleeing French police. I couldn't verify the story. It sounded less probable than his address. But then I wasn't one to talk. After my relationship with Sara gave in to the various stresses besetting it, I decided to bury myself in a place where I'd be able to write and live inexpensively. I ended up in Puebla, Mexico, where I'd landed a job at the Universidad Autonomia teaching English. The place was dirt-cheap and I was convinced that no one would find me there. That was before I realized that no one was looking. I was working haphazardly on a futuristic novel about a ruined, waterless Melbourne, a stony Fatehpur Sikri sucking up the filthy dregs of a dying river. In the first scene, a bloke wearing a suit is standing on a city street nursing a tombstone in his arms. It occurs to him that the tombstone is as light as a bouquet of flowers. In the last, the same guy is on a boat looking back at the city. The buildings lining the bay, all bathed in a weird, sub-aquatic glow, look as if they are made out of obsidian. What was going to happen in-between was still a mystery to me. I had an elaborate pictorial representation, a mess of lines and arrows linking places and people, real and imagined, but the words, as yet, refused to come.

GERALD MURNANE

Gerald Murnane was born in 1939 in Coburg, a suburb of Melbourne in the Australian state of Victoria, which he has seldom left. His fiction, however, is full of a range of landscapes, both inner and outer. He has written of Paraguay, Romania, various regions of the U.S., and, perhaps most significantly, Hungary. He learned Hungarian in his fifties, has translated Hungarian writers such as Gyula Illyes and Attila Joszef, and regards Hungarian as an almost sacred tongue. One of the most significant honors he has received was being invited to a dinner in Melbourne commemorating the fiftieth anniversary of the suppressed Hungarian rebellion of 1956. Murnane's obsession with horse-racing is reflected in his book *Tamarisk Row* (1974), and his early training for the Roman Catholic priesthood comes to the fore in *A Lifetime On Clouds* (1976), which has been compared to the early work of James Joyce and Philip Roth. His characteristic fictional mode reached fruition in *The Plains* (1982). In *Landscape and Landscape* (1985) and *Inland* (1988), Murnane refined the metafictive style of *The Plains* into a deeply personal imaginative terrain. He showed he was not just an cerebral writer but a profoundly emotional one. *Velvet Waters* (1990) displayed Murnane's talents as an experimental short-story writer. *Emerald Blue* (1995) was thought to be his last work of fiction; however, Murnane has entered a new period of productivity, heralded by the appearance of his collection of essays, *Invisible Yet Enduring Lilacs,* in 2005, and by his forthcoming novel *Barley Patch*. Murnane won the Patrick White Award in 1999 and is the winner of a special citation in the New South Wales Premier's Awards in 2007. Celebrated by small but intense coteries of admirers in Australia, the U.S., Canada, and Sweden, his fiction is slowly gaining recognition as one of the most remarkable bodies of work Australia has produced.

From *Barley Patch*

Must I Write?

A few weeks before the conception of the male child who would become partly responsible, thirty-five years later, for my own conception, a young man aged nineteen years and named Franz Xaver Kappus sent some of his unpublished poems and a covering letter to Rainer Maria Rilke, who was by then a much-published writer although he was only twenty-eight years of age.

Kappus, of course, wanted Rilke to comment on the poems and to advise him as to who might publish them. In an answering letter Rilke made some general comments, not especially favorable, and declined to discuss the matter of publication. However, Rilke did not fail to advise the young man:

> Nobody can counsel and help you, nobody. There is only one single way. Search for the reason that bids you write . . . acknowledge to yourself whether you would have to die if it were denied you to write. This above all—ask yourself in the stillest hour of your night: *must* I write?

I first read the above passage in June 1985, soon after I had bought a secondhand copy of Rilke's *Letters To A Young Poet,* translated by M. D. Herter

Norton and published in New York City by W. W. Norton & Company. When I first read the passage, I typed it onto a clean page and then put the page into one of the folders of notes that I used for my classes in the unit that was called Advanced Fiction Writing. Once each year thereafter, I read to the students of that unit the advice of Rilke to the young poet. I then urged the students to question themselves from time to time as Rilke would have had them do. I then said it would be no bad thing if several at least of the persons present were to decide at some time in the future, in the stillest hour of their night, that they need no longer write.

I never afterwards heard that any former student of mine had suddenly decided to write no more or that he or she ever put into practice or even remembered Rilke's stern advice. In the early autumn of 1991, however, four years before I ceased to be a teacher of fiction-writing, and on a bustling afternoon rather than during a still night, and without even putting to myself Rilke's recommended question, I myself gave up writing fiction.

Why had I written?

When I stopped writing, I could have said that I had been writing seriously for more than thirty years. Some of what I had written had been published, but most of it had been stored as manuscripts or typescripts in my filing cabinets and will be there still when I die.

My pieces of published writing were called by publishers and by almost all readers either *novels* or *short stories,* but to have them thus called began in time to make me feel uncomfortable, and I took to using only the word *fiction* as the name for what I wrote. When I stopped writing at last, I had not for many years used the terms *novel* or *short story* in connection with my writing. Several other words I likewise avoided: *create, creative, imagine, imaginary,* and, above all, *imagination.* Long before I stopped writing, I had come to understand that I had never created any character or imagined any plot. My preferred way of summing up my deficiencies was to say simply that I had no imagination.

I was seldom embarrassed to have to admit this. The word *imagination* seemed to me connected with antiquated systems of psychology: with drawings of the human brain in which each swelling was named for the faculty residing there. Even when I looked into some or another novel by a contemporary author much praised for his or her imagination, I was far from being envious: a powerful imagination, it seemed, was no preventative against faulty writing.

For many years I wrote, as I thought, instinctively. I most certainly did not write with ease: I labored over every sentence and sometimes rewrote one or another passage many times. However, what might be called my subject matter came readily to me and offered itself to be written about. What I called the contents of my mind seemed to me more than enough for a lifetime of writing. Never while I wrote did I feel a need for whatever it was that might have been mine if only I had possessed an imagination.

I was never merely a writer of course; I had been a reader since long before I became a writer of what I called fiction. Many writers of novels or short stories have claimed to be, in their own words, voracious or insatiable readers. I would describe myself as an occasional or selective reader. As a child, I spent more time on devising what might be called imaginary landscapes than I spent on reading. Of course, many of the details of those landscapes owed their existence to my having read certain passages in certain books. As a child, I seldom read what were called children's books, partly because I hardly ever saw such books and partly because I was capable of reading adults' books from an early age. My parents always had on hand several books borrowed from what was called during my youth a circulating library. As well, they bought each month two magazines filled with short stories. One magazine was *Argosy*, which came, I think, from England. The other was *The Australian Journal*, which included not only short stories but part of a published novel. The rule in our household was that my mother would first read each of those magazines so that she could tell me which stories, if any, in each issue were not suitable for me. I would then be allowed access to each issue, provided that I undertook not to read the stories deemed unsuitable. These, of course, I always read first, hoping to learn from them some or another secret from the world of adults. I learned from this furtive reading of mine only that my mother did not want me to read descriptions of what might be called prolonged, passionate embraces and that she did not want me to know that young women sometimes became pregnant even though they were not married.

A person who claims to remember having read one or another book is seldom able to quote from memory even one sentence from the text. What the person probably remembers is part of the experience of having read the book: part of what happened in his or her mind during the hours while the book was being read. I can still remember, nearly sixty years later, some of what I read as a child, which is to say that I can still call to mind some of the images that occurred to me while I read as a child. As well, I claim that I can still feel something of what I felt while those images were in my mind.

I wonder whether I should be surprised that I can still recall the influence on me of certain pieces of popular fiction that I read in the 1950s, whereas I recall hardly anything from the hundreds of hours when I was studying the books prescribed for each of the three years of the major study in English that was a part of my bachelor's degree in the late 1960s. During the years from about 1970 to about 1990, I read about a thousand books, mostly of a sort that could be called literature. When I last looked through the pages of the ledger where the titles and the authors of those thousand books are recorded, I learned that twenty or so of the thousand had left on me some sort of lasting impression. A few moments ago I was able to scribble in quick succession, in the margin of the page where I wrote by hand the early drafts of each sentence on *this* page, the titles and authors of nine of the twenty or so books mentioned in the previous sentence. And just now, while I was typing the previous sentence, I remembered a tenth title and author. The date when I decided not to go on reading one after another book of a sort that could be called literature—that date was only a few months before the date when I decided to write no more fiction. When I made the earlier decision, I intended to confine my reading in future to the few books that I had never forgotten; I would re-read those books—I would dwell on them for the rest of my life. But after my decision to write no more fiction, I foresaw myself reading not even my few unforgotten books. Instead of reading what could be called literature and instead of writing what I called fiction, I would devise a more satisfying enterprise than either reading or writing. During the rest of my life I would concern myself only with those mental entities that had come to me almost stealthily while I read or while I wrote but had never afterwards detached themselves from me. I would contemplate those images and yield to those feelings that comprised the lasting essence of all my reading and my writing. During the rest of my life, I would go on reading from a vast book with no pages, or I would write intricate sentences made up of something other than words.

Before I began to write the first of the two preceding paragraphs, I was about to report that a few images had come to my mind while I was writing the last two sentences of the paragraph preceding that paragraph. The first of the few was an image of two green paddocks and part of a homestead shaded by trees that first appeared in my mind in 1950, while I was reading the first story I read of the series of short stories published in *The Australian Journal* about a fictional farm named Drover's Road, or it may have been Drovers' Road. The author was, I think, a woman, but I have long since forgotten her name. The same few chief characters took part in each story; they were members of the latest of the several generations of the family that had lived at the farm, whichever name it had. I have forgotten the names of the chief characters, both male and female, but I felt just now something of what I felt towards a certain female character whenever I read about her: I wanted no sadness or anxiety to be visited on her; I wanted the course of her life to be untroubled. The character in question was young and unmarried, and I wanted her to remain so for as long as I went on reading about her.

While I was typing the first few sentences of the previous paragraph, I was unable to recall any details of the images of persons and faces that I had had in mind while I read as a child the series of short stories referred to. At some time while I was typing the last two sentences of the previous paragraph, I found that I had given, so to speak, to the female character mentioned the image of a face that I first saw during the early 1990s when I looked into a book I had recently bought on the subject of horse-racing in New Zealand. (I recall no reference to horse-racing in any of the short stories in which the young female was a character, but after I had given, so to speak, a face to the character, I recalled that the place called Drover's or Drovers' Road was reported as being in a fictional New Zealand; and as soon as I had recalled this, I saw in the background of my mind, far behind the image mentioned earlier of the two green paddocks and part of a homestead shaded by trees, an image of snow-covered mountains almost certainly derived from a photograph in the book mentioned in the previous sentence—a photograph of part of a so-called stud property where valuable racehorses were kept for breeding).

Not far away (according to the scale of distance that applies in my mind)—not far away from the two green paddocks and part of a homestead is an image of a two-story building intended to be an English farmhouse several centuries old. I have always assumed that this house is surrounded by green paddocks or fields, as they might be called, but only one such green expanse has been of interest to me. It reaches from the vicinity of the house to a steep hill in the middle distance. Near the summit of the hill is a grove or a clump of trees. In the book of fiction that first caused me to see this hill in my mind, the original hill is called *Tanbitches*. Somewhere in the book is the explanation that the name of the hill is a variation of the phrase *ten beeches*, the trees near the summit being beech trees.

Sometimes I seem to recall that the variation was explained as being merely the sort of change that happens over time to an often-used phrase. At other times, I seem to recall that *Tanbitches* was said to be a remnant of the dialect formerly widespread in that part of England. Regardless of which explanation I seem to recall, I always feel again a semblance of the unease that I felt whenever I saw in my mind, as a child-reader, an image of the hill with the trees on it and heard in my mind at the same time the quaint-sounding name of the place.

I should have felt not unease but pleasure. I should have been pleased that I could refer to a prominent place in my mind by using what was more a codeword than an obvious name. I was already aware as a child that the landscapes or the human faces or the melodies or the panels of colored glass in doors or windows or the set of racing-colors or the aviaries of birds or the narratives or descriptive passages in books or magazines—that the origins of the seeming-persons and seeming-places lodged in my mind had each a certain quality that first took my notice and afterwards compelled me to memorize the item affecting me. I am no more able now than I was as a child to apply a name to the quality mentioned in the previous sentence. I have sometimes supposed that I could only find an apt word for the quality if I could devise one or more terms as yet unknown but suitable for inclusion in the English language. (At other times, I have supposed that every item in my mind is a term in a language that has not yet been translated into English.) I should have been pleased to be able to hear in my mind the word *Tanbitches* whenever I saw in my mind a green field sloping upwards towards a hill with a clump of trees near the top, but the word made me uneasy, and I believe today that my unease caused me for the first time as a child-reader to think of a story, as I would have called it, as having been made up, as I would have said, by an author.

I seem to recall that I was disappointed by the similarity between the plain English of the phrase *ten beeches* and the would-be quaintness of the word *Tanbitches,* however its origin might have been explained by the text: that I wished the hill—if it could not have a plain English name—might have been known by a word so outlandish that not even the author could explain its occurrence. I may not be exaggerating if I claim to recall that I preferred the hill in my mind to remain nameless rather than to bear the name assigned to it by the author.

The author in question was named Josephine Tey. The book was *Brat Farrar,* which was published in monthly installments in *The Australian Journal* in either 1950 or 1951. At the age when I read every piece of fiction in every issue of the *Journal,* I was not at all interested in authors, and yet I recall myself speculating sometimes about Josephine Tey, or, rather, about the ghostly female presence of the same name that I was sometimes aware of while I read *Brat Farrar.* I would not have enjoyed speculating thus. I would much rather have read the text of *Brat Farrar* in the same way that I read other works of fiction: hardly aware of words or sentences; interested only in the unfolding scenery that appeared to me while my eyes moved past line after line on the page. But the word *Tanbitches* would cause me to stop and sometimes even to suppose that Josephine Tey had erred: she had failed to learn the true name of the hill and so she had given it a name of her own choosing—*Tanbitches* was only a word that an author had imagined.

I had another cause for thinking sometimes about the personage named Josephine Tey when I would rather have been admiring the image of the two-story house or the image of the green field rising to the wooded hill, or when I would rather have been feeling towards the images of persons who seemed to live in that scenery as though I lived among them. I seem to remember that *Brat Farrar* was called a mystery novel and that the plot turned on the return to the family home of a young man claiming to be the long-lost heir to the estate. The claimant, so to call him, was invited to live in the family home although none of the people already living there was yet entirely sure of the truth of his claim. I recall three of these people. One was the claimant's brother, who may have been named Simon and who may have been a twin; another was the claimant's sister, or perhaps half-sister; the third person was an older woman known always as Aunt Bee. The three siblings, if such they were, had no parents that I can recall. Aunt Bee was the oldest of the chief characters and by far the most powerful of those who lived in the two-story house. Whether or not she was their aunt, she seemed to have authority over the three purported siblings. The young woman especially confided in Aunt Bee, consulted her often and almost always followed her advice.

For as long as I had the text of *Brat Farrar* in front of my eyes, and often at other times, I did as I was compelled to do whenever I was reading much of what I read during the 1950s or whenever I was remembering the experience of having read it. I felt as though I myself moved among the character.
I was unable to alter the course of the narrative; anything reported in the text was a fact that I had to accept. However, I was in my way free to alter or to modify the course of events. The text of a work of fiction, as I seem to have understood from the first, reports in detail certain events from certain hours in the lives of the characters but leaves unreported whole days, months, years even. A narrative would often include, of course, a summary of a lengthy period of time, but a mere summary hardly restricted my freedom.

I was free, first of all, to observe and admire. I could watch openly while my favorite female character rode on horseback to the far side of some land-scape described in the text and even further, or while she fondled or fed her pet animals or birds, or even while she sat reading some work of fiction and perhaps feeling as though she herself moved among the characters. I was free also to influence the life of my favorite female character, but within strict limits. In 1953, for example, while reading *Hereward the Wake* by Charles Kingsley, I was distressed by Hereward's abandoning his wife, Torfrida, for another woman. From my standpoint as a shadowy presence among the char-acters, I knew I could never reverse Hereward's decision. And yet, I was able in some mysterious way to add to whatever remorse he might have felt from time to time; I became, perhaps, one more of the lesser characters whose disapproval conveyed itself to Hereward. More to my satisfaction, I was able to convey—wordlessly, or so it seemed to me—my sympathy to the cast-off Torfrida and even to suppose that this was of help to her.

In my life as the ghost, so to speak, of a fictional character—as the creation of a reader rather than a writer—I could say or do no more than my creator was able to have me say or do, and my creator was a child. He was a most precocious child in some ways: in his reading of adult books, for example, and in his intense curiosity about adult sexuality, so to call it. In other ways, he was an ignorant child. When he sent a version of himself into the scenery that included the hill with the trees on it and the two-story house, he wanted no more than to have that version fall in love with one of the female charac-ters and she with him. And although he could have said that he himself had already fallen in love with many women in what he would have called the real world, he knew about girls' or young women's falling in love only what he had read about them in fiction.

A reader of *this* work of fiction may be wondering why I had to insinuate a version of myself into the scenery of so many novels or short stories when I might have chosen from the male characters in each work a young man or a boy and might afterwards have felt as though I shared in his fictional life. My answer to that reader is the simple statement that I had never met up with any young male character with whom I could feel the sympathy needed for such a sharing. And the most common reason for my failing to sympathize with young male characters was that I could not comprehend, let alone agree with, the policy of these characters towards young female characters.

Sometimes I tried to live in my mind the life of one or another male character of fiction. I believe I tried, while I read the first of the monthly installments of *Brat Farrar,* to take part, as it were, in the fictional life of the young man who had arrived at the two-story house claiming to be the long-lost son. If I did so try, then I might well have persisted for longer than I usually persisted. I recall that I suspected from the first that the claimant was an imposter and, therefore, no kin of the young woman. This would have left me free to fall in love with the young woman, who had attracted me as soon as I had begun to read about her. At the same time, my representing myself as her brother or half-brother would have obliged me to disguise my true feeling for the time being—or, if my claim was accepted, perhaps indefinitely. Far from being a hindrance or a hardship, this would have been much to my liking; for me, the process of falling in love needed much secrecy and concealment and pretense. To fall in love with a young woman who had to allow for the possibility that I was her brother or half-brother—such an event would have allowed me to set going all that I considered necessary and appropriate during a courtship: the young man's confiding in the young woman day after day for month after month, if necessary, until she had learned every detail of his life-story, of his daydreams, and of what he might have called his ideal female companion, and until she had come to understand that he was different indeed from the many coarse-minded suitors that she would have read about in fiction who could hardly wait before they tried to kiss and embrace their girl-friends; the young woman's responding to the young man's confidences by reporting in equal detail her own history, especially those periods of her life when she believed herself to be in love with one or another boy or young man; finally, the young woman's falling into the habit of asking the young man, whenever he took his leave of her, where he was likely to be and what he was likely to do during his absence, thereby allowing the young man to suppose that the young woman daydreamed often about him while he and she were apart, so that he did not deceive himself whenever he seemed to feel her presence about him while he was alone, and to suppose further that she was waiting for him to declare his love for her.

Before I began to write the first of the six previous paragraphs, I had intended to report more of what I recalled about my feelings towards the character of Aunt Bee, as she existed in my mind, and more about a further reason that I had for thinking sometimes about the personage known as Josephine Tey when I would have preferred simply to look at the unfolding scenery that appeared to me while I read. I had intended to report that I was jealous of the influence that Aunt Bee had over the young female character that I looked forward to courting in my mind. If the young female had a fault in my eyes, it was her unquestioning admiration of Aunt Bee.

I sensed that Aunt Bee disapproved of my interest in the young female character and that she contrived to keep me from being alone with her. Even though I conducted myself towards the young woman with unfailing seemliness, as though I truly was her brother or her half-brother, still Aunt Bee seemed to suspect me of wanting to make advances to the young woman if only it could be arranged for the two of us to be alone together. Of course I wanted to be alone with the young woman, but for the time being I planned only to have long, serious conversations with her during our meetings.

The publication in serial form of the whole novel surely took at least six months, during which time I would have seen myself often in my mind as a version of the character of the claimant, and even more often as a version of myself inserted, so to speak, into the scenery of the novel. During the two weeks while I was writing the previous two thousand words of this text, I recalled a number of my experiences as a child-reader of the text of *Brat Farrar*, but not once did I recall any scene in which any version of myself was alone with the young female character. I attribute this to the influence of Aunt Bee. Not only did the young female character consult the older woman at every turn, but I believe that I, whether as reader, seeming character, or intruder-into-the-text, was rather afraid of Aunt Bee.

If only I had been able, in spite of Aunt Bee, to spend some time alone with the young woman and had prepared beforehand not just the substance of what I was going to tell her about myself, but also the scenery in which

I was going to explain myself. I have little doubt that Josephine Tey would have described in detail more than one view of the countryside visible from that two-story house, but all I recall today is the distant hill with the clump of trees and the name that I could not accept. The scenery mentioned two sentences ago was of my own making. As soon as I had understood that the two-story house stood among green English countryside, I would have felt free to arrange throughout that countryside my own preferred distant views or hidden nooks. And so, I recall more than fifty years later that I hoped often to sit with the young woman in an upper-story room that had been fitted out as a parlor and the windows of which overlooked a distant moor or fen. I cared nothing for what might be called geographical veracity; I wanted to have the young woman see in the distance the sort of place where she and I might have strolled together as innocent friends if only we had known each other during childhood, or the place where we had, in fact, strolled if I was, in fact, her brother or half-brother. Five or six years before I first read *Wuthering Heights,* I had decided that a moor was an eminently suitable place for a male and a female child to be alone together and to talk together until the image of each became in the other's mind the utterly trustworthy companion that he and she had always longed for. As for the fen, I thought of it as no more than a shallow swamp that two children might have walked around in complete safety. I believe I might even have decreed—I, the willful reader—that the inexpertly named hill with the coppice near its summit was the source of a tiny stream that trickled downwards in rainy weather until it became, if the rain kept up, what the English call a brook, which I understood to be a watercourse shallow enough and narrow enough for a child to be able to wade across or even to jump across. Since my early childhood, I had been much afraid of large bodies of water or of fast-flowing, murky rivers and drains, but much interested in shallow ponds or swamps or small creeks that filled or flowed only during seasons of rain. Walking with my uncle across his dairy farm during many of my school holidays, I would have liked to inspect certain green places among clumps of rushes where the soil might have been still spongy and damp, but my uncle always reminded me that these places were infested by snakes. The equivalent indoors of my interest in shallow or trickling water was my longing to have access to an upper-story window. At the time when I was reading *Brat Farrar* I had never been inside a house of more than one story, although I had often daydreamed of watching unobserved from an upper window not only persons close by but also distant landscapes. At least five years before I read *Brat Farrar,* I had been taken for the first time to a house where one of my mother's older sisters lived with her husband and her four daughters in a clearing in the Heytesbury Forest in southwestern Victoria. My mother and my aunt, and even the four girls, my cousins, often amused themselves by recalling in my hearing that I had walked into one after another room during my first minutes in their house and had looked behind the door of each room. In reply to their questions at the time, I had said that I was looking for stairs. Their house was hardly more than a cottage, but something about the angle of the roof must have suggested to me as I approached that a few upper rooms or even a single attic might have looked out over more of the forest than I could have seen if I had stood among its nearer trees. I found no stairs, of course, but I found later on the back veranda something that caused me to forget my disappointment. My two oldest girl-cousins, one of them my age and the other a year older, were the owners of the first doll's house that I had seen anywhere but behind shop-windows. The house was of two storys, and seemed to be fitted out with items of tiny furniture. I could not inspect the house: its owners would not allow me or my younger brother to approach it. I tried to explain that I wanted only to look into the house and not to touch it, but the girl-owners were unmoved. My brother and my mother and I were to stay overnight. One of the girl's beds was moved from the tiny bedroom onto the back veranda so that my brother and I could sleep head-to-toe in it. I can only suppose that my mother slept in one of the girl's beds in their room and that two at least of the girls had to sleep head-to-toe, which might have explained in part why the older girls seemed to dislike their visiting cousins, especially me who begged to see into their doll's house or, failing that, to join in their games or their conversations. During the early evening, I felt sure that the owners of the doll's house would take it to their own room at any moment, but the doll's house was still on the back veranda when my brother and I were preparing for bed. I could not believe that the owners had forgotten it. I supposed either that their mother had forbidden them to take the thing into their crowded bedroom or, more likely, that they, the girl-owners, had left it on the veranda in order to entrap me; they knew I was anxious to inspect the house and, probably, to handle some of the items in it; they knew also the rightful position of every bed and pillow and chair; in the morning they would find proof that I had handled certain things; they would convey this proof to their mother and even, perhaps, to my own mother. Having foreseen these possibilities, I became cautious. I forced myself to stay awake until half an hour after I had heard the owners of the doll's house going to their room for the night. Then I slipped out of bed and knelt beside the doll's house and tried to look in through an upper window. A certain amount of moonlight already lit up the back veranda, but while I knelt and peered my head kept the upper story in darkness. I hesitated but then dared to slide the whole doll's house far out onto the veranda, hoping that nothing inside had been moved from its rightful position. Then, while the faint moonlight shone through the windows on one side of the upper story, I stared in through the windows on the other side. I thought that my doing so might reveal to me some secret that my girl-cousins had been keeping from me—perhaps on some bed in an upper room lay a tiny doll with only a thin night-dress covering her female parts. In the event, I had seen in the upper rooms only neat furniture. No doll that my cousins owned was small enough or dainty enough to belong in the house. It was not only I who had no right to poke my fingers through the windows; I began to think of my cousins as hardly worthy to own the house, which I had stopped thinking of as a mere residence for dolls.

Three or four years after my visit to the house in the clearing in the Heytesbury Forest, I first read in a comic book belonging to a boy-cousin of mine, about a character named Doll Man. Some or another unremarkable citizen of a vaguely American city was able, when the need arose, to compress the molecules of his body and to become a doll-sized man. On the night when I had looked into the doll's house, I fell asleep as though my own molecules had somehow been compressed so that I was able to lie comfortably in my chosen bed in an upper-story room overlooking a clearing in the Heytesbury Forest and to hear already in my mind the shrieks of the giant female personages who would look in on me next morning through the window.

I reported at the end of the second paragraph before the previous paragraph that I was often afraid of the character known as Aunt Bee in the work of fiction *Brat Farrar*. I reported even earlier that I sometimes resented the influence that Aunt Bee was allowed to exert over one at least of the other characters in the work. While I was reporting those matters, I seemed to recall from more than fifty years ago my having once or twice doubted whether the one character in a work of fiction should be allowed to possess so many qualities deemed admirable by the narrator as Aunt Bee was allowed to possess in *Brat Farrar*. Of course, terms such as *narrator* and even *character* were unknown to me at the time. I simply observed what happened in my mind while I read. And although I was afraid of Aunt Bee, I must sometimes have been aware that the cause of her appearing as she did in my mind was no more than that a personage known to me only as *Josephine Tey* had chosen that she, Aunt Bee, should appear thus.

I would like to be able to report here that I once, even once, supposed that Josephine Tey, whoever she might have been, ought to have written differently about Aunt Bee. I suspect that I had already accepted, more than fifty years ago, that a writer could not be compelled to deal fairly with his or her characters; not to mention readers.

OUYANG YU

Ouyang Yu graduated from La Trobe University with a doctoral degree in Australian literature and has had thirty-seven Chinese and English books of fiction, poetry, literary translation, and literary criticism published since his arrival in Australia in 1991. His first English novel, *The Eastern Slope Chronicle* (2002), was shortlisted for the 2003 NSW Premier's Awards and won the Festival Award for Innovation in Writing at the 2004 Adelaide Bank Festival of Arts. His his sixth book of English poetry, *New and Selected Poems,* was published by Salt Publishing in London in 2004, and his eighth book of English poetry, *The Kingsbury Tales: a Novel,* is forthcoming with Brandl & Schlesinger. His fifth book of Chinese poetry, *Er du piao liu* (Second Drifting) was published in Beijing in late 2005. His fourteenth book of translation, in Chinese, of Robert McCrum et al's *The Story of English,* was published in 2005 by Baihua Publishing House in China; other published translations in Chinese include *The Whole Woman* by Germaine Greer (2002, Baihua Publishing House, China) and *The Shock of the New* by Robert Hughes (2003, Baihua Publishing House, China). Ouyang Yu's first book of creative nonfiction, *On the Smell of an Oily Rag: Speaking English, Thinking Chinese and Living Australian,* is forthcoming in late 2007 from Wakefield Press, and his second novel, *Loose: A Wild History,* is forthcoming in the U.K. from Bluechrome Publishing. He is professor of Australian literature and director of Australian Studies Center in the English Department, School of Foreign Languages and Literature, Wuhan University, China, as well as visiting professor at the Institute of Comparative Literature and Comparative Culture, Nanjing University, China. For more information, please visit www.ouyangyu.com.au.

From *The English Class*

Living under English

1.

"My name is Ma Tian. I come from Taiyuan. Let me explain my name first. You may think I am horse in a field, Ma for horse and Tian for field, but my middle-school classmates used to call me Horse Sweet because Tian sounds exactly like Tian for sweet. When I turned it the other way round like a foreign word, to make me Tian Ma, they started calling me Sweet Horse until one day someone mispronounced it Swift Horse. I grabbed the opportunity and started calling myself Swift Marr. Now that's how I got this name and please call me Swift Marr or more simply Tian Ma, a heavenly horse, whichever way you prefer it. In any event, I would like to thank you all for giving me this opportunity to be with you and, in particular, I'd like to thank Mr. Fu for thinking of such an ingenious way of practicing oral English."

"I come from Harbin in Heilongjiang Province. I'm Zhenya. Have you been to Harbin? If not, come to my place one day. It's really beautiful. Very Russian, I must say. In winter, ice everywhere and there is an annual winter ice festival.

In summer, the Pine Flower River is a pretty sight to see. I don't know what else I can say because of my limited English but I want to learn from all of you."

"I'm Jing. I'm from White Sand but I'm not a local. As a matter of fact, I come from a small town not far from this city. I drove my truck a few days ago to this university with all my belongings, a box of clothes, a bag of books, and a friend from the same team. He drove my truck back to the factory. I think my aim in learning English is simple. I want to catch up. I have lost so many years mucking around, altogether ten years, some in the countryside and some in the factory that I just mentioned. In the meantime, I felt I have grown doubly old. I envy some of you who come fresh from the middle school, having lost no time in your learning process, straight from middle school to university. I've said what I wanted to say. Thank you. Before I go, can I say something about my friend's name Tian Ma? With your permission, I remember a poem by the Persian poet Omar something whose surname I've forgotten but he said in a poem:

> How time is slipping underneath our Feet:
> Unborn Tomorrow and dead Yesterday
> Why fret about Them if Today be sweet!

"For this reason I think being sweet is actually very good. I am finished with my presentation now."

Designed to improve the students' spoken English, the morning presentation continued as Mr. Fu had planned. In this classroom, with walls newly white-washed, a smiling Mao's portrait on the front wall, a poster bearing Lenin's remark "Study, Study and More Study" on one side wall, and another slogan on the facing side wall, bearing Mao's famous remark, "Keep a daily upward learning curve!" which Mr. Fu himself had translated from Mao's virtually untranslatable, "haohao xuexi, tiantian xiangshang," Fu was in his element. Watching how one student after another went to the podium in front of the blackboard to please him with their performance, he made comments at the end of each presentation, three every morning. After a number of these, he had a pretty clear idea who was good at what, and what level of English each of them had reached, which seemed consistent with the examination results he had gone through before he hand-picked his students. Experience told him that it was hard to predict what each one of the students would become, career-wise, in the future, as the potential of each individual was great and varied. "The only thing you know is that you don't know anything," he reminded himself. He had already forgotten where he had come across this remark and who had made it. In particular, he liked the looks of some of the girls in his class—Zhenya, for example. Her full name was actually Alexander Sergevic Zhenya, possibly born of mixed White Russian and Chinese parentage, although she looked more Chinese than Russian, with a large round moon face and small round eyes, extremely white skin, a little tired perhaps because of the over-long train journey, over forty-eight hours. He remembered that after her presentation he made a comment to the effect that she should try to improve her English by eliminating her Northern accent. Her face immediately blushed a deep red, which made him feel a little sorry for having been so forthright. He was most impressed with Tian Ma, the heavenly horse: he excelled in spoken English and had earned more than 90% on his English examination. From Ma's file, he understood that his father was a Professor of English at a university in Shanxi. The connection was unmistakable. You couldn't expect someone from a working class background to achieve that score, could you? Take Jing. He wasn't sure about Jing, although he'd had an interview with him and after a long deliberation decided to accept him. He didn't know why, but had made the decision on instinct. Something told him that this was no ordinary person. Jing's results in English were average, and he seemed pretty average across the board—except when it came to poetry. Was it sympathy that moved you to accept him? Fu dismissed the suggestion. Or does he remind you of your own humble background as a peasant boy? Well, that Fu couldn't deny it. Still, he trusted his instincts, his gut feelings. It was the whole person, the way he talked, the things he talked about, and the poetry that he managed to recite, that somehow impressed him. If there was anything else that impressed him, it was the guy's eyes, which seemed to have a penetrating effect on Fu that lasted a long time after Jing was gone. Otherwise, this was a pretty ordinary fellow, no different from any other factory worker in his overalls, even in his manner of speech. A couple of days ago, one student had reported to him that she heard Jing use dirty language on campus; she wondered if it was because he'd come from a factory background. Fu didn't tell Jing about this but he kept a close eye on him. He wanted to wait and see how he developed, along with his classmates.

Fu felt a little hot. He pushed open the window that faced the lake. A breeze came wafting in, carrying frog croakings, insect chirpings, and a whole raft of fragrances: lotus flowers and mountain flowers, mixed with some wild grasses that he could not name. The lake was shivering in semi-darkness, occasionally sending out a faint lapping sound. The hill stood black and still to the side, concealing half the sky from view. At the foot of the hill was a big pond overgrown with lotus leaves, reflecting a bunch of feeble stars scattered across its surface, wrinkled from time to time when there was a fish coming up for air. What a beautiful autumn, Fu sighed. To familiarize himself with the English class he was to teach, Fu took out a piece of paper with all the names of the students on it and took a last look at it before he went to bed:

Bao Hongjun
Cen Zhengyi
Dang Jie
Hu Chenggeng
Jing Ying
Liu Ya
Ma Tian
Wei Hua
Xin Shen
Yang Guizi
Yu Hu
Zhao Feiyan

Zou Ganmei

Alexandra Sergevic Zhenya

Some of the names made him wonder about his students' family back-grounds. Did Hongjun (Red Army) come from a family of old revolutionaries, and did Zhengyi (Justice) come from a family with a legal background? You could almost tell at what era the names had been given. Take Ganmei (Expel-ling the Americans), who must have been named in the early 1950s during the Korean War. Some names had an artistic twist, such as Yu Hu (Jade Kettle), which, by the sound of it, reminded one of a line from an ancient poem that ran, "yipian bingxin zai yuhu" (a piece of icy heart is in the jade kettle). Fu was trying to match the faces of his students with their names, but found it hard, aside from the few that he had already taken note of. His memory was failing him; he was dog-tired after four classes that morning and the long prepara-tion for the next day. He turned off the light and went into sleep with a sense of expectation.

.

You are now faced with a most serious problem, because of which you have not been able to write a single word for the last few days. You know that this whole English thing is for real—it happened some twenty years ago. You knew every one of the people involved, and to write about it would be as easy as turning your palm out. However, for obvious reasons, you can't do it, have to reinvent it, come up with different things, different people, different places—unless you wait and outlive them all. It's not hard to imagine a situa-tion whereby real people from real life come to you at the launch of the book and make claims about misrepresentations. But even if you change the whole thing, won't they still pick up the clues, see something of themselves in the story? Besides, student life at a university isn't particularly interesting. It gets repeated on a grand scale year in and year out, not only nationally but inter-nationally. Perhaps the only difference is that this university no longer exists.

What if you die when you finish writing this book? What if you die halfway through? As the rest of the world is having a holiday, you are sitting on the couch near the window, your iBook on your lap, your fingers on the keys, hitting them from time to time, trying to make connections to the past, a recent past that exists nowhere except in your own mind, your own memory or imagination, or both.

Technically, how are you going to structure the middle part of this novel around twenty or so people in an English class, a class that takes four years to finish? You could approach it the way Jing once did in a novel he wrote about the last year before he finished his university degree in English. It was called *On the Eve of Graduation,* and it was never published. Eventually, by the time Jing came to Australia, he had lost it. Perhaps this novel is about the moment, the lived moment that will pass, the moment that combines a moment lived in the past, retrieved from memory or simply imagined, moments combined and put together for no other purpose than being put together in a coherent or incoherent mess, like life itself, finally to be sorted out by an editor with an eye on the market, beyond the author's control.

Ultimately, read or unread, you are alone. So why not do your own thing and be happy about it?

TIM RICHARDS

Tim Richards was born in Kerang, Victoria, on June 3, 1960. His family moved to Hampton, the dreamy Melbourne suburb that features in his fiction, on the day John F. Kennedy was assassinated. Educated at Hampton High, Melbourne University, the Australian Film, Television and Radio School, and Deakin University (where he was Gerald Murnane's student), his first published fiction appeared in the U.K. periodical *Wisden Cricket Monthly* in December, 1979. After leaving film school in 1989, Richards wrote television sketch comedy as a staff writer on all eight series of *Fast Forward* and three series of *Full Frontal*. In 1997 and 1998, two cycles of surreal football stories, "Endgames," appeared in the *Melbourne Age*. Richards's autobiographical trilogy *Approximate Life* was published in three volumes by Allen & Unwin, and was comprised of *Letters to Francesca* (stories, 1996), *The Prince* (a novella, 1997), and *Duckness* (stories). This unusual trilogy has been hailed by critics from Australia, the U.S., and Sweden for its humor, irreverence, uninhibited originality, and perceptive insight into the ways we both lack and make meaning in the world today. Though vexed by publishers' current distaste for story collections, he continues to concentrate on that medium, and the bulk of his stories are best described as bizarre autobiographical fantasies, or "autobiographical expressionism." Some critics have described his fiction as cool, anxious, and cerebral, and the story included here may be seen as an early attempt to warm things. Script-editor on the feature *Looking for Alibrandi,* and current recipient of an Established Writers' grant from the Australia Council, Richards still lives in Hampton, and works as a script consultant, mainly for the New South Wales Film and Television Office.

Isnis

Travelers who don't know the Kust region or its history would be hopelessly confused by the signs where the Birzek and Kust highways intersect. Having followed an arrow indicating the road to Kust, the traveler finds himself making a long, winding descent into Hedut. For the people here, this misdirection is an endlessly funny joke, part of a six-hundred-year tradition. On the way to sack Kust, Mir Hamir's great army was confused by a sign at the same crossroad, their error leading them to be ambushed by Damu Sur, who had gathered his forces by the Hedut River. Heduts will tell you this story as if the ambush happened last month. "Don't forget, Mir Hamir's army made the same mistake. But for that, we'd still be under their yoke."

First heard, this historical awareness is impressive. But after meeting more Heduts, you realize that this knowledge is little more than folkloric cliché. They can tell you nothing about Mir Hamir's army, how it was assembled, or what its military objectives were. Nor do they know how a vast army coming from the hills could be ambushed by a force one third its size gathered on the river plains. Further enquiries will tell you that the Heduts don't really care, that this anecdote is a convenient rationalization of an indifference to geography and the needs of travelers. I had come forewarned, but if you were really headed for Kust, only to find yourself twenty kilometers down the wrong road, baked by the sun on the outskirts of Hedut, you might wish that Mir Hamir's army had been equal to its bloody task.

Nowadays, the river so frequently romanced in eighteenth-century Azark poetry is not much more than a trickle, and the cotton fields and textile manufacture that made Hedut's valley the jewel of the Kust region are practically extinct. Seeing the winds of change, my newly married grandparents and their siblings left just before the Gistul Dam was completed in 1949. Most made for Russia, some to Canada. My maternal grandparents had their hearts set on cool New Zealand, before settling in Melbourne in 1951.

The city Zoltan and Sesmina abandoned had a population of nearly one million. Even with recent Kurdish resettlements, there is now less than half that, unless you include the countless dogs left to roam Hedut's waste-littered streets. Having fought off one hound only to rush headlong into another angry beast, I might have become dog meat on my first day but for the intervention of an ageless, one-eyed man, Neshum, who then accompanied me to my hotel opposite the statue of the cunning, victorious Damu Sur.

"You speak Azark as my grandparents spoke it," he told me. "You never hear dialect spoken by young people."

I explained that I had been taught Azark in Melbourne by my mother's parents and their friends, and that this was my first visit to their homeland. Perhaps he could remember Zoltan Zulla, or his wife Sesmina, who was a Zhor before she married.

His toothless smile testament to a hard life, Neshum said that Zhor was the most common family name in Hedut. Several cousins were Zhors. But he knew nothing about my grandparents. Give or take a few months, he was the same age I was, twenty-seven.

.

Azarks are known for their love of vividly colored interiors, but lurid alternations of gold and red couldn't mask the fact that the Riverside Hotel's dining room had seen better days. Only half the lights worked, which was a blessing given the built-up grime on the red plastic tablecloths. With just six diners— all male—in the room, the waiter was determined to seat me with a dodgy pair who looked like they were plotting to bomb the regional administration. Telling him that I couldn't stand cigarette smoke, I was directed to an ill-lit table beside the kitchen.

The only Azark dish I've ever fancied is hezchuk. When made by Grandma, hezchuk was a thick, heavily spiced stew of rice, vegetables, and beef or chicken. Chunkier than risotto, hotter than paella, a heaped plate took a week to digest, even if you were a nervous kid with a fast metabolism. I still crave Grandma's hezchuk any time I go a month without.

"This is a pale imitation of the hezchuk they eat at home," she'd say.

Fifteen minutes after my order, the waiter returned with a tub of hezchuk, and begged me to stand my spoon upright in the center—a time-honored tradition. While the consistency couldn't be faulted, this was the blandest dish I'd ever eaten, and I could only suspect that the waiter misunderstood my request for a strongly spiced stew. Though edible, the meat was sinewy, most likely goat or camel. I could hardly fail to notice that fellow diners were watching my every mouthful.

Finally, the pair of men I'd avoided previously approached my table, and without waiting for an invitation, took the seats opposite.

"Good?"

"Yes, very," I lied.

The elder of the two bearded men then asked what brought me to Hedut.

That was a question I'd been trying to avoid. On several previous occasions, I'd given the answer, "Family business." I was researching my grandmother's paternal grandfather, who left Hedut during the middle of the nineteenth century to become chief adviser to the Sultan in Kust. I'd heard two different stories. The first had him beheaded for having a tryst with one of the Sultan's wives. Another said that he'd been executed under suspicion of being a Czarist spy.

"Why trouble the past? Be thankful you still have a head."

They'd obviously joined me to ensure that no portion of my huge hezchuk went uneaten. With each mouthful, they asked me to confirm that nowhere in the world could a humble man eat better.

By the time I returned to my small, dusty room, I knew I'd be shitting goat for a week. Maybe the men were right. There was no point in me being here.

Then, from the next room, I heard a woman's voice. For nearly an hour, she sang melodic songs with the most extraordinary delicacy, and I didn't know whether to enjoy this concert or resent it. In all the years I'd been forced to learn Azark, and expected to memorize the most inane phrases and poems, no one mentioned the unique beauty of Azark song.

Shortly after my neighbor fell silent, a savage dogfight started in the laneway below my second-floor window, but I can't say how long it lasted, having fallen to sleep imagining beasts who wanted nothing more than to rip into travelers who don't know their own minds.

.

My mother died suddenly while I was in Sydney failing to resurrect a two-year love affair with a dope-addled book illustrator. Mum was fifty-three years old, and though she'd worked fourteen-hour days all her adult life, she'd never had an illness worse than a cold. My father was so devastated he asked someone I barely knew to call me with the news.

Nearly two years later, lugging my pack down the potholed road into the faded city of Hedut, I could make no more sense of my mother's life or death than the doctor who wrote the certificate. She was meant to nurse my children, and their children. Now it would never happen.

I spoke the truth when I said that I'd been a bad son, that I'd never respected my mother the way I should have. Dad said that she'd never seen it that way, or wished me to be any different. In thirty years of living and working together, my parents hadn't exchanged a harsh word, or used sarcasm, yet he echoed Mum's closest friends when describing her as an unusual woman. She was an Azark to the nth degree.

Born in Melbourne to Azark parents, my mother managed to be more Azark than they were, though a brief honeymoon in Byron Bay would be the only time she ever left the state of Victoria. For thirty years, Mum and Dad worked hundred-hour weeks to make sure their Elwood milk bar remained the most prosperous small business in suburban Melbourne.

"If we weren't here, our regulars would go somewhere else." My mother behaved as if this was the certain outcome of violating an unwritten contract she and dad had entered with each customer. At the funeral, one said that Mum had memorized the bar-code on every item. Whenever I complained about the pointlessness of being so obsessive, she'd shrug and say, "That's how Heduts are."

"You're not Hedut. You're an Australian. Try to behave like one!"

I must have said this a thousand times. Mum gave me everything she had to give, and I repaid her with embarrassment. If it wasn't her awful Azark meals, or her choice of peasant clothes, it was her determination to see things opposite to how normal people see them. Her constant point of reference was a city in a river valley she only knew from stories her parents told her. We couldn't take things for granted the way Australians did. Heduts knew how quickly the wheel turned. One day, my great-great grandfather was the Sultan's trusted advisor, the next, kids were using his head for a football.

"We know something Skips don't," she'd tell me in the thickest Australian accent. "Australians don't know Isnis."

Isnis was something I never understood. Even now, I wouldn't claim to be on top of the concept. It's the sort of special understanding that only comes with having lived in one place for thousands of years. You wouldn't be far wrong if you described Isnis as a kind of ancestral ventriloquism.

"One day, you'll stand by the River Hedut, feel a cool breeze billow through the valley, and you'll know Isnis and its importance," she'd say with a confidence that came from never having visited the beach across the road, let alone a valley nine thousand miles away.

"We didn't force your mother to learn Azark," my grandmother told me after the funeral. "We wanted her to be Australian. It was her who begged us. She asked to hear the stories, and wanted to know how to tell them in our language. If she hadn't met your father when she did, she would have had us arrange a marriage to an Azark."

Though it's impossible to credit now, my father dropped out of law school to marry my mother and take over the running of his in-laws' milk bar. His dad repaired refrigerators, and he asked Bob to come along one Sunday to help haul away one of the big dairy cabinets. According to Grandpa, his boy took one look at Mira Zulla, her raven hair covered by a blue silk scarf, and that was it.

Looking at the faded color photographs of my parents as they were in the mid-1970s, I struggle to see what Dad saw. Mum had the same square jaw she inherited from her mother, and would bequeath to her own children. According to Dad, her eyes were a long journey worth taking. "There's no need to travel the world when a girl has eyes like that."

Whatever Dad's parents thought of this arrangement, they wouldn't stand in the way of love, or the trade-off that saw Mira Zulla convert to Christianity provided that her children were brought up to speak Azarki. Though my friends know me as Kev, I was "christened" Memim Harris. Named after her grandmother, my sister Sesmina would call herself Min right up to the time—the week of her thirteenth birthday—when she tripped while crossing the path of an oncoming train.

In her grief, my mother rediscovered Islamic ritual, and I, who thought that no true grief could differ from my own, ridiculed this retreat. Was there ever a time when I wasn't trying to hurt Mum's feelings, or blame her for my own failings?

"If Hedut's so great, why don't you go back there?"

"That's why we work hard. So you'll have the choice when you finish school."

"What would I want with a shit-heap five-thousand miles from nowhere ?"

Dad steered clear of these arguments, but if he heard me insult Mum, he'd pull out the big gun, and ask if that was the last thing Min would have wanted to say to her mother. One way or another, there was a train coming for us all.

With Min gone, and me the last of my generation, it was impossible to mount a case against Azark lessons. I picked up the language easily enough, but the history and myths were fragmentary, and made no more sense to my teachers than they made to me. I wanted to be like my friends and play cricket on Saturday mornings.

At university, I studied History and Philosophy for no other reason than to irritate a mother who'd wanted me to study law. I made a point of becoming intimate with the flashy, fleshy girls mum was certain to dislike, women who'd sooner kill themselves than make the dusty pilgrimage to a crumbling metropolis in Azarkstan. So I was always disheartened when Mum expressed an unexpected fondness for these girls, choosing to see only their most positive qualities. Worse, these lovers loved my mother, and were at a loss to understand my constant harping.

"When you meet the right girl, you'll know," Mum would say, hoping she'd live to see that day. Mum wasn't always right about things, but she had most people well-sussed, and they knew it. They saw it in her eyes.

When I told Dad that I wanted to travel to Azarkstan, he made no comment except to say that Mum had put money away for "just such a journey." I said that I was thinking of re-shaping my doctoral thesis to deal with my great-great-grandfather's experiences as adviser to the Sultan, and needed to see if there were enough documents to make the enterprise worthwhile. This was no more a lie than the story I'd been telling myself, that I needed to do something special to honor my mother's memory.

.

My mission, so far as there was one, involved searching the Hedut Library collections for mention of my great-great-grandfather, the incomparably wise Tazir Ali. This was unlikely to be a simple matter. Volunteers had been managing the library's collection for the best part of four decades. Just finding the building without being molested by dogs was likely to be the hardest part of the bargain.

As I closed the door to my room, a key turned in a nearby lock and I looked up just in time to see a woman in full purdah scuttle away. Following her down the stairwell, I heard some of the same joyful, melodic singing I'd heard through my wall the previous evening, but when I reached the foyer, the melodies and their singer were gone. One thing that had already become clear was that Hedut women had a gift for invisibility.

Though dogs shadowed me on my fifteen-minute walk to the library, they made no demands I couldn't handle. Once in a while, they passed the corpse of a recently killed comrade in the gutter, and sniffed a little before continuing to roam, regularly leaving the footpath to weave through the flow of motor-bikes and Soviet-era sedans.

Everything I'd read about the library gave me reason to believe that it would be in shambles, and on that score, I wasn't disappointed. The first man kind enough to offer assistance was functionally illiterate, and only by a series of accidents did I find the basement room where the nineteenth century documents were stored in a crowded, apparently random arrangement of cabinets. After squeezing between two of these, I was startled to come face to face with a voluptuous middle-aged redhead, who immediately addressed me in English.

"You'll need gloves. This is a breeding ground for scorpions." Without pausing, she reached into her bag to produce flesh-toned rubber gloves identical to those that made her own hands look like five-fingered condoms.

Bath-based Alice reminded me of Mrs. Kingston, an equally buxom, bound-lessly enthusiastic woman who taught European History at Scotch. I hadn't been alone in having a massive crush on her. Like me, Alice was conducting genealogical research, and, like most genealogists, was eager to speak about it. Though her great-grandfather was a key figure in the oriental opium trade, the family wealth derived from his wife, who managed an infamous brothel that supplied heavily pregnant women to "discerning gentlemen."

"Why is it that the worst scum are always described as 'discerning gentlemen?' These days they'd be wanking themselves silly in front of their laptops, but in those days men would travel a long way for pleasures that met their requirements. But you, you're here to find something you won't find. You have that look people have when they've no idea what they're looking for."

Mention of a great-great grandfather who lost his head to the Sultan for reasons never fully explained didn't wash with Alice. Noting my use of a formal Azark phrase, she placed a gloved hand on my shoulder and moved close enough for me to feel her breasts against my arm. Her primary interest was to examine my jaw-line.

"You're Azark on your mother's side. It's the women who pass on the jaw. For some westerners, it's too geometric, but I find Azark men very attractive."

If Alice hadn't released me just then, I might have passed out.

"But the women are a mystery. Is your mother mysterious?"

I said that Mum was dead, but I never thought of her as mysterious.

"Well, how would you know? Men only exist to be mystified. Do you look like her?"

People said so, since the square jaw dominated all else.

For Alice, that inheritance mattered more than documents. Family history was a speculative science that had more to do with probability theory than old photographs and birth certificates. Documents would only tell what they wanted to tell. You were better off to seize the past and belt it into a shape that suited your personality.

"We don't want to know our ancestors," she told me. "We want to abduct them. I keep my great-grandparents tied up in the spare bedroom, and only let them loose when they need to pee. That's how family history works."

I was given no time to process this point before she told me that everything I was looking for was in the cabinet just to my right, but I wouldn't find it very satisfactory.

"How do you know? There's no index."

I can't say how Alice knew what she knew, if she'd really seen scorpions or just liked the feel of latex, but half the documents in the second drawer pertained to my ancestor, the incomparably wise Tazir Ali, and the circumstances of his death at the Sultan's hands. Alice was also right in predicting that I'd find the official version unsatisfying, since it lacked the romance and treacheries of the versions I knew.

Entrusted by the Sultan to resolve a diplomatic issue to do with the education of the Russian ambassador's twin daughters, Tazir recommended a close friend to take on the role of private tutor. When this friend stole the eldest twin's virtue, the Sultan gave Tazir a choice. The perpetrator would lose his head or walk free. If he went free, Tazir would be required to take his place.

You might like to believe that your wise ancestor would choose the honorable path, but Tazir Ali was so pathetic when insisting that his friend be punished that the Sultan reneged on the bargain and had them both beheaded.

While this was a fine anecdote to amuse dinner-party guests, it was hardly a matter that merited four years of close investigation and analysis. The most profound discovery was finding that Heduts used irony in much the same way as Australians do, and the phrase "incomparably wise" was a common insult. Most likely, Tazir Ali had been given the task of finding a tutor for the twins to atone for previous stuff-ups. And Alice was probably right. If I'd needed Tazir to be the Czar's man in Kust, I wouldn't have troubled myself to learn otherwise. My needs had nothing to do with distant ancestry.

After hearing my report, Alice said that she'd first come across Tazir's name as someone who'd been involved in supplying pregnant women to her great-grandmother's brothel. More likely than not, he'd acted as an agent for the Sultan, who was well-known for treating pregnancy as an invitation to clear the decks in his harem. Azark men weren't known for being honorable.

.

Insisting that she accompany me back to my hotel, Alice didn't cover her bottle-red hair. With that, and a chest that would draw attention even in a town where women were more to the forefront, I felt like someone walking headlong into danger.

"Shouldn't you cover up?"

"I've been coming here for years. The Heduts know me. You're not embarrassed, are you?"

She knew very well that I was embarrassed, just as she knew that I was horny. At the risk of sounding like a conservative mullah, the female form looks uncommonly enticing when you've gone several days without seeing it. Alice would have recognized straight away that I was a young man with mother issues, and must have known that I'd worry about whether a mission to honor my mother could permit me to sleep with a handsome woman of my mother's age.

She directed me down a riverside path where roaming dogs and pedestrians were few, though the trickle that called itself the Hedut River could hardly be seen through thick brambles.

"I suppose your grandparents described Hedut as a jewel of the Orient."

"They made it sound like a place no sensible person would leave."

Laughter sent a shimmer through her huge bosom.

"When a southerly blows through the valley, there's no chill like it. If the wind blows from the north, you'd swear you were in a furnace. Either way, the dust is impossible. This is as good as it gets," she said, clasping my hand with hers, a gesture that might have seen those hands amputated were it witnessed by a person of true faith.

"Now that you know about Tazir, how long will you stay?"

I didn't know, and Alice would have seen that the absence of a Plan B left me vulnerable to someone who knew what they wanted.

When we left the river path for the street leading to my hotel, Alice released my hand, but didn't hesitate to smile at the men whose eyes nearly exploded when they saw her. Their heads soon turned to the ground lest they be struck dead by lightning.

As we paused out the front of the Riverside, two dogs engaged in a frenzied rut, something the Englishwoman refused to ignore.

"They don't like them."

I thought she meant the idea of getting barreled from behind in the central business district, but she was referring to the local attitude to dogs. "According to legend, the first dogs came from this valley. Heduts now feel required to let them fuck and shit wherever they like. Do you think that makes it a good place to be a dog?"

I couldn't say. The dogs looked neither happy nor well fed. And the sex act didn't seem to offer a satisfaction that you'd want to write home about. Alice then asked for my room number, "in case we both find ourselves with nothing on," and I offered it with the ambivalence I used to feel when I first took to masturbation. In doing so, I probably demonstrated that I'd inherited Tazir Ali's "incomparable wisdom."

.

Still thinking about Alice's breasts as I headed upstairs, I was interrupted by a familiar voice approaching from the other direction. This song was, if anything, even more heartfelt than those I'd heard the previous night. Just before my neighbor and I crossed paths on the landing, the singing stopped.

"Keep going, it's beautiful," I said in Azark.

"Do you know the song?" she replied.

When I said that I didn't know any Azark songs, she used American-accented English to say that she didn't either. "It's 'Bachelorette' by Björk. I translated the lyrics myself."

Feeling dumb for not recognizing the tune, I smiled, but said nothing.

I'm Mira," she said, and drew her veil to one side to reveal a smile of singular beauty, an earthquake smile that threw my world out of whack in an instant.

Though I spluttered something about Mira being my mother's name, I couldn't imagine a Hedut who looked less like Mum. For the first time ever, I introduced myself as Memin, but Mira Katt was more impressed by me being Australian. She'd known Memins, but never one from my corner of the world.

"Women can't dine in the dining room, so I'm getting the kitchen to send something up. Want to join me?"

"Isn't that risky?"

"No one has to know," she said, with a hint of mischief in her eye. "Besides, I'm Lutheran. When Grandpa got a job at the brewery in Madison, that was it for us and Islam."

Knowing little about Lutherans, and not a lot more about Midwestern girls, I promised to join her in twenty minutes.

·

Twenty minutes can seem like nothing, and it can seem like forever. This serve was long enough to brush my teeth, and it might have been long enough to get a call through to Dad if I returned to the lobby. Dad would be keen to know that most of the stories told about the valley being paradise were bullshit, but that wasn't what I needed to say.

As I said before, Dad was set to become a lawyer before he met Mum, and he would have had a better idea than me what I needed to find in Hedut. He'd always been a quiet man, who drew strength from Mum and her ability to let him believe he was running the show. That was the one joke they never tired of.

Dad must have known that Mum's fantasies were more precious to her than the reality, that her Hedut was a language she invented to explain her love for her parents. In that sense, Mira Zulla was a poet, and Dad didn't need me to tell him that, or that Tazir Ali was a low-life, or that the only decent things that came out of this place were the people who had the sense to leave, and the idea of Isnis.

Maybe his dreams and mine weren't so different. I had fantasized about meeting a beautiful, shy Hedut girl. She would tell me so little that I'd be forced to reconstruct her history and thoughts from a series of nuanced glances. When I put my speculations to her, she would smile as if to say, "You're warm," or, "You're closer than you think." Song-filled Mira was no more the shy, grateful girl I'd dreamt about than she was my square-jawed, resolute mother. Nor could I imagine what it was like to know a happiness so uncontainable that it had to be voiced in song.

·

With her long dark hair draped across the red silk blouse she wore with blue jeans and sneakers, Mira Katt was the pocket-sized all-American girl, only twice as pretty. Suddenly incapable of speech, I cursed myself for not bringing a handful of flowers.

"The food shouldn't be long. The hezchuk here is sensational."

No way would I contradict an Azark princess. Maybe the Riverside's hezchuk was sensational compared to those she'd known in Wisconsin.

As soon as I sat down, Mira began a rapid, warmhearted interrogation. How had I learned to speak the Hedut dialect? How did my family get to Australia? Might my grandparents know hers, who left Hedut for America at roughly the same time? Why did my grandparents allow their daughter to marry an Australian? What had the Harrises thought? Is it possible for a half-Hedut to see himself other than Hedut? And what kind of profession was historian for a man who might want a wife and family? Don't you want that, Memin?

Until then, I hadn't thought that a twenty-seven year old could be expected to know what he wanted.

"You've studied too much philosophy. Philosophy's worse than smoking crack," Mira told me.

When I told her the sad tale of the incomparably wise Tazir Ali, she was unsurprised. Among Azarks, Heduts were famed as shady dealers. Even the fact that there were eight different words for trust suggested a basic uncertainty.

She'd grown up as a small, exotic brunette among statuesque girls with northern European names like Selma and Gretchen. To a child enduring endlessly cold winters, Azark myths seemed pure and romantic. Mira begged her parents and grandparents to tell her everything they knew about the beautiful valley where dogs came from. Only when she'd mastered the Hedut dialect did she realize how little depth and resonance the stories had.

"Did your parents tell you about the legless man who breeds butterflies?"

"Yes. The story begins well, then it peters out."

"That's it! The stories peter out. The stories prescribe the history of this place."

Following a hard rap on the door, I tiptoed to my hiding-place in the bathroom, where I couldn't fail to notice the black lace bra and underpants drying on the towel rail. Dad once said that Hedut women were famed for their skills in the bedroom, and I took that to be ironic, but now I couldn't be so sure.

"Memin, it's OK, you can come out now."

Mira had emptied half the hezchuk into an enamel camp plate, and I saw that my spoon was standing upright, exactly as it was meant to. She smiled and said a brief grace before inviting me to tuck in.

This hezchuk was so unlike the meal I'd eaten the previous evening—so superior to anything I'd eaten at home—it was impossible to believe that it was prepared by the same chefs.

"How is it?"

"It's incredible."

With Mira pausing to watch me eat, I struggled to divide my attention between the food and her fabulous smile. I then admitted that I'd eaten hezchuk the previous evening, but it tasted nothing like this.

"I add herbs and spices. Without them, it's just goat stew."

"What are they?"

Mira took a mouthful and chewed slowly, keeping me on tenterhooks.

"Do I look like a girl who'd surrender ancient family recipes on a first date?"

I ought to have said she was the kind of girl who could disrupt the gravitational pull on large planets, but I was stuck on her mention of "a date." I knew that Americans were very particular about dating, and that a first date was a moment of some significance, not least if the girl suggested there might be more dates to follow.

"You haven't told me what brings you here."

"*The Cat in the Hat,*" she said.

I hadn't seen a cat the whole time I'd been in Hedut. The dogs must have run them out of the place.

"That's part of the trouble I'm having," she told me. "I'm a translator for a firm that wants to publish Azark editions of the Dr. Seuss books."

I couldn't imagine a higher calling.

"You'd think so. But the Azark language has so few monosyllables. The word for cat is *enchuznut*. The word for hat is *kheela*. I spent today with a local trip-hopper, and he thinks it will be hopeless. Azark's all trip, no hop."

Was that what she thought? That it was hopeless?

"It's going to be a challenge."

"Exactly."

As we scraped clean our plates, we agreed that a good beer with hezchuk like that would be a bliss beyond endurance. Mira then grabbed some paperbacks from her suitcase, and we spent the next hour in Seussville with the Cat, Fox, and assorted Knoxes.

Though *Green Eggs and Ham* would be a problem, I thought *The Lorax* might be a good starting point.

"I was thinking *Horton Hatches an Egg*."

"That's my all-time favorite," I told her. "My mum loved that one."

I asked Mira if she would read it to me, and she was retrieving the book from her case when there was a series of loud knocks on the door of the neighboring room.

"Are you expecting someone?" she asked.

"No, I don't think so," I said, immediately picturing the generously shaped Alice with "nothing else on." When I thought she'd given up, a voice called, "Kev, it's me, Alice. Are you there?"

"We've had a nice time, but I'm keeping you."

I felt awful about standing Alice up, especially after the things I'd thought about doing with her, but Mira's smile had smashed that man to bits.

"No, you're not keeping me. Not unless you want to."

"I'm tempted."

Looking deep into Mira's eyes, I saw depths that were inexhaustible. Those eyes could take a man anywhere, and if they took me to Wisconsin or some brightly-colored place inhabited by Yings and Knoxes, my father and grandparents would understand. It wasn't as if they didn't know the form.

"Hey, you were going to read to me. There's an elephant with an egg that needs hatching."

THOMAS SHAPCOTT

Thomas Shapcott is one of Australia's most prolific and honored writers, acclaimed for his poetry, fiction, and belles lettres. He was born in 1935, a twin. He left school at fifteen but eventually completed an M.A. at Queensland University. He was originally a qualified public accountant, in practice with his father, but wrote poetry hidden beneath tax forms. His first book, *Time On Fire,* was published in 1961 and won the prestigious Grace Leven Prize, at that time the only poetry award in Australia. He has since published fifteen poetry titles, most recently *The City Of Empty Rooms* (Salt, 2006). He sold the accountancy practice in 1978 to take up writing, and in the 1980s he began to publish novels, including *White Stag Of Exile* (1984), a memorable story of the Hungarian diaspora. To date he has published seven adult novels, three children's novels, and three collections of short stories. From 1983-1990 he was Director of the Literature Board of the Australia Council, the country's chief arts funding agency. In 1997 he was appointed inaugural Professor of Creative Writing at the University of Adelaide. He retired in 2005 and is now living in semi-retirement in Melbourne, married to the poet Judith Rodriguez. He is an editor, librettist (two operas for which he provided libretti have been performed in Australia, with music by Colin Brumby), reviewer, and literary critic. He has published two books on the Australian artist Charles Blackman, and his collection *Twins in the Family: Conversations with Australian Twins* (2001) reflects his personal interest in this subject. A travel/family history *A Circle Around my Grandmother* is due for publication in 2008. Shapcott was made an Officer in the Order of Australia in 1989, and was awarded the Patrick White Prize in 2000. He was also awarded the Gold Wreath in the Struga (Macedonia) poetry festival in 1989, the first Australian to be so honored.

From *The Waterfall Pool*

ONE
HAL COLLINS

1.

Albin Setheni is dead. He has to be. Three years is too long for anyone to be
a missing person. And besides, I have my own reasons to suspect the worst.
If that's what you would call it. His shack is empty, has been all this time. I
suspect no one has even been onto the property, at least since the police and
detectives and photographers and that mob came and did their futile exer-
cises. I think I did not expect them to find anything. With Albin, that would
have been too easy. Besides, there were other factors.

At the inquest, and all the questionings by the police, because I was Albin's
closest neighbor, naturally they quizzed me. Did they quiz me! But I told them
what I could. Almost everything. Some things, well, I just did not want to put
anyone else through all of that, and besides, there was nothing I could prove.
Not a thing. And Linus certainly had enough cause to do his old man in, if
that was what it was—and I'm the last man to go making claims or accusa-

tions. No. Better to remain quiet about all of that. I have no reason to set the cops off on what might well be a wild goose chase.

Linus has disappeared, too, but nobody seems in the least concerned about Linus. Just as Albin was hardly, well, a concerned parent. I have a touch of sympathy for Linus.

After three years I suppose the case is closed, at least as far as the authorities are concerned. I've never bothered to enquire. Albin Setheni left no family—other than Linus, and I don't know what they do about estates. He was probably intestate, anyway. So there the old shack still sits. And rots. All that work of Albin's, now feeding the white ants and the weather.

I wander over to his farm every once in a while, but it is all too depressing. Makes you realize just how temporary things really are, once there is nobody to care. His place was special, once. Janet and I were drunk with it, and with Albin, in those first years. We'd never met anybody like him. Charismatic, that is the word these days. But charismatic does not quite get the nuance of it, of Albin. Charismatic suggests light and life, energy and outreach. Albin was none of those things. Moody, rather, a lot of the time. And when he did laugh, or even smile, you felt included, as if you were part of him, or of what he was holding in to himself most of the time. Albin in a sense let you feel the darkness of things; but he could also let you see the light, the wonder, the damned otherness of life.

Yes, I was hooked for a long time. And even Linus, when he did turn up, and I have a lot of heart for Linus, a lot of sympathy, even Linus and his anxieties or whatever, cannot fully quench the sort of magic, the aura, his dad seemed to hold around himself.

Perhaps Linus even envied that.

The whole place is a fire trap. I've written to the Council, the authorities about this. It seems the insurance people want everything to stay as it was, I don't know why. Case unresolved, or something. Albin had that sort of capacity to create this circle around himself and all he touched. There is a reluctance to interfere. I wonder does someone—Linus?—pay the rates and taxes? Or are they holding off until everybody forgets the incident, so they can auction it off for unpaid rates. Then what? Put the remainder in some Trust Account and hope nobody claims it.

I do wonder what did happen to Linus. He has to be the only claimant. Perhaps they are both together somewhere reconciled, though the image that recurs is Master and Slave. Linus as Master. The Young Bull exacting homage.

Wherever Albin is, he is no longer here and it's difficult even to think of him alive. Janet sometimes says it could be possible! I think not.

The body, his body, was in some ways the least important part of Albin. Not that he didn't have an attractive enough body—ask Janet. But what is body, after all? It was the man inside the body, it was Albin, pure mind, pure spirit if you like. Sometimes, now, I think: pure turbulence. I wonder was he haunted? Certainly, thinking back on all that, I half believe that was it. Albin was too unsettling. I liked that. At least, I thought I did. If I were to find the body; well, speculation; but if I were to find him: what would be my response? I have never thought of him being still alive; not really. But if he were, and were to turn up again, suddenly, like Linus did: I think I would curse him. I would embrace him. No, too much of that. I would probably see him with altogether different eyes. That would be curse enough. The Albin I knew has been changed utterly by the Albin I discovered. The other Albin.

2.

The way it began was simple enough. When I bought this farm the flower business was already established, and Janet and I were full of ourselves and the future in it. We were still in our thirties. All the real contracts were established and old Roger Hamilton, since he had that heart attack, was not up to keeping the place in operation. It was very much a one-man band, as far as he was concerned.

At least, after his wife Judit passed away. And I've got to hand it to Roger: he had built up the business from nothing. He had planted two acres of *Leptospremum* initially, and it was in demand as filler, as background, for floral arrangements in some of the big hotels down in Brisbane, and on the Gold

Coast. And when the fashion moved to *Protea* for feature items, he put in that second acre on the flat below the slope where the *Leptospermum* seemed to thrive. He also was canny enough to plant the little grove of firewheel trees. Their flower stalk fetches a fortune in Japan now. But it was the extensive plantings of *Gypsophilia* that became his masterstroke: he exported his produce quick-frozen to Japan and Canada. It wasn't only his heart attack that threatened to put paid to everything: air freight charges rose steeply and all the fuel and transport costs just skyrocketed. I think old Roger got out just in the nick of time. But we bought in at a good price: the land itself is now worth all we paid for the business, and more. I'm not complaining.

Judit came out from Hungary in 1948 on the same ship as Sir Peter Abeles. You know; he started TNT. Judith always called him Emil, and pronounced his surname AH-bel-esh with the accent on the first syllable. Hungarian, you know. But she was the one who got TNT to pick up the flowers to transport them to Brisbane. She was a dynamo, that woman. Old Roger missed her a lot. After she died, I think his heart really went out of it. But by then they had their own little refrigerated van. He used to get young Renzo Tedesci to take deliveries down to Brisbane. I still do that.

Janet loved the idea: flower farmers. Much more interesting than being a librarian, though she knew all the right reference books. We must have the best botanical library in Queensland. Well, New South Wales exactly. Though the house is very close to Stanthorpe Township, the land is actually over the border. It's only a few kilos. She looks after the mail-order division now, and it has built up better than I predicted. As she keeps reminding me. Bulbs are her specialty. Janet has secret resources that surprise me sometimes. Janet is the sort of person you should not take for granted.

When we moved in there was not a lot of new work to do: the acres of flowering shrubs needed a bit of tending: mulching and pruning mainly. The *Gypsophilia* area had been allowed to sprawl and that damned couch grass was getting in. But, overall, we had it pretty easy. When I was working at the Agency in Toowoomba (and we had a branch in Stanthorpe), I had gotten to know Roger Hamilton pretty well and I took an interest. The snap-freezing and the packaging interested me: I could see the possibilities. I was the first one Roger offered the business to when he was forced to call it a day.

Fortunately my dad helped me with the initial outlay, and we paid him off in two years flat. How's that for business?

When we moved into the farm Janet was all for modernizing the old house, but I said it would do for a while, and now of course these Colonial Queenslanders are all the go. I had the floors sanded and polished, even the big verandas, and I'd say at one fell sweep we almost doubled the value of the place. That's my trump card with Janet. Now she's the one who's all for "period charm."

Albin Setheni was the next block along from us. He didn't have a phone—and certainly not a mobile, not Albin! He only got the electricity connected when we had been living here six months. Don't think he was too pleased, either. It was after Sky—that was his girlfriend, or whatever—had left. She had a little kiddie. Don't think it was Albin's, but that's not the sort of thing you ask. Or, at least, I didn't. It was probably Janet told me that. Not Albin.

They had been living there for nearly a year, in that little shack Albin had built himself. Old timber from derelict farms or barns, a foundation and porch of bricks—sandstock, most of them. And the corrugated iron roof that I imagine he swiped from an old dairy somewhere. A real cocky job, you ask me. But inside: well, once you were inside, Albin had made it sort of special. Stanthorpe gets a lot of casuals; it's the fruit growing area of Queensland: apples, stone fruit.

I first went over there shortly after we moved in. A phone call, with a message for him. Roger had warned me about that, and it was no problem, the shack was a five-minute drive from us, and neighbors should be neighbors.

I pulled the Jeep up outside his front door, but there was nobody home. I was about to scribble a note to give him the phone number to ring, when I saw them coming up from their dam.

The three of them were starkers. I had not met Albin at that stage. But he was clearly the tall bloke with the tawny head of hair and a long wiry body brown as a berry (what berry is brown like that? His skin was like milk coffee).

Beside him Sky was almost white. She was a lot shorter and that long blonde hair was wet from their swim, and clung around her little face like a sort of cap. She was carrying little Sun and her breasts bounced as she walked up hand in hand with Albin. They looked the real Adam and Eve. Aren't bodies beautiful, I thought. Perhaps that was the moment when I fell under the spell. When I lost the necessary caution that preserves us from ourselves. She was quite unconcerned to be naked, and so was he. I guessed him to be a little older than me—late 30s perhaps—but all muscle and sinew.

When they saw me he waved. He was carrying a big straw hat in his other hand, and he put it on. Somehow that one item of clothing made his naked-ness even more visible. He was brown all over and his hair, down there, was only a sort of intensification of that brownness. His cock and balls dangled down, all lax and easy as if they were never used to being covered in cotton or wool. Sky's pubic hair was like the silky tassel of a corncob, but I will not go on. They were, well, beautiful.

"Hi. I'm your new neighbor, Hal Collins. We live in Roger Hamilton's place now. He sold us his flower business. And I've got a phone message for Albin Setheni."

"Thank you," he said. His voice was grave, strangely so, considering how openly nude he was. "That is me."

Sky and the baby had wandered inside, but I was introduced to them in due course. We had a cup of some sort of herbal tea out on their porch.

First impressions count. Albin turned out to be a man in his early forties, but he had the body of someone ageless: an athlete, a Phys. Ed. instructor, a god. That gravity about him. He offered smiles rarely, but like a sort of bene-diction, and it was almost dazzling. Restraint, that's what I thought: this man has a wonderful restraint. And I wondered what was at the back of it. Imme-diately I caught that his accent was not Australian. Well, with a name like that, hardly a surprise. And yet he seemed so much at home in his particular space, as if he had always been there, just there. When I went inside the house—the shack—a bit later on, everything confirmed that impression: there were dried arrangements of leaves and branches, in vases, in bottles, on the mantelpiece and on the table there were pebbles, too, smooth ones from the riverbed, and an opened eggshell quartz with its brilliant hidden core. I knew at once that this was no mere cowcocky, no hopeful fruit farmer; this was a man who cared. At that stage, I had not seen his drawings.

We talked about the flower farm and he commended me on all the natives. "People only begin to appreciate the Australian native plants," he insisted, but I didn't have the heart to contradict him and tell him that, back in the eighteenth century, Joseph Banks had taken *Grevillea robusta* back to England after his first visit and that they caused a sensation, even in their juvenile growth. Book learning (thank you, Janet) can sound like a lecture, and Albin had his own mind on things. I was right to guess this.

Before I left I invited him—them—up to our house, to use the phone, to let us return the courtesy of a cuppa (not that we had herbal teas around, but I guessed, again rightly, that stronger stuff might suffice). Albin said it would be good for neighbors to know neighbors. Sky was breast-feeding little Sun, but she had put on a pair of shorts by this time. Albin was still entirely unclothed, and was so natural like that I did not even really notice. Except that he had taken off the straw hat. When he did so I realized how becoming that one item of ornament was. I think I imagined him with a jade pendant hanging from his neck, falling among the sparse hairs on his chest. But the thought of trousers on him: it made me itchy. I don't think I even wondered at that. Some bodies just seem to be in accord with themselves and their owners. Albin was like that.

Janet and I had never indulged in skinny-dipping; it was not really our thing. But somehow Albin and Sky had acted so natural about it all that I was completely won over, taken in. It seemed like normality, as if our civilization were somehow a sham, a cover-up. That was Albin's achievement. In his way, on that afternoon, he seemed a divine messenger. But I exaggerate.

Let's say I was able to accept the way he presented himself. I accepted his terms, as it were.

When they did walk up to our place, later that afternoon, they were all dressed in ordinary gear: Albin had khaki shorts and a white T-shirt, but no footwear. Sky had a loose blouse (which allowed her very buoyant breasts to move freely; well, she was feeding the child) and Sun wore a little cotton outfit, but no nappy that I could see. Janet met them and introductions were made. By the time I got in from the back paddock they were all sitting on the side veranda and deep in conversation. I felt, for a while, almost an intruder into their circle. Janet was quite at home. The perfect hostess, I thought. But she was more relaxed than that.

"Albin has been telling me how he found the place—their property. He has been living there two years. He says he doesn't find it lonely at all, even though he does not have a car, or even a pushbike."

"I walk," he said, and I could see his feet were wide and perhaps flat. I agreed.

"When I was in primary school," I said, "we never wore shoes or even sandals, except on Sunday, to church."

"Good for the feet," Albin said, "but my church is the open air. My church is that piece of land down there," he pointed, "especially down at the creek and the waterhole. I worship there. My whole body is a tribute, you know that? I am at one with my body there." I think we were silent for a bit. Janet smiled and looked as if she would agree with them, but she started shuffling plates and saucers, but I was not going to let Albin change the subject.

"I could tell that," I said, "when I saw you walking up through the grass from down your back gulley. You carried your body like, well, like it all belonged." Albin laughed. "Your man caught us unprepared."

"We were in the nuddy," added Sky, pulling her nipple out of Sun 's mouth and shifting her over to the other side. "I think Hal felt he was poking his nose into our private affairs."

"Nothing is private," Albin said. "Least of all our body. Know me, know my body. It's the best way. Everything else is artifice. I think I worship the sun, even though in this country the sun can be capricious. Perhaps we deserve that. But I also worship the moon, and the grass and the water. Especially the water. Water is ninety percent of our body and though we cannot live entirely in the water, yet water has good lessons that we must heed. My body in the water knows we are other than a walking biped."

"I used to be a competition swimmer," I said. Janet looked to me as if I had spoken some sacrilege. But I was not daunted. "If you like water, Albin, you also must be a swimmer."

He smiled at that, one of those rare smiles.

"I learned to swim because my father threw me into the icy water. That was in Sweden. I thought I would die, but it taught me to swim, immediately. And ice water. Here in this country the water is like a woman's body, so warm. Ice water is more stern, but also more bracing."

I knew it was not the moment to drag him into reminiscences. I caught Janet's eye as if to ask, "Is he being sexist, or what?" but she rose from her cane chair and began putting things into the tray. Sky had finished feeding the baby by now and she wriggled up and, with Sun on her hip, followed Janet into the kitchen. I knew there would be a further interrogation, even if couched in sweet politeness.

Albin rose and shook my hand. His grip was firm, as one would expect. It felt almost claw-like: bone, rather than muscle. A handshake, particularly a first handshake, is one of those tests. I wondered how he interpreted my own hand—my own body. The office years, the business of relearning all the old gardening techniques. But I did not feel I had anything to be ashamed of. In fact, I think I felt well-satisfied with myself. Firm handshakes are part of the deal in an agency, particularly with farmers. Albin's handshake was something different. Bony, yes, but also not exactly that hearty farmer's grasp. It was as if he were asking something of me, rather than asserting, or insisting. He held my hand, also, just that moment too long. I felt uncomfortable. But I also felt, strangely, powerful, purposeful. How wrong could I be?

From THE DIARY OF ALBIN SETHENI

EVERYTHING IS GIVEN EVERYTHING IS A GIVEN
THIS LAND IS A GIFT TRULY IT IS A GIFT
AND FOR ONLY A SMALL PLANTING IN THE HIDDEN SPACES
ALL IS GIVEN TO ME
AND I THANK THE SKY AND THE SUN AND THE WATER

THAT CARRIES ITS HIDDEN TURBULENCE IN THE WATERFALL
POOL
AND OF COURSE I THANK MY FRIEND, THAT STRANGER,
WHO WILL NOT DISTURB ME EVER
BUT WILL LEAVE ME PEACEFUL IN THIS HIDDEN PLACE
WHERE I SHALL LIVE QUIETLY
AS NEVER BEFORE
AND WHERE I INTEND TO RETURN TO THE NATURE
OF ALL THINGS
AND RECOVER PERHAPS INNOCENCE

+++++

THE WATERFALL HAS COME TO LIFE THEY SAY WE HAD TEN YEARS
OF DROUGHT BUT WITH MY ARRIVAL THE SACRED WATER
AND THE SPRINGS REVIVE
THE WATER FLOWS AND I AM COME INTO MY OWN

+++++++

I AM NOT ALONE. PEOPLE ARE NEIGHBORS
AS ARE HORSES AND A COW I SOMETIMES HEAR LOWING
BUT I HAVE BUILT MY SHELTER
AND THE WOOD SPEAKS TO ME OF USAGE AND CONVERSATIONS
IN OTHER TONGUES AND I HAVE A ROOF OF CORRUGATED IRON

+++++

THIS IS NOT A GREEN WOOD BUT I HAVE COMFORT
AND AS I ALWAYS KNEW WATER SHOWS ME
HOW TO BE MYSELF
THE TREES ARE MOSTLY RAGGED
BUT NEAR THE WATER THEY GROW THICK

AND HAVE A GREENNESS THAT THE SUN DOES NOT
PENETRATE
I WALK AMONG THE TREES
AND DISCOVER HIDDEN PATHS
A LEAF SOMETIMES GUIDES ME
OR THE SOUND OF THE WATERFALL.

+++++

I HAVE GREETED MY NEIGHBORS. I LIKE THEM
AND I WILL BE GENTLE TO THEM THEY HAVE WATER
AND IT IS MY INTENTION TO TAP INTO THEIR WATER
FOR WHICH I WILL ALLOW THEM ENTRY
EVEN INTO MY WATERFALL POOL WHICH IS SACRED
AND THEY HAVE INSTRUCTED ME IN REGULATIONS
AND THE TYRANNY OF THE LOCAL COUNCIL
I WILL BE OBEDIENT
OBEDIENCE IS THE FIRST LESSON

+++++

MY CLOTHING HAS LEFT ME
AND THE AIR ON MY SKIN REJOICES
THIS IS TO BE IN LOVE
THIS IS TO BE AN OWNER
OF ALL THIS PLACE
OWNER

+++++

SKY IS WITH ME SHE HAS COME AFTER THE TIME OF LABOR AND I
HAVE GIVEN HER A TRUE NAME
AND THE GIRL BABY WHO IS SUN LIKE SUN SHE CAUSES HER
MOTHER TO CIRCLE AND WORSHIP
I UNDERSTAND WORSHIP

THE FATHER IS SOMEWHERE THAT DOES NOT MATTER
SKY IS DEFENSELESS
AND I WILL BE HER DEFENSE
I GROW STRONG AGAIN
AND I BEGIN TO FEEL PROSPEROUS

+++++

IN THE HOUSE ALONG THE ROAD THERE IS A TELEPHONE
AND MY NEIGHBORS SAID THEY WILL TAKE ANY MESSAGES
I HOPE FOR NO MESSAGES BUT THEY WILL COME
AS MY SMALL HIDDEN CROPS MATURE THEY WILL COME
THAT IS THE NATURE OF THINGS
BUT I WILL HIDE SKY FROM SUCH INTRUSIONS
SHE IS SO LOVELY AND LIKE ME SHE REJOICES
IN HER BODY IN THE GIFT OF HER BODY
WE BATHED WITH THE BABY IN THE ROCK POOL
AND SKY PLUNGED UNDER THE WATERFALL IN THE DEEP PART
SHE IS WHITE AS A LILY FLOWER
EVEN IN THE SACRED PLACES SHE IS GOLD AND WHITE

+++++
THIS SEED POD IS CALLED A KURRAJONG
LIKE SKY IT IS AN ENCLOSED SPACE WHICH INSIDE IS BEAUTIFUL
I OPENED THE SEEDPOD TO REVEAL THE TREASURE
SMALL POLISHED GOLD SEEDS IN THEIR GENTLE COCCOON
AND I OFFERED THIS TO SKY WHICH SHE ACCEPTED
I THINK I AM IN LOVE

+++++

THE TONGUE IS THE SOURCE OF ALL SENSATION
THE TONGUE IS CLOSE TO OUR INNERMOST WISHES

SKY WAS ASLEEP
WITH THE BABY AT HER BREAST
HER FULL SWELLING BREAST LEAKING MILK
AND SATISFACTION FOLLOWED MY TONGUE
AND WAS GENTLE
TOMORROW WHEN SHE IS AWAKE I WILL TEACH HER MORE WAYS
WHERE THE TONGUE CAN DISPORT AND DISCOVER

+++++

I BROUGHT IN A LEAF
LOOK, I SAID TO SKY, LOOK AT ITS PERFECTION
AND ITS IMPERFECTION.
THE WAY IT CURLS GENTLY IN A SLIGHT ARC
WHICH IS LIKE THE WAY MY COCK CURLS THE WAY IT IS SMOOTH
BUT NOT SMOOTH
THE WAY IT HIDES A SECRET SMELL
NEVER TO BE FORGOTTEN
AND, NEAR THE TIP, A LUMP WHERE SOME INSECT
CONTRIBUTED ITS OWN IMPERFECTION WE ARE ALL PART OF
EACH OTHER
I THINK SKY UNDERSTOOD

+++++

SKY WAS DOZING, LOLLING SO ALL HER MUSCLES
RELAXED AND THE BABY LOLLED WITH HER
NAKED AND I KNEELED DOWN IN HOMAGE I EXPLORED
MY TONGUE PAID HOMAGE
IT EXPLORED
UNTIL SKY WOKE UP
SHE WAS FRIGHTENED
BUT I SAID NOTHING IS FRIGHTENING

EVERYTHING IS ITS OWN CELEBRATION
I SHOWED HER THE DRAWING
NO LONGER THE BUSH SEEDPOD OR THE BUSH LEAF
BUT THIS IS YOU, I SAID.

+++++

SKY HAS LEFT ME
SHE VANISHED AND TOOK EVERYTHING
I WALKED DOWN TO THE POOL SINGING TO HER
AND TO HER MEMORY
CHILD WOMAN, MOTHER WHO IS NOT CAPABLE
OF BEING A MOTHER
WHO WILL NOT GROW UP
WHO WILL NOT ALLOW HERSELF TO EXPERIENCE THOSE THINGS
WHICH A GROWN-UP REACHES FOR AND TOUCHES AND HAS TO
EXPLORE
SHE IS GONE
AND I AM NOT ANGRY
THOUGH I AM DESOLATED.

+++++

THE YOUNG MAN WHO LIVES NEARBY
HE CALLS HIMSELF HAL AND HE HAS EYES
THAT ARE TOO INNOCENT
THOUGH HE THINKS HIMSELF A MAN, AND EXPERIENCED.
I LIKE HIM BECAUSE OF HIS INNOCENCE
WHICH IS IGNORANCE MERELY
AND MUST BE TAKEN
IT WILL BE A NEW LESSON TO TEACH HIM
AND I THINK HE IS READY TO BE TAUGHT. WE HAVE BATHED IN
THE WATERFALL POOL WITHOUT HIS CLOTHING HE IS SALLOW

HE IS MORE VULNERABLE THAN HE REALIZES
HIS HAIR IS WIRY AND THICK BUT HE IS VULNERABLE I LIKE
THAT.

+++++

THERE IS A WOMAN. SHE IS NAMED JANET
SHE IS MORE KNOWING. SHE DOES NOT TRUST ME.
SOMETIMES I FEEL I MUST COVER MYSELF
CLOTHING IS SO IRRITATING TO THE SKIN
BUT SHE WILL COME, ALSO, TO THE POOL
PERHAPS WITH HER MAN BUT SHE WILL COME
AND I WILL SEE THEM BOTH NAKED
AND THEY CAN GAZE ON ME
IT IS TIME FOR THE TRUE NATURE OF LIFE TO BE WITH US
IT IS TIME TO TAKE THEM INTO THE SACRED WATER
I WILL BAPTIZE THEM

+++++

SURPRISE AFTER SURPRISE
AFTER THIS LIFETIME LINA RETURNS
AND IS WITH ME
TRULY WITH ME
I COULD NOT HAVE BELIEVED SUCH A THING POSSIBLE
HER BODY IS WITH ME
HER BODY IS WONDERFUL
HOW CAN I HAVE EVER DESERTED HER BODY
HOW CAN HER BODY HAVE EVER EXISTED WITHOUT ME THOUGH
I KNOW I AM BOASTFUL AND MY PRIVATE NOTEBOOK WILL NEV-
ER
INSCRIBE THE NAME OF THE WITCH WHO POSSESSED HER
WHO IS DEAD

WHO IS DEAD WHO IS DEAD
AND LINA IS LIVING AND WITH ME
IT IS A MIRACLE THAT COULD NOT BE IMAGINED I COULD NOT
EVEN WISH TO IMAGINE BUT HERE IN THIS VERY SECRET PLACE
MY FOREST
SO FAR ACROSS THE WORLD FROM EVERYTHING
SHE HAS HAPPENED
I COULD NOT BELIEVE IT
AND I DO BELIEVE IT NOW
A WHOLE BOUQUET OF FLOWERS IN A CLEAR GLASS JAR
DESCRIBES OUR REUNION, OUR UNION,
AND OUTSIDE IN THE MORNINGS A MAGPIE
MAKES THE MOST IMPOSSIBLE MUSIC
I BELIEVE EVERY NOTE

+++++

THE BODY IS THE HARP THAT GOD PLAYS UPON
THE BODY IS THE FLUTE THAT HEARS GOD'S BREATH
THE BODY IS THE CLARINET THAT TAKES THE TONGUE OF GOD
INTO EVERY NOTE
THE BODY IS A DRUM AND GOD KNOWS HOW TO PLAY
TO PLAY TO PERFECTION.

+++++

WE HAVE HAD OUR YOUNG MAN.
IN THE POOL THE THREE OF US VENTURED
AND LINA KNEW WHAT HE WAS WISHING
EVEN THOUGH HE SAID NOTHING.
I KNEW WHAT HE WAS WISHING
BECAUSE I SAW THE WAY HIS EYES
WERE LIKE A FINE PENCIL OVER THE SPACE OF A PAGE

CURVING THE WAY LINA'S BODY WAS CURVING AND AS HOT AS
HER MOVEMENTS.
WHEN WE WERE ALL JOINED
IT WAS LINA'S TRIUMPH
BUT MY VICTORY
I HAD HIS BODY AS I HAD LINA'S BODY
AND HER BODY WAS A PART OF ME
HER BODY EXTENDED ALL OF ME AND I TOUCHED HIM, MY FIN-
GERS LICKED HIM
EVEN AS MY TONGUE POKED IN HER EAR AND MY OTHER HAND
AND ITS FINGERS
TOOK POSSESSION OF HER BREAST
AND TUGGED HARD AT THE AUREOLE AND NIPPLE
AND HE CALLED OUT IN AN ECSTACY
SUCH AS HE HAD NEVER KNOWN
AND LINA CRIED OUT ALSO
AND I REJOICED
TO FIND GOD IN THE SPIRIT OF THESE WATERS AND THE BODY OF
ORDINARY MORTALS

+++++

HE WANTED ME TO BURN MY DRAWING
WHICH HAD BEEN TRIBUTE
JUST AS SKY HAD WANTED ME TO DESTROY
THE PAGE THAT CELEBRATED HER INNOCENCE
AND THE PETALS OF HER MOST INTIMATE FLOWER.
HE WAS OFFENDED
ONLY BECAUSE HE WAS NOT ACCUSTOMED
TO THE SIGHT OF HIS BODY AND ITS LITTLE IMPERFECTIONS
ITS PLACES OF AMUSEMENT AND UNIVERSAL PRIVACY HE WILL
NEVER BE ADULT.
I BURNED THE BIG DRAWING BUT HE DOES NOT KNOW

THIS PAGE.
HE HAS A PRETTY BUTTOCK BUT IT IS NOTHING
HE DOES NOT DESERVE IT HE THINKS LINA MAY ADMIRE IT BUT
HE WANTS HER TO SEE
THE FRONT PART, WHERE HE IS MORE CONFIDENT. WE ALL POS-
SESS THESE THINGS. THEY ARE NOTHING UNLESS WE REALIZE
THAT GOD IS IN THEM
BUT, MORE REMARKABLY, GOD IS IN OUR TONGUES.

+++++

IT IS NOT POSSIBLE. I SHOULD HAVE UNDERSTOOD
THAT LINA WAS JUST A LOAN GIVEN TO ME
FOR SHE WAS NEVER GIVEN TO ME
SHE EXACTED A PAYMENT
FOR EVERYTHING
EVEN HER DEATH.
MAN IS A CREATURE ALWAYS CAPABLE OF LEARNING
ALWAYS READY FOR THE NEXT LESSON
AND IF HE IS NOT READY
HE WILL BE DEFEATED.

+++++

AND NOW THIS. LINUS.
LINUS. LINUS. LINUS.
THE MAN FROM THE NEXT FARM, HAL, HE IS
APPREHENSIVE. I AM WAITING.
HAL IS ALWAYS FEARFUL
HE IS A FRETFUL MAN
HE HAS NEVER GROWN INTO ADULTHOOD
I SHOULD SCORN HIM

FOR MAKING ME DESTROY MY DRAWING
I SHOULD PITY HIM
BUT I HAVE TO ASK MYSELF HOW MUCH IS MY OWN DOING? LINUS
WILL SHOW ME PERHAPS
HOW MUCH IS MY OWN DOING
HOW MUCH IS IRRETRIEVABLE
HOW MUCH IS THERE IN LIFE TO BE NEGOTIATED
HOW MUCH IS DOWN PAYMENT
HOW MUCH IS LAID WASTE.

IT IS CURIOUS THAT, AS I WAIT AS I HAVE NEVER WAITED, I THINK
IN TERMS OF COMMERCE. AS IF GOD
WERE NOT IN THE SACRED WATER BUT IN NUMBERS
AND GOLD AND THE THOUGHT IS ALWAYS GRUBBING
INTO OUR GUT. WHAT FURTHER PAYMENT
IS THERE TO BE MADE?

CHRISTOS TSIOLKAS

Christos Tsiolkas was born in 1965 to Greek immigrant parents in working-class Melbourne. He is the author of the novels *Loaded* (1995, filmed as the feature *Head On* by Ana Kokkinos in 1997), *The Jesus Man* (1997), and *Dead Europe* (2005—all Random House Australia). *Dead Europe* won the *Age* Fiction Book of the Year Prize in 2006, and the 2006 Melbourne Prize for Writing. In 1996 Tsiolkas collaborated with Sasha Soldatow on *Jump Cuts: An Autobiography* (Random House Australia). In 2001 he published a monograph on the 1974 Fred Schepisi film, *The Devil's Playground,* for the Australian Screen Classics series. Tsiolkas is also a playwright and scriptwriter. His theater works include the collaboration *Who's Afraid of the Working Class?*, which won the major prize from the Australian Writer's Guild in 1999, as well as the plays *Fever, Viewing Blue Poles,* and *Non Parlo di Salo* (co-written with Spiro Econompoulos, with whom Tsiolkas has co-directed short films). Tsiolkas has also written on film, pop culture, and politics for magazines such as *Cinema Papers, Rolling Stone, Overland, Outrage, Arena,* and the online journal *Senses of Cinema.* Ever since the appearance of his first novel, Tsiolkas has been recognized as a taboo-breaking, innovative, ambitious writer. *Dead Europe,* his most important work, has been described as "breathtakingly good" by Ian Syson, influential former editor of the leftist journal *Overland.* As Syson says, "*Dead Europe* tells the story of Isaac, a Greek-Australian photographer invited to Athens to help celebrate the culture of the Greek diaspora . . . From Greece, Isaac travels step-by-step across post-Communist Europe and finds that in each country he visits the cultural certainties once taken for granted are out of joint." We are pleased to present three excerpts from this truly significant novel.

From Dead Europe

To a saintly man
—So goes an Arab tale—
God said somewhat maliciously:
"Had I revealed to people
How great a sinner you are,
They could not praise you."
"And I," answered the pious one,
"Had I unveiled to them
How merciful you are,
They would not care for you."
—Czeslaw Milosz

ANTE-GENESIS

The first thing I was ever told about the Jews was that every Christmas they would take a Christian toddler, put it screaming in a barrel, run knives between the slats, and drain the child of its blood. While Christians celebrated the birth of Jesus, Jews had a mock ceremony at midnight in their synagogues, before images of their horned God, where they drank the blood of the sacrificed child.

"Is that really true, Mum?" I demanded. I could not have been more than five years of age. My mother had been reading to us from an illustrated book of mythology. Her hair in those days was long and raven black; it cascaded down across her shoulders and her breasts. I would weave my fingers through it as I lay between her and my sister as she read to us. Mum had been reading to us about the gods of antiquity and I had demanded to know what had happened to them when Christ was born.

"They all went up in smoke and only God remained."

"And where did God come from?"

"He was the Jewish God," she explained, "but the Jews refused to accept his Son as their Saviour and for that they turned against him and followed Satan instead. They killed Christ and for that God will never forgive them."

"Is that really true, Mum?" I asked again.

She suddenly burst out laughing. I knew then that it was make-believe.

"That is what my father told me and what his mother had told him. Maybe it is true and maybe it isn't. Ask your Papa. He knows about Jews."

"What do you want to ask your Papa?"

The three of us looked up as my father entered the bedroom. In all of my childhood memories, my father is a giant, strong and lean and handsome, towering above me. He had just finished showering, and came out buckling the belt on his jeans. His skin gleamed like that of the gods in the plates of the mythology book.

I breathlessly recited what my mother had just told us about the Jews. He frowned and spoke harshly to her in Greek. Her face had crumpled. My hand instinctively reached out to her. My father sat on the bed and patted his thigh and I crawled across my mother and jumped onto his lap. I could smell the poppy-seed oil in his wet hair.

"What's this?" It was a regular test of my knowledge of the Greek language and I was anxious to do well. He was pointing to the center of his face.

"Nose," I answered in Greek.

"And this?"

"Mouth."

"And this?"

"Eyes."

"And this?"

"Hair."

"And this?"

I was confused. I had forgotten the word for "chin." He whispered the word and I repeated it to him. He then made a slicing motion across his throat.

"And if I do this, what would you see? What would come out?"

I was silent. I had no idea how to answer.

"Blood," my sister yelled out eagerly in Greek.

"That's right," he said, now speaking in English. "Jews have my eyes and my nose and my hair and my chin and we may all even share some of the same blood. I grew up with Jews, I studied with Jews and Jews were my friends." He looked across at my mother.

"Your mother is a peasant. Scared of everything she doesn't know. And she knows nothing about Jews."

Sophie and I were quiet. We knew that for my father the word "peasant" was one of the worst insults. The word conjured up images of dark, cowed faces, of evil old crones and decrepit, toothless old men.

"I'm sorry." My mother's voice was low, chastened.

My father ignored her. He opened a bureau drawer, pulled out some money, and folded the notes into his pocket.

"Where are you going?"

"Out."

"When are you coming back?"

"When I'm ready."

I understood that he was still angry. He kissed my sister and me and, without looking at my mother, he left the house.

I picked up the mythology book and started flicking through the pages.

"No more," my mother said, shutting the book, "I'm tired."

I must have pleaded for one more story. She turned her fury on me and shouted at us both to leave her alone. Scrambling across the bed, my sister and I fled the room, slamming the door behind us. We must have put on the television. The set was new, the black and white images as crisp and sharp as the white shirts my father wore, the black shoes that he shone diligently every morning. We must have watched television till my mother had done what she needed to do to calm herself and then she would have emerged from their room, she would have kissed our brows, and then begun to make us breakfast.

I wasn't to hear about the Jews again until I was eleven and my father started making plans to move us all back to Greece. For a whole summer all he talked about was Europe. He told us about Paris and Berlin, real cities, he explained, cities in which there were people in the streets day and night. He spoke about his own home, Thessaloniki, how it was the most beautiful city in Greece. His words painted pictures for me: I could see the crowded, dirty port with the ruined castle looking down onto it; I could imagine the tiny alleys and the sloping-roofed stalls of the old Hebrew markets, the crammed terraces of the old city. He said how he would take me on a walk under the Alexandrian Arch that was over two thousand years old. "Imagine that," he kept repeating, "two thousand years. What does this country have to offer that is that old? Nothing. Fucking nothing. We are going back to real history. Greece is free again."

I knew that my mother did not share his excitement about returning, even to a Greece that had just booted out the colonels. She had lived most of her life in Australia, and she countered his excitement with concerns about money, about how we children were to cope with learning the language. He brushed her worries aside. He ridiculed her fear of flying.

"There's nothing to fear, he smiled. Aeroplanes are safer than cars."

"They terrify me."

"Peasant," he chided, but there was a smile on his face and he kissed her on her lips. "I'll hold your hand the whole time," he promised. He lowered his voice to a whisper. "You are so beautiful, I'll have to hold on tight to you in Greece. They're real men there, they'll want you."

I was blushing.

"Shut up, Dad."

My father winked at me as my mother laughed and pulled away from his grip.

"What if we get hijacked?"

That summer the news was full of images of military-fatigued Arab men holding hostages to ransom. I found their camouflaged faces, with only their steely black eyes visible, both terrifying and alluring.

"There's nothing to fear from the hijackers," he counseled her. "Just remember, if the plane gets hijacked don't say a word in English. Just speak in Greek. They won't harm us then, they'll let us off immediately. They know we Greeks are their friends. Their comrades," he added.

"Why do they hijack planes?" I asked him. "What do they want?"

"What the fuck do they teach you at school?" He softened his tone. "They want their land back. They're fighting to get their land back. The Jews have stolen their land."

Blood and land. Thus far, this is what I knew about the Jews. Jews were blood and land.

But with the coming of autumn, all talk of Europe ceased and I soon realized that we were not going. It may have been that Dad had lost another job. I can't remember and I didn't mind. The idea of travel had excited me but I did not want to leave either my friends or my home. Mum and Dad took us for a camping holiday to the prehistoric forests of the Grampians; climbing the abrupt ferocious mountains that jutted out of the desert landscape, I forgot all thoughts of Europe, of crowded, never-sleeping cities.

My father died before I reached Europe. We buried him in a civil ceremony; he was adamant he would not be buried as a Christian. My mother pleaded with Sophie and me to agree to an Orthodox funeral but we stood our ground. When I had been just a boy, around the time my mother had told me the heinous lies about the Jews, I remembered a morning when the house seemed to shake from the screams my parents were hurling at one another. Sophie and I peeked into the kitchen to see that, instead of their work uniforms, my father had on a shirt and tie and my mother was wearing her best dress. Dad was drunk, almost paralytic: he was slurring and stumbling. My sister and I clung to each other, terrified. We listened to the argument. Someone had died. The man who had died did not want to be buried by the Church, did not want anything to do with the priests. My father was adamant he would not betray his friend's last wish. He threatened to upset the funeral, to insult the family, the priests, everyone. My mother did not want him to shame her in front of the congregation. "You have to have respect, husband," she was crying, "you have to show respect." My father was also in tears: "They're all fucking hypocrites." "Maybe," my mother had answered simply, "but your friend is dead, it's the living that now matter." My mother got her way. Dad passed out on a kitchen chair and Mum took us off to school. But I never forgot the force of my father's fury, nor the conviction in his voice when he called them hypocrites.

Sophie and I would not be shaken from our determination to bury my father as he wanted. "Please," my mother beseeched us, "do it for me. What does it matter? Your father is dead." She was on her knees, she was banging the floor with her fists, she was tearing out her hair. I could tell that Sophie was wavering. I remembered that my mother was a peasant.

"His soul would never forgive you."

We got our way. My father is buried in unconsecrated ground.

For his headstone we ordered a small rectangular stone inscribed with his name and the dates of his birth and death. Underneath, in Greek, we had the words: husband, father, worker. We asked the cheery Croatian stonemason to carve the hammer and sickle into the stone but the burly old man refused. On the day of the burial my sister and I painted the symbol crudely on the stone in her scarlet Max Factor nail polish. Like blood, it washed away in the first rain.

On the third anniversary of my father's death, I took my lover to his gravesite. I crouched and pulled out the weeds around the headstone. I had not long returned from Europe. On my last night in Thessaloniki, my cousin Giulia, the daughter of my father's brother, had placed a small red pin in my hand. It was my father's Greek Communist Party membership badge, she told me. He never wore it. He didn't dare. It had been hidden behind a portrait of my grandfather and grandmother. My aunt discovered it and was going to throw it away but my cousin saved it. For you, she told me, I saved it for you.

I took that pin with me across Yugoslavia beginning its descent into civil war, through Hungary and Czechoslovakia just emerging back into history. I traveled with it through Italy, Germany and France, flew with it from London to Melbourne.

Colin watched me as I dug a small hole in the ground, placed the badge in the pocket of earth and covered it over with dirt.

"Steve's buried here in this cemetery."

"Who?"

"Steve Ringo."

I said nothing.

"I'm going to visit his grave. Do you want to come with me?"

"No."

I didn't dare look at him. I was furious. Colin walked away and I sat cross-legged on the ground, took a joint from my shirt pocket and lit it. Steve Ringo had been the first man Colin had ever loved. At nineteen, Steve had been arrested for manufacturing and dealing amphetamines. He emerged from seven years in prison with dual faiths: the teachings of the Christian God, and the doctrines of the Aryan Nation. He was the only one of Colin's lovers to show any interest in Mum's child. He forced the teenager to learn to read. "He was adamant," Colin had explained, "that the kid wouldn't end up like him."

"He couldn't read, he was fucking illiterate. He made me read from the Bible for half an hour every evening. He forced me, told me he'd bash my lights out if I didn't do it. So I did, it took me a fucking year but I read the whole thing."

On Colin's fifteenth birthday Steve got him drunk on bourbon and took him to a tattooist mate who carved a swastika on the boy's right arm. Faded to a watery blue, the swastika was still there. I wanted to erase that tattoo. I hated the barrier it placed between myself and Colin. I hated its history, I hated its power.

"You have to get rid of it, you fucking have to get rid of it," I screamed at him when we first got together, "I will not go out with you while you still have that evil on your body."

He was pleading with me to stay, crying.

"I can't," he whispered. "This is my history and this is my shame."

And I stayed. His shame and his tears made me stay.

Colin believed in the Old Testament God, in punishment and vengeance and sin.

"What happened to Steve Ringo?"

"He went back inside and OD'd in jail. I never saw him again."

I finished the joint and was looking at my father's name carved in stone. I suddenly laughed. How did it happen, Dad, I said out loud. How did all this happen? When Colin came back he found me laughing and crying. He offered a hand and pulled me up. Our arms across each other's shoulders, we walked to the car.

That night Sophie asked us to babysit the kids. While I cooked dinner, Zach curled up in the hollow between Colin's armpit and broad chest, and my lover read to him from the old mythology book. He was reading the ancient Egyptian creation myths when Zach interrupted him.

"Uncle Colin, didn't God make the Earth?"

"Some people believe that," I hollered from the kitchen. "But I don't."

The boy ignored me.

"Is He the same God as Zeus?"

"No. He is the Jewish God. Zeus is the ancient Greek god."

I lowered the flame and went into the lounge room. Zach was looking in bewilderment at Colin.

"The Jews created God," he explained. "They called Him Jehovah—now he is our God."

"Who are the Jews?"

I found that I was holding my breath, waiting for Colin's answer.

"They're God's chosen people," he said simply, and began to read again from the book.

I had promised Zach that he could stay up late and watch *Star Wars*. He was so excited that he had to go and piss twice before we could start it. Lying between Colin and me, his legs were shaking in anticipation as the first bombastic notes of the score thundered through the stereo. Colin read to him as the yellow letters scrolled across the screen.

"A long time ago in a galaxy far, far away . . ."

The boy turned to him, his face flushed, his eyes shining. "Uncle Colin, he asked, does that mean Europe?"

APOCRYPHA

High in the mountains, where the wind goes home to rest, lived Lucia, the most beautiful woman in all of Europe. Now one must not simply dismiss this claim as an exaggeration, a parochial and ignorant testament from the villagers and Lucia's kin. It is true that most of the village had not traveled far beyond the mountain ridges which formed their world. But the fame of her beauty had spread wide, from village to village, from village to town, from town to city, until carried in whispers through the roaming of commerce and war, it became a legend that began to cross even borders. Word of Lucia's beauty circulated slowly, but it did circulate, and men and women began to swear by the moon-milk complexion of her fair skin, her slender long hands, the coal-black hair that swam down to her waist. By the time of her thirteenth birthday Lucia's myth had spread so wide that travelers would go miles out of their way, circumnavigate the precarious mountain ridge, to stop at Old Nick's café, order their coffee or chai, and sit in hope of glimpsing the radiant girl.

But Lucia's father had no intention of allowing any man to covet his daughter. He himself began to be enamored of the exquisite cast of her delicate face, intoxicated by the emerging abundance of her young flesh. His wife, noticing the stark hunger in her husband's eyes, kept a vigilant watch on her youngest daughter. Between the twin sentries of her father's ravenous desire and her mother's fearful jealousy, Lucia spent most of her days cloistered in silence. She was forbidden to go to school, as were all her sisters, and she was only allowed outside the family courtyard if escorted by her fathers or her brothers. To speak to any man, or even to a boy who was not a relative, was a sin to be punished with the most savage of beatings. She was allowed basic formalities with male relatives but even then she was ordered to not look them directly in the eye and to keep her face lowered at all times. Her mother's eagle gaze immediately noted any indiscretion on Lucia's part, and the punishment that followed was always swift and harsh. Both her eyes were blackened when she had laughed at her cousin Thanassis's impious joke. Her father's belt drew blood from her back when he whipped her on hearing that she had spoken to Baba Soulis's boys after church one Sunday. While thrashing her, Lucia's father would be deaf and blind to her agonies and her laments, exhausting himself with his brutality. Only afterwards, his rage spent, would he crawl on his knees in front of her, kissing her feet, pleading for, demanding apologies, licking clean her bloodied hands or brow or back. Watching all this was his increasingly terrified wife, who silently crossed herself and implored the saints that a suitor would come soon to take away this treacherous daughter. And if the saints won't help, she added, then let Black Death take her.

It should not be thought that Lucia was oblivious to the effects of her beauty. Her sisters, her brothers, her own father had shown enough devotion for her to understand that her looks were indeed powerful. She may have been forbidden to glance at men, but she took any opportunity that arose to break this command. When the priest fed her the communion wine she looked him boldly in the eye, causing his hand to shake; when her older brother hoisted her on his shoulders for a ride, she threw her skirts over his head; when she kissed the cheek of her just-wed brother-in-law before the altar, her whole family was shamed. Fotini, the eldest of the sisters, had been betrothed to Angelos, the oldest son of the widower Kapseli. Fotini's dowry had cost the family dearly—fifteen of their finest nanny goats, their cherished store of carpets and blankets. But the Kapselis family owned vast fields along the valley and it would be a prosperous match. When the marriage vows were completed and the families lined up in the church to kiss and bless the married couple, Lucia kissed Angelos twice chastely on his cheeks, but whispered her blessing close to his ear. The youth blushed and shivered and almost fainted. And immediately underneath the thick black cloth of his grandfather's Constantinople suit, his erection flared. As the remaining guests kissed him and shook his hand they could not help but notice the awkward lump pressing against them. An initial sniggering, then laughter, and then howls of mirth followed the newlyweds outside the church. That night, on returning home drunk from the celebrations, her father's savagery had been so fierce that Lucia lay bleeding and unconscious for days. She was locked in the cellar, with the wine and the snakes, and only her mother was allowed to see her. And even she was forbidden to speak to her. Silently brushing her blood-matted hair, stroking her bruised face, Lucia's mother nursed her daughter back to life, forcing her to eat wet bread, splashing water on her lips, all the time imploring God and the Saints and the Virgin to find a husband for her daughter. And if there were to be no one to the liking of the feverish possessed man who paced the floor above them, contorting in knots of guilt and self-disgust for the damage that he had inflicted on his most prized possession, if there were no acceptable suitor to be found, the mother prayed, let the Devil take her.

"We should marry her to Michaelis Panagis."

Lucia's father snorted, drank from his wine, and climbed into bed next to his wife. She turned her back to him. She smelt alcohol, sweat, and sex on him. The embers in the kitchen fire were waning and she could hear her two daughters in the bed next to them quietly snoring. Lucia was still banished beneath the house. The boys were asleep, four of them on the one bed, in the room across the courtyard. Her husband touched her shoulder and she lifted her nightdress and slightly raised her leg. He entered her quickly, fucked her like a hare. He began snoring as soon as he had finished. She shook him awake. Lucia was not responding to her ministrations, was sickening. She must be married.

"We should marry her to Michaelis Panagis," she repeated.

"We have two others to marry off first."

"No, she insisted, Panagis is a good marriage. He'll bring wealth. It will be easier to marry the others after that."

"He's a bastard. I won't give my Lucia to any bastard."

"You won't give Lucia to anyone."

Michaelis Panagis was the child of the idiot Panagis and his Albanian whore, Maritha. It had been assumed that Panagis, who still dribbled and slurped when he spoke, would never find a wife, but his father had returned one morning with a young Albanian girl whom he had purchased across the mountains and whom he offered to his son. Within two years they had three children. As people could not believe that the idiot Panagis had it in him to sire a child, it was assumed that all three offspring were bastards, children of the Albanian whore and her father-in-law. They were all sickly children, living in filth and poverty, but the youngest, Michaelis, had surprised the village by disappearing when little more than a child and emerging years later fat and rich from his travels abroad. He had worked in Egypt and in America and on returning to the village he had paid for a pew and a gold icon for the Church of the Holy Spirit. Now every Sunday the idiot Panagis and the whore Maritha sat in front of the congregation, ignoring the envious glares behind their backs. Michaelis had built a huge house high above the village. Though he was still insulted behind his back, there was no one in the village who did not greet him with a friendly word, who did not offer him the choice of any of their daughters.

"In the name of God, Husband, he has money."

He was silent.

"She is dying. It's a curse. It's a curse because you want to sin against your daughter."

The force of his fist on her face was so loud in the quiet mountain night that it woke the sleeping girls, who began to cry. He left his wife moaning, pulled on his trousers and descended the cellar stairs.

Lucia was lying still on the solid dirt ground. Her face was pale and her eyes dark hollows. He crouched before her and she hardly stirred from her stupor. He touched first her cheek, then her shoulder. He felt the firm curve of her breast. She did not stir but her frightened eyes looked straight into his soul. He closed his eyes, whispered his love for her and pulled her listless hand towards him. Quickly he stroked himself with her cold velvet hand and he spilt over the black dirt. He was crying.

"If he will take you, Daughter, you are to marry Michaelis Panagis."

He grabbed the child and kissed her harshly on the lips and face. Lucia pulled away.

"You are the most beautiful woman who has ever lived. Satan take you."

He raised himself and pulled up his trousers.

"Don't forget I am with the saints, Lucia. I am a saint for not raping you."

He climbed the stairs and locked the cellar door.

"What is the use of being the most beautiful woman in the world if I'm barren?"

The moon was high in the sky, and a slight breeze brought forth a keening from the pine trees that echoed through the mountains. Lucia and Michaelis had been married four years and she had yet to produce a child. The envious whispers and jealous curses that used to follow her along the paths of the village were now replaced by mutterings of pity and self-righteous joy.

Curse the damn lot of you. Lucia found sleep impossible; her dreams were filled with nightmares of demons and dead children. She cursed her father, her mother-in-law. She blamed her sorrow on the evil done to her by years of jealous occult mischief. She cursed her envious sisters and her embittered cousins. Surely it was one of them who had cast a spell on her womb? They were all bitches, jealous ugly bitches.

Every Sunday Lucia offered another promise to God should he make her pregnant, and every Sunday afternoon she and her mother would work together to undo the damage of the Evil Eye. Her mother would drop a touch of oil into the vial of holy water and she would read the villagers' gossip and spite in the dispersion of the oil. Then Lucia would pray in hope of undoing the evil; she would send down her own curses to the women who envied her. But still nothing stirred inside her. And every month when she felt her body flushing out her blood, she cursed the names of every woman in the village, spitting out each one.

But still nothing stirred inside her.

As she lay there, sleepless, there was a scratching on the door and she went cold. She held her breath. From the outbuilding she could hear bleating from one of the goats. Then the scratching continued. She shook Michaelis awake. "Michaeli, there's something outside."

Her husband jumped out of the bed, reached for his hunting knife and opened the door. Two shivering figures stood under the moonlight.

"What in the devil are you doing here?"

Lucia hid under the quilt. She knew one of the men at the door. It was Jacova, who worked as a tanner in Thermos; it was to Jacova that Michaelis sold the skins of the wolves and the minks that he hunted. Beside the Hebrew was a young boy, his eyes large and black. She could not hear the whisperings between her husband and the Hebrew.

"Don't let them in, Michaeli," she prayed. "Don't you dare let them in." But her husband beckoned her to rise and to bring out some wine. She pulled a shawl across her shoulders and, without looking at the strangers, she made her way into the dark cellar to fetch a pail of wine. She placed two glasses in front of the men and she and the boy sat apart on a bench near the dead fire while the men talked to each other in whispers. They did not dare light the lanterns. Lucia peered through the shutters at her mother-in-law's house across the courtyard. No one stirred. She came and sat back on the bench.

She looked the boy up and down. She had never been so close to a Hebrew and was surprised at how ordinary he seemed. His features were not so different from those of her brothers. His brow was wet, as indeed it would be if he had just completed the long walk from Thermos up into the mountains. She could smell his fear, and the keen hint of his trade, the bitter reek of pelt and leather. Though still only a child, he was developing the strong forearms of his father. He was destined to be a handsome man. She smiled at him but the boy blushed and immediately looked down at his feet. Lucia smiled to herself. She was still beautiful.

"I will forget him. If you take him he will be as your son."

Lucia strained to hear more of the conversation.

Michaelis shook his head.

"It is too dangerous, Jacova. The Germans are everywhere and all the region knows that Elia is your son. We cannot hide him."

Lucia nodded to herself. Good. Good answer, husband. All the harpies in the village will be lining up to denounce us.

"Michaeli, I have known you a long time. Yes, the Germans are everywhere, that is why my wife and daughters and I must flee. But up here in these mountains there are many hiding places. You can hide the boy. And this war will not last. Once it is over, once the Germans have gone, the boy is yours to keep."

Lucia shook her head in disbelief. The man was a fool if he thought that they would be taken in. Everyone knew that the Hebrews could not be trusted. Even if the Germans were to be conquered, nothing would stop Jacova returning and claiming his son. No, throw him out, Michaeli, throw out the Hebrew and his bastard child.

Michaelis turned to Lucia.

"Up near the summit of the mountain, near where you graze the goats, in what condition is the old church?"

"Michaeli, stop this nonsense. Old Voulgaris, Basili Leptomas's youngest, they all graze their herds up there. We could not hide the child."

"We could, beneath the stone. The old monks had a room beneath the church. No one is fool enough to venture there. We could lock the cellar during the day and the child could roam free at night. We could do that."

Lucia stared across the table to where the older Hebrew was sitting. Jacova was looking only at Michaeli, a glimmer of hope shining in his eyes. The boy was staring at her. In the darkness his face was dark and only the white in his eyes was visible. Lucia shuddered.

"We cannot do it, Husband. If they catch us . . ."

Michaeli ignored her. He was looking hard at Jacova.

"And what will you pay us if we decide in your favor?"

The father nodded to his son. From underneath his tunic Elias took out a small parcel wrapped in black silk. Jacova took it from him, pulled away the silk, and opened the lid of a square wood box. In the dark room, the gold and the jewels sparkled like fire. Lucia drew a breath. Michaelis's eyes grew wide and delighted. Lucia rose from the bench and stood beside her husband. The men and the boy had disappeared. From the box she took out a small band, gold and studded with glittering silver stones, which she placed on her finger. She took a ruby brooch and held it close to her lips. All the time the boy's gaze did not leave her enraptured face.

"Ours?"

"All of it, yours."

Lucia placed the jewels back into the box. Michaelis closed the lid and placed the box on his lap as if he feared the Hebrew would regret his offer and snatch it back.

"He will work hard for me."

"He works hard for me now."

Jacova placed his arm around his son.

"You will treat him fairly?"

"Of course."

Michaelis rose from the table. He gave the box to his wife and beckoned the boy to come with him. The father and son were allowed a moment to say farewell and then Jacova began his trek back down the mountain. Lucia watched as her husband and the boy walked into the black night for their ascent to the summit. She cursed her useless womb, pounding her fists on her stomach, and then fell to the ground and began banging the stone floor. Her anger was so ferocious that on reaching to brush aside a wisp of hair that had fallen loose from her headscarf, she found that she had torn a clump of hair from her head. In her fury and hatred she had not felt the pain. Her face twisted into a terrible grimace, spit falling from her mouth as she banged her head on the stone, until she finally exhausted herself from curses and lay trembling on the floor. Again she could hear the breeze spinning among the trees. Giving up her curses, her prayers to God spent, she now turned elsewhere.

—Satan, give me my own child. Give me my own child, Lord, and take away the demon Hebrew you've let into my house.

As soon as Lucia uttered her prayer, a peace descended. Slowly she rose from the floor and, gathering her hair tight under her scarf, she dried her eyes. The dawn was beginning. She went to light the fire and prepare herself for the day ahead.

The Book of Lilith

"Every Christmas the Jews would steal a Christian toddler, put it in a barrel, still alive, run knives between the slats, and drain the child of its blood. Then they'd drink it. That's the first thing I ever got told about the Jews."

"I can't believe your mother told you that shit."

"I must have been about five when she told me. She made it sound like a fairy tale . . ."

". . . some pretty fucked-up fairy tale . . ."

". . . I know, I know. Dad told her off when he heard her talking about that sort of stuff. He told us it was uneducated peasant bullshit. He sat me down and gave me a history lesson. He explained where the Jews came from, told us that the Bible was their history, told us about the Holocaust. He even explained what the Ashkenazi and the Sephardim were. Being Dad, of course, he put his own Marxist spin on it. He always said that the tragedy of the Holocaust was that the Nazis destroyed the Jewish proletariat. And he told us that the Bible was all crap and not to believe in any religion."

"He was never religious?"

"Maybe when he was a kid. But, nah, he hated religion. His religion was communism. And heroin."

"My mum hated religion too. Typical Aussie, she taught me jack-shit. I had to go to school before I heard about Jesus. I believed in the Easter Bunny but I hadn't heard of Jesus."

"So how was she when you became a Christian?"

"I was never a Christian."

"I thought you were . . ."

". . . I was fascinated by religion; I read the Bible because Steve made me. I'm glad he did. It made me fall in love with reading history. I know, that's not very Aussie of me. But I hardly knew any Christians. Just Steve and some of the kids at school. I knew the Catholics, the Orthodox, the Muslims. But they didn't give a fuck about religion except for some fasting at Ramadan or Easter. That was all religion was for them."

"I know exactly what you mean. It's all ritual, no theology. When I got older I yelled at Mum, said: Your bloody Jesus was a Jew, how could you tell me the things you did? He was a Jew."

"He wasn't."

"He was."

"Listen to me. He was born a Jew but he came to Earth to announce a new Covenant, to replace the old Covenant between Moses and God."

"Now you do sound like a Christian."

"I just fucking hate that liberal bullshit that claims we're all brothers, that it's all the same religion . . ."

". . . it's the same bloody God . . ."

"Listen, all I'm saying is that if you're a Jew, you claim to be a descendant of the twelve tribes of Israel. Your law is the Law of Moses. You are the Chosen People. That's it. Your God doesn't give a fuck about anyone else. It's all there in the Torah. If you're Christian you believe in the resurrection of Christ, the Trinity and the new Covenant. If you're Muslim then Mohammed was God's last Prophet and you submit to the word of God as written in the Qu'ran. They are not the same thing. I can't stand New Age Christian preachers trying to humanize the Bible. I can't stand secular Yank Jews brandishing their copies of the Constitution as equivalent to Holy Writ and thinking they can be both Jewish and nonbelievers. Fucking bullshit. At least the Muslims are bloody honest. You can't be democratic and monotheistic. Choose. It's one or the other."

"I disagree. That's too hard, much too hard. You can be ecumenical. You can have a rabbi, a priest, a mullah . . ."

". . . and they go into a bar . . ."

". . . You can have them get together, acknowledge differences but also accept similarities. Find common ground. Otherwise you are talking perpetual war. I can't agree with you".

"Listen, your mum didn't make that up about the Jews, not the blood libel. It's a fact. It's in the Gospels, I can't fucking remember exactly where, I think it's in Matthew. The Jews answered Pontius Pilate: let His blood be on us and our children. If you're a Christian, you have to accept that obscenity as fact. Your dad was wrong. Your mother wasn't speaking as an illiterate peasant but as a believer. That's the source of blood libel and I don't give a fuck how many bourgeois theologians attempt to explain it away by theorizing about the politics of the early Church and the Roman state. What are you? What do you believe? Do you believe that the Jews killed Christ? Or do you believe that the Jews are God's Chosen People and his only people? Or do you submit to the word of God as revealed in the Qu'ran and unless you do you are doomed to Hell? This might offend your fucking democratic wishy-washy liberal pieties, but religion is war."

"Why are you so angry?"

"Because people are cowards."

"Who came first? Abraham or Moses?"

"Jesus Christ, I can't believe this. And you're the one who went to fucking university."

"They don't teach religion at university."

"They should."

"Why?"

"It's history, it's politics."

"You sound like a bloody fundamentalist. Bullshit. God is dead. That's what you learn at university."

"Right, He's dead, is He? Go ask Khadijah and Bilal next door. Go ask your mum. Go ask the fucking Israelis and the Palestinians or the Hindus and the Pakistanis if God is dead."

"You haven't answered my question."

"Abraham was before Moses. He was after Noah. Isaac, your namesake, was his son whom God demanded he sacrifice. Abraham was prepared to do God's will. His other son was Ishmael, the bastard son he had with his slave, Hagar. The Jews come from the line of Isaac. The Arabs claim they are descended from Ishmael."

"Fucking perfect. Slavery and blood feuds. And that's religion? You can fucking keep it."

"That's history, mate, that's politics. Blood and servitude."

"So you're arguing that if you are going to believe in God, you have to believe fundamentally? You believe in Noah and the flood, Sodom and fucking Gomorrah? The Resurrection? That Mohammed received the word of God? That's your argument?"

"Yes."

"And Adam and Eve?"

"Yes. Adam and Eve and Cain and Abel. And Lilith."

"Who?"

"Adam's first wife."

"What? That's not in the Bible."

"It's apocrypha. I like Lilith. She gave God the finger."

"Who the fuck was Lilith?"

"First there was the Word. And the Word was Wisdom. Then there was God, Yahweh, and he created the heavens and earth and all that walks and lives and is on the earth. He created Adam after his own image and placed him in Eden. Then when Adam came of age he wanted a partner. So God passed all the female animals past him and Adam slept with them all but none of them satisfied him."

"You're making this up."

"I'm not. It's one version of her story, anyway. You want me to continue?"

"Go."

"So God created Lilith from the earth, as he had done with Adam, and he created her in Wisdom's image. Sophia. You should know that word. It's Greek."

"Hang on. And is Sophia another god?"

"Yes."

"But isn't there only one God?"

"Moses told the Jews they could only worship the one God. But they had many gods before that.

"So Lilith and Adam get together?"

"Yes. And they had children, which are now the demons that roam the earth. But Lilith wasn't satisfied with Adam and she left him. She wanted to be equal to him. She flew to the Red Sea and there gave birth to more demons."

"Fuck. What happened to her?"

"She's still on earth. She departed Eden long before the Fall and, as she hasn't eaten off the Tree of Good and Evil, she's immortal. She will live to the end of time and God allows her to eat the blood of uncircumcised children. That's our first mother. Blood, you can't escape it. All religions know this."

"But they're fairy tales."

"Or they're truth. It all depends on faith."

"But you must agree that they are of their place and time. You can have faith in God or Christ without having to accept all that superstitious shit from millennia ago."

"You can argue and disagree about the meaning of the words, but no, I don't believe you can pick and choose from religious moral codes as if faith is some kind of supermarket of beliefs. I'm with the fundamentalists. You make your choice. You make your fucking choice. You are either a believer or not. God makes his meaning and his character clear in the Torah, in the Bible, and in the Qu'ran. He is not a God of love, he is a God of justice."

"So for me to believe in God, I have to believe that loving you, making love to you, being with you, is a sin and I am damned to Hell forever?"

"Yes. You can ask God's forgiveness, but if you remain with me, you are damned."

"So do you believe in this God?"

"I don't know. But I'll tell you this, my love, if there is the one God, I still choose you. I choose you above God. I've made that choice and I'll live with that choice. I choose Lilith and the demons, I choose Lucifer, who too knew love. I promise you, Isaac, if God is the righteous prick from the Bible, I choose Hell over Him. Fuck him. I choose to be with you. I choose Hell."

BRENDA WALKER

Brenda Walker was born in New South Wales in 1957, growing up largely
on the North Coast of the state. Her mother, Shirley Walker, was one of the
first feminist critics to attain prominence in Australian academia. Brenda
Walker has also written widely on questions of gender and their relation to
both the theory and practice of fiction. She studied at the University of New
England in Armidale and, after getting a Ph.D. in English at the Australian
National University, moved to Perth in 1984. She now lectures in English at
the University of Western Australia. Walker has co-edited three books: *Katharine Susannah Prichard: Centenary Essays* with John Hay in 1984, *Poetry &*
Gender with David Brooks in 1989, and *Elizabeth Jolley: New Critical Essays*
with Delys Bird in 1991. In 1996 Walker edited *Risks,* an anthology of short
stories. She also contributed to *Motherlove,* edited by Debra Adelaide, and
has published influential articles and reviews in the field of contemporary
Australian women's writing. Fremantle Arts Center Press published her first
novel, *Crush,* in 1991. It won the 1990 T. A. G. Hungerford Award for Fiction
and was short-listed for the Western Australian Premier's Award. Subsequent novels were *One More River* (1993) and *Poe's Cat* (1999). Walker's most
recent novel, *The Wing Of Night* (2004), concerns the aftermath of the First
World War, which is perhaps the most traumatic event in Australia's modern
history. The South Australian academic Gillian Dooley has commented that
The Wing Of Night "is as much about what could be happening in the present
and will happen in the future" than simply the past. This marks the difference between Walker's conception of the historical novel and many of her
Australian contemporaries, and foreshadows her shift back to the present in
the excerpt presented here.

Vast Partings out in Space

Allie and Ash were watching TV in the breezeway on the farm when the terrorist's ex-wife came on. It was a week for ex-wives; Ash had just read a newspaper interview with the ex-wife of a gangster. These women talked about their husbands in the kind, abstracted way that lost wives often do. He was harmless, he just ordered all those shootings. Men flew apart in cars and cafés all over Melbourne. The terrorist was a vulnerable person. He was looking for a family, in the dirt and ammunition of Afghanistan. He had a family, as the TV interviewer pointed out. But he left them and went looking for a different family, a bigger one with louder guns. And the wives didn't know. They didn't question their harmless, their vulnerable men. The gangster's ex-wife said, "I had to sleep beside him every night." So she didn't want to know.

The terrorist's ex-wife was pretty. Ash knew better than to comment. Allie wasn't frivolous, and the prettiness of the terrorist's wife, the noticing of this prettiness, showed a deplorable frill in Ash's personality, a willingness to turn aside from the main game, an excess. And there was nothing excessive about Allie, who took a Jeep with a weak battery and an axe out every morning and searched for dry wood, dragging it out of the sand and salt and chopping it into pieces for the hot water system. There's money and electricity on the farm. There's a telephone. You can pick it up and order a new hot water system in the city and an electrician will drive out and fit it. It's even easier to get a new battery for a Jeep. But these are things Allie would never ask for; asking would draw attention to some city-ness in her. So would cleaning out the house. She might end up in an ordinary home which just happened to be in the bush, instead of a scuffed jumble of rooms walled in harsh torn metal fly mesh and piled with meat safes and long elegant family tables tipped on their sides and painted with whatever had been lying in old tins in the machinery sheds, thick crinkled drips of nasty blue or orange halted in mid-slide down the legs and scraps of floor covering nailed to the top.

Allie had her point to make, Ash knew. Behind the sheds fifty years of vehicles sat in a rough line, from a Ford with a broken axle to last year's Audi, which died in a paddock, the back seat stuffed with sheep, and was dragged into place by the Jeep. To Ash it looked as if hundreds of people had driven there over the years, stepped from their cars or leaped from their trucks, landing in a brief squat in the dirt, or else having thrown a leg over the back of an English motorbike, a Norton or a BSA, and pulled off a pair of heavy gloves and thrown them on the fuel tank, and walked away, out on the salt pans, gone forever, all the people, still walking, as far as she knew, out on the salt, their keys unclicked in the ignitions. And the sheep, scrambling out of the open windows of the Audi, their little hooves marking the turquoise dust as they struggled to follow the drivers, the riders, over the bright flat salt.

Ash had a theory about Allie, who grew up in a sweeter climate and traveled to school each day with her father in a very big car. Her father was a surgeon. Her name wasn't always Allie, then. Yes, sometimes she was Allie, sitting in the front with the driver to spite her father, who was some distance away in the back seat, alone. She despised her father for a number of reasons, chiefly because he was devoted to his work, not her. When she became Alexandra, the surgeon knew he was forgiven, briefly forgiven, and his little girl got in the back seat with him and the driver, relieved, could concentrate on the road. Allie could switch to Alexandra in a blink. Ash doesn't ever want to sit with Alexandra, who surely ruled whatever schoolyard she was headed for. She could cope with Allie and the old TV with the pretty face of the ex-wife of the terrorist, an ex-wife who is kind, not stupid, and who seems to be entirely visible on the screen, no gearshifts into a different register, no sudden strain in the motor of her personality. Perhaps this had something to do with being an ex-wife.

Allie and Ash are married to two brothers: a country brother, a city brother. Ash is keeping Allie company for the week. They had matching babies, little sons. The men have taken the children to the football in the city. The boys will visit their grandmother in her high apartment. Ash's son is looking forward to the game. Last year it rained on the crowd and water collected in the cuff of his raincoat and he drank it secretly and told Ash about it in a whisper later. They had to be a little careful. He was in danger of being called a sook, a mummy's boy. These are among the insults the gangster's ex-wife aims at her husband in the newspaper interview. A sook, a mummy's boy. Weak and soft, except in the small matter of contract killings.

Things are not going so well with Ash's husband. She tried to talk about it to Allie, but Allie became Alexandra and said that sometimes the family thinks you must be very unwell. The word unwell gave Ash a shock. Allie is big on family, as long as it doesn't include her father the surgeon, who she hasn't spoken to for seven years. After the conversation with Allie, Ash took a potted cyclamen to the children's grandmother, her mother-in-law. Her mother-in-law was famous in the family for shooting birds. When she lived in the bush each dawn began with rifle fire. The galahs were her enemies, they picked the leaves from the eucalyptus beside the machinery shed. But she was reasonably good with people. Ash didn't mention the problem with her husband and she didn't need to. As she left the apartment her mother-in-law reached up to be kissed. We are Ruth and Naomi, she said. Ruth and Naomi in the story in the Bible.

On the TV the terrorist's ex-wife said he had a heart of gold. He'd do anything for anyone.

Time for bed, the sisters-in-law agreed.

It was a bright clear winter. Ash drove from windmill to windmill, checking the water-troughs so the sheep wouldn't go thirsty. When they died foxes dragged their bones far and wide. She found a tangle of dirty tapes in the glove box of the Jeep: British music, Traffic and Cream. A hammer banged about in the tray. It was used for finishing off sheep that were too weak to survive. There were no seat belts, her son pressed hard against her when the back wheels slipped sideways in sand and they came to a halt in a crescent of tire tracks. The trick is, she told him, to relax into the slide. He asked if there was a trick to everything and she told him yes, to shut him up. Her skin was hot with fear. Out in the distance the animals left their small shelters by the fence and staggered in the direction of the water. There were vines spiked with thorns in patches on the ground but no trees, just low scrub and the distant blue shine of salt on the surface of the earth. While Ash drove out to the stock and the water Allie cleared the shit pump. There was a cesspit at the side of the house. The liquid at the top of the pit had to be pumped out and hosed away. When the pump was clogged Allie put on gloves and heavy overalls and cleaned it out. Each night Ash slept alone in the bed her husband had slept in before he went to boarding school and stars, clouds of stars, shone through the window. Allie and Ash had taken their children to the Observatory near the city and the astronomers had put them in a Faraday cage: a kind of large box that screens out electromagnetic fields. Inside the cage is an electrical blankness, a vacuum of energy. It can never be perfect, electricity is always able to leak in. Ash imagined herself in the closed-off blankness of the Faraday cage. It was the opposite of a sheep paddock, where the horizon lies at knee height, in the far distance, and the whole upright human body is exposed to the great white bowl of the sunlit sky. She tried to make herself comfortable in her husband's childhood bed. You are unwell, she said to herself. Allie didn't know how unwell, nobody knew how unwell Ash was except her GP and a surgeon in the city, who happened to be Allie's father.

He knew who she was, of course. After they finished the medical discussion he stood to show her to the door. He was a tall man, square-shouldered, very old, very good at what he did. Which was just as well, because Ash still had to decide whether she will agree to him cutting up her body, very soon. Ash wondered about the limits of his patience and his self-control. He broke at the door. And how is she? he asked. How is Alexandra? Ash said that Alexandra was well and happy and busy with her little boy. She had a garden, said

Ash, full of vegetables and marigolds, and a pet galah called Leroy who never left her shoulder.

When Allie and Ash drove up into the hills to an open night at the Observatory, Ash was already sick, although she didn't know this at the time. It was a long drive; they had to be well clear of the city to see into the sky. Her son had a bottle of cordial in his schoolbag, a backpack that Ash had to empty out before they could take it with them. Ash found pieces of quartz at the bottom. Lunchwraps and *The Guiness Book of Records* and half a Burger Ring. That's for you, mummy, he had said. Dan asked me for it and I said I'm saving that for my mum but you can have half. Dan is his cousin, Allie's boy. The roads divided in places that weren't marked on the map. They drove and drove; headlights showed a narrow space through old trees, grown hard and close against the road.

There were seventy, perhaps as many as a hundred people gathered for the tour of the Observatory. Someone lit a cigarette and the match showed the line of an eye-socket or a nose. Then everything was quickly black. The furthermost dark shapes moved on up a track. Gravel slid and finally steadied under their shoes.

A little night-vision came to Ash, under the structure of the telescope. Then everybody began to climb. The steps were lit dimly at ankle height. It was cold. Ash could see why the astronomers had scarves and beards. One of them explained what he was doing as the great dome of the Observatory slid open to the sky.

There was no eyepiece, no pirate telescope as Ash had imagined. Stars appeared on a screen like a TV in a bare room to one side of the dome, where the astronomer sat alone each night, holding a chocolate bar in gloved hands, with little to do except wait for the moment when he wanted to eat chocolate more than he wanted warm hands. Ash thought of Rilke: who dares to lean his forehead against the night as on a bedroom window? It was as easy as watching TV, for the astronomer. He told them about slow explosions among the stars; how every atom in our bodies has been through many vast partings, out in space.

They looked at the planets, which were a dirty white in the soft blackness of the sky.

Ash walked quickly down the track, holding her child on her hip. He was light enough to carry. The gravel was unsteady underfoot. She took small edgy steps, listening to the footsteps of Allie and Dan behind her.

Inside the main building, hospitable astronomers took everybody down to their Faraday cage. There were wall-sized photographs of galaxies and a display about an early, Parisian attempt to map the whole of the night sky. It didn't matter that it was abandoned.

Later, in the dark car, Allie opened a bottle of Bundaberg rum and the women passed it backwards and forwards on the long drive back to the city. Ash grew drunker, warmer, until everything seemed to connect and they were all part of this, the night, the alcohol, the children and each other and the galaxy.

Ash couldn't sleep. She got up and put wood in the stove and found an old aluminum saucepan, pitted with black speckles, and a jug of milk. Shelves held books from the days when her mother-in-law lived on the farm. She found Kipling and the Bible and an old nursing textbook that told her that her condition was a menace to life. How good it was to read this, after the bland phraseology of current medicine. Even Allie's father expressed concern, he did not speak of active menace.

There was a fault in Ash, which she freely recognized, which she turned over in her mind as the sky lightened and the foxes moved with confidence over the green and stinking pasture by the shit pump, out to their burrows in the salt. Ash was dreamy, indecisive. She couldn't even decide if the terrorist was a vicious mercenary or a poor boy led astray in a foreign land. She couldn't decide to wrap up her son in the night and put him on her hip and walk away from this family. Would she be following ghosts and sheep and foxes out over the salt? She couldn't decide whether to see Allie's father, the surgeon, and ask him to cut up her body immediately. She couldn't decide to save herself. The milk warmed on the stove, under an elastic skin. She poured it into a big frail octagonal cup that must have been here when her mother-in-law was a bride. She settled into a wicker chair with the Kipling and read story after story. Take my word for it, writes Kipling, the silliest woman can manage a clever man; but it needs a very clever woman to manage a fool. Was she clever or silly? Ash had no idea. She'd been like this all her life, it seemed. Surveying different positions until decisions just cancelled themselves and she floated stupidly, freely, and reached for a book, where characters act on one another, and live.

Once Ash took Allie to a concert; something she would never see in the bush. The *Requiem* was somber, full of flats, or so the program said, written in the last months of Mozart's life and commissioned by someone who wished to plagiarize it. He thought he was being poisoned and perhaps he was. The music was unfinished when he died.

The soloists followed the score in bound books, so they seemed to be attentive readers, remote, lost in the act of reading. Sometimes the tenor closed his eyes and smiled privately; sometimes he looked across to the audience as if they were a landscape, or the sea, as if he was sitting on a headland with a book. Then he started to sing. One of the violinists was shaking her head as she played, her shoulders swaying. When she took the violin from under her chin she pressed her fingers deeply behind her collarbones. How Ash loved the way they lost themselves in art.

Her son called to her from a bedroom at the far end of the house. The hallway was beautiful in the darkness, you couldn't see all the broken cornices. Ash sat on the edge of her son's bed. He was asleep again. His cousin slept too, an arm's length away. She remembered the moment when the back wheels of the Jeep went from under them and she told him that you must never correct a slide. The shelf between the boy's beds was stacked with old videos. She pulled one out. She almost remembered watching it. Yes. She remembered the escape from the Death Star, the forced obedience of the machinery of flight, the speed and perfect accuracy of it all, the relief, afterwards, the sweet blackness of space.

Roberta Williams, quoted in "Laid Low by the High Life," *The Weekend Australian,* June 2-3, 2007, page 21.

Jodie Sparrow interviewed on *60 Minutes,* Channel 7, May 27, 2007.

Rainer Maria Rilke, "Straining so Hard Against the Strength of the Night," *The Selected Poetry of Rainer Maria Rilke,* ed. and trans. Stephen Mitchell (London: Pan Books, 1987) page 127

Rudyard Kipling, *Plain Tales from the Hills* (London: Macmillan, 1931) page 14.

MICHAEL WILDING

Born in England and an Oxford graduate, but long the quintessential writer about academic and daily life in Australia, Michael Wilding was a longtime lecturer in English at the University of Sydney, and has written scholarly books on John Milton, British fiction, and Australian social fiction, writing with particular acumen on Christina Stead. Wilding is associated with a group of innovative writers including Frank Moorhouse, Murray Bail, and Rodney Hall, all of whom combined a traditional Australian's yarn-spinning with the influence of American postmodernists such as Barth, Barthelme, and Coover. The major themes of his fiction include bohemianism, suburbia, the Beat and Hippie generations, and rogue manhood. Wilding is a genial ironist with a savage bite and unexpected doses of compassion.

The Prisoner of Mount Warning

Back in the 1970s, Charles Dorritt worked on a bibliographical survey of the alternative press. Thirty years later, recovering from a nervous breakdown by doing a creative writing course, he announces that he is publishing his memoirs of recruitment by the intelligence agencies, torture, and sex-slavery. Plant is called to lunch by some survivors of those times, all of whom seem deeply concerned that the revelations should not appear. They hire Plant to have a word with Dorritt. Plant pursues him through the dope lands of northern New South Wales. A past era of magic mushrooms, free love, American friends, and an alternative newspaper of deep level inauthenticity begins to emerge, something no one but Plant is keen to see revealed.

In Dorritt's account it was a privileged world. A secret garden. An idyll he had strayed into and never wanted to leave. He had visited them in their rambling house in Balmain. The grounds down to the water. The boatshed. The towers and turrets. He had always wanted to live somewhere with towers and turrets. A castle somewhere. He had always wanted to live beside water, to wake in the morning and walk down lawns to the water's edge, barnacles clustering on the boatshed piles, fish silently moving in the dappled light and shade. Angela sat on the old stone wall and fished. The smell of fresh coffee wafted across the lawns, mingling with hibiscus and frangipani, honeysuckle, jasmine.

"Of course I didn't see all of that at first," he explained.

When he arrived it was just a gate in a fence. He knew there were reaches of the harbor around but it was not a suburb with which he had any familiarity. Old sea captains' mansions, run down, divided up into rooming houses. Pokey dockworkers' cottages. An air of unemployment and criminality pervaded.

He gave his sharp barking laugh.

"Appropriate, really," he said. "Now it's all movie people and accountants and drug dealers."

They were sitting around a big table when he arrived. Some of them, anyway. Drinking coffee. Rolling joints. The record player playing Bob Dylan and Leonard Cohen, Maria Muldaur and Linda Ronstadt. It may have been the kitchen table. But it had the air of a boardroom. Directors' meeting. Council of war.

It used to be the fashion. The kitchen table. It became the central icon for houses like that.

"Funny, really, how they all did that," Dorritt reflected. "Sat 'round the table in the middle of the morning. Or the afternoon. Or the evening for that matter."

A bowl of fruit, maybe. Bananas, oranges, apples. Nothing he especially wanted to eat. The peaches and mangoes had always been taken. If they were ever there. The idyll of eternal spring in eternal autumn suggested they were there. Or had been. But he never recalled seeing them. Not in Balmain.

And the newspapers and magazines.

"It was always the same," said Dorritt.

Or nearly the same. The poetry magazine people would have piles of poetry magazines on the table. The political editors would have political magazines. And newspapers. International papers. Some still rolled and sealed and unwrapped. And books too. Maybe the small press publishers had more books scattered on the table and the political editors more newspapers.

Only the poets had poetry. "So if the conversation became too difficult you could just pick up something and read it."

"Too difficult?" said Plant.

"Oh, too political, too abstruse, you know. Or too embarrassing. Personal stuff. That sort of thing."

And did it?"

"Did it what?"

"Become too political. Or too personal."

Dorritt reflected. He pushed his glasses up from his nose onto his forehead. That way he would look at whoever was talking and not see them. Just a smudge. A sort of undifferentiated blur where their features used to be. Face and nose and that sort of thing.

"To be honest," he said.

Plant waited.

"To be honest I find most conversations difficult. Really. One way or another."

"So you did a lot of reading."

"I came across a lot of publications I might otherwise have missed," he said. "Little magazines I hadn't heard of. Fugitive pamphlets. Ephemera. It was good in that way. It meant I could be more comprehensive."

"Sitting in embarrassment at the kitchen table."

"It wasn't always embarrassment," said Dorritt. "Sometimes it was . . ."

He took off his glasses and rubbed them with a tissue he had found in his trouser pocket.

"Magical," he said. "Quite magical."

He finished his polishing and peered at the glasses before putting them back on.

"And beautiful," he said, smiling, his shy, nervous, almost endearing smile. "It seemed so beautiful. At first."

"It was like a William Morris vision. All these pre-Raphaelite girls wandering past in robes and shawls, all the colors, drapes and cushions and art work. That was when I realized."

"Realized what?" Plant asked.

"Life is art."

"Uh-huh."

"Your life should have the beauty and design of art. Every little detail. The cups you drink from, the chairs you sit on."

Plant looked at Dorritt, furry and fuzzy in his beard and greasy hair and dull browns and khaki.

"And they were living it. Producing this paper, espousing these politics."

"Espousing what politics?" Plant asked.

"Oh," Dorritt sighed, a long, deep sigh, like the deep withdrawing sea. "It was really hard to pin them down. They were for revolution, of course. A total revolution. Art and life. Like William Morris. Culture and politics."

"All that smudgy printing and erratic typesetting."

"Yes," said Dorritt. He gave his irritating smile, that one of possessive love for everything he had ever encountered and catalogued.

"Hardly the Kelmscott Press," said Plant.

"How could it be?" said Dorritt sharply. "Time goes on. Art changes. Different conditions produce different aesthetics. You couldn't have had hand-set type and hand printing."

"Why not?" asked Plant.

"It wouldn't have been right. It would have been anachronistic."

"Of course," said Plant.

"The problem was, they just weren't very helpful. They were terribly nice. When you got used to them. But you could never pin them down. Like how often did the paper come out?"

"When it's ready," Rose told him.

"But when's that? Every month? Every other month?"

"Something like that," said Rose.

"That's the difference between twelve issues a year and six."

"Is it?" said Rose.

"Yes. Which should I put down?"

"Twelve seems an awful lot," said Rose. "We sort of work on an issue and it takes the time it takes. And then in the fullness of time it's delivered."

"Who's the editor?" he asked.

"The editor?" said Angela. "What do you mean who's the editor?"

"Well, who's in charge? Who decides what goes in?"

"You do have a schoolteacher's vision, darling," said Angela. "Why should anyone decide?"

"Surely someone has to."

"We are all editors," said Angela. "Everyone has edited and all shall have prizes."

"What sort of prizes?"

"People who ask questions," she said.

"I don't understand."

"They're a great prize," said Angela. "Hook one of them and who knows?"

"Who knows?"

"You could be set for life. We could keep you in a goldfish tank and whenever we needed some questions we'd be able to go down and open the lid."

He laughed nervously.

"Or like a chook box. We could give you some scraps of paper and a pen and you could write down your questions and leave them in the straw. We'd come and collect them every morning. What have we got today? Wow, that's a big one, that must be a double-yolker."

She looked at him carefully.

"Mind you, you'd have to keep on producing them. We couldn't have you going broody. We couldn't keep feeding you handfuls of grain if you didn't deliver. Stop delivering questions and that would be it. Put you in a chook raffle. Wring your neck and pull out your feathers. Pop you in the boiler."

Her teeth flashing at him in the glorious sun.

"It was one of those households where there were always visitors. People coming to stay. People passing through. I found it very confusing. Especially at first. I didn't know who was who. I would ask about the paper and they wouldn't know. Normally it wouldn't take me long. I'd visit someone, some magazine, talk to them. It might only take half an hour. A bit longer. But a couple of hours at the outside. Then I'd have to write it all up, of course. That took time. Listening to the tapes and transcribing them. Sometimes I'd have to go back. If something wasn't clear. Some detail. If I couldn't catch what they said. Or I'd realize when I wrote up an entry that some detail was missing. Or contradictory. That sort of thing. So I might have to go back. Just briefly. But that was it, usually. And I'd done a lot of the basic work in the library. So I had a sort of skeleton of information.

"But with these, I didn't even have the skeleton. Like how often it came out. Or how to subscribe to it. Let alone who edited it. Who was responsible for what. Layout. Design.

"I could never seem to pin anyone down. If I did it was the wrong person. Someone just passing through who didn't know anything about it. Or worse, someone who had nothing to do with it, really, but talked as if they did. They'd rave on and then I'd realize it was pointless.

"The girls were nice. But they were very vague. And the men, they were always going off somewhere. Or busy. I could never get them to sit down and talk. That was why I had to keep going back. At first. I'd make an arrangement to interview them and they wouldn't be there. I'd sit around and wait. Talk to someone else. Rose. Or Angela. No one seemed to mind. There were always people sitting round the table. Making coffee. It was quite pleasant, actually.

"Except I'd given myself a timetable. To get it all done. Otherwise it could have gone on for ever."

He laughed.

"Maybe that's what I should have done. Dragged it out. Made it a research project for life."

He shook his head.

"Funny how when you're young you're so conscientious. Don't you think?"

Plant made his non-committal noise. He wasn't sure that he did think. Not that.

"I was terribly conscientious," said Dorritt. "That was why I'd been so shattered about my thesis. I'd been meticulous with that. Absolutely meticulous. And then Professor Oates had said it wasn't good enough. That's when he hired me for the survey."

He took off his glasses again and rubbed his eyes.

"So I was determined to be meticulous about this. And they were making it hard for me. Not deliberately."

He paused.

"Or maybe it was deliberate. Sometimes I thought they were deliberately avoiding me. Deliberately avoiding answering questions. It was hard to tell. The girls were so nice about it. About everything. But it was getting embarrassing. Going round there all the time and getting nowhere. I felt I was intruding."

He laughed again.

"I suppose I was, really. And I started feeling like an outsider. And it's not nice feeling you're an outsider all the time. That's what it was getting like. Sitting round that table."

"And then I went round there one day and they'd gone. Moved out. Totally new people there. I couldn't believe it. I think it was a women's collective. They weren't friendly. They all had short hair and wore dungarees. And their dogs barked at me all the time."

"I suppose it all might have ended there," Dorritt said. "Or that part of it. I still carried on with the project, of course. You've no idea how many little magazines and small presses were springing up then. It was like a renaissance. A cultural rebirth. And I was in the middle of it. I couldn't believe my luck, sometimes. There were the bad things, of course. My thesis, for instance. And the way the *Rites* people had just vanished. That upset me. But if I didn't think about those things, it was fine. That was what I was learning. Not to think about the bad things. Not repress them. Just not think about them."

"Is there a difference?" Plant asked.

Dorritt laughed. His nervous, ingratiating, immensely irritating laugh.

"I don't know," he said. "Perhaps there isn't. Perhaps that was the cause of my problem. An underlying cause. I don't know."

He became lost in reverie.

"So you stopped thinking about them."

"Yes. I might never have seen them again. I mean, I had enough information to give some sort of entry on them. I could look through the back issues and list contributors. And the sort of things they wrote about. I'd picked up copies. It would have done. It wouldn't have been as complete as I wanted it. But it would have done. I'm not an obsessive."

He laughed, challenging Plant to dispute.

"And then their 'Back to Nature' issue came out. 'Birds in the Bush.' With them all naked on the cover. Rose. And Angela. And the rest."

"And it hit you where you lived."

"Yes," said Dorritt. He giggled. "Something like that."

"Stirred up the juices."

"I was young," said Dorritt. "I had normal desires. Urges."

"I don't doubt it," said Plant. Or did he?

"I saw it in a newsagent's. It quite took my breath away."

He raised his glasses to his brow again, rubbed the back of his head with the palm of his hand, breathing deeply.

"We weren't used to that sort of thing at that time. Till that time, anyway," he said.

"So?"

"So? So I bought a copy, of course. And then I looked for the address."

"After you'd feasted on the cover."

"No, straight away. I opened it up straight away."

"And?"

"Oh yes, there was an address. Not a street address. A post-office box. But it was still an address. A post-office box at Byron Bay. So I knew where they were. The district, anyway. I figured it couldn't be hard to find them. Somebody would know. It's not a big place. It was even smaller, then."

"So you set off in hot pursuit."

"Yes," said Dorritt.

He giggled.

"Just like you did after me," he said.

Dorritt descended on them. From his point of view it was more like ascended. They were the world he aspired to. Girls in sarongs gently ministering around him. Creativity on every wall. Posters, screen prints, photographs. Mobiles hanging from the ceiling. And amidst it all, the paper. The word made material. Columns of words. How to be an urban terrorist. How to cure your own marijuana. How to achieve new consciousness. How to raze and destroy the bad old world.

He tracked them down. Using his research skills.

"I thought I'd put them to some practical use," he said. "My research skills. They didn't seem to have done me much good with my thesis. Not that that was my fault. That was sabotaged by my supervisor. Though I only realized that later. When I'd got my confidence back. When I realized I had these skills and they worked. And they did work. That was how I tracked them down."

Huxter had looked out of the window when the taxi turned up. Dorritt saw his thin white face, peering through the glass like a fish in an aquarium.

"He didn't look pleased. But he never did, really. Only on rare occasions."

Dorritt withdrew into silent reflection. Or something.

"What sort of occasions?" Plant asked, to prod him along.

Dorritt shuddered. Then he reassembled his smiling, ramshackle face and continued.

"No one came to the door. So I knocked."

Still no one came so he tried the handle. It was locked. He left his rucksack on the veranda and walked round the house. Round the water tank. Round the woodpile. The back door was locked too.

"But I'd seen Huxter's face so I knew they were there. I knew he was there, anyway. So I just sat on the old couch on the veranda and waited. I got bitten by midges."

In the end they cracked. Or Rose did. The door suddenly opened and she was there. Smiling at him.

"I thought I heard something," she said. "But we were sort of"—she smiled suggestively, fingered the button of her blouse as if to do it up, and undid it—"otherwise engaged."

"That's all right," Dorritt said.

It wasn't. The thought that she might have been making love to Huxter hurt like a wrench in the stomach. Irrationally. What claims had he? How could it be jealousy? Envy, perhaps? But it was more proprietorial than that, the way it hurt.

"You'd better come in," she said.

He followed her in.

"Take a seat."

The ever-present kitchen table. The bowl of fruit. Not just bananas now but passion fruit, mangoes, the nectarine and curious peach, fruits of this other Eden, this perpetual fruiting paradise.

"Cup of tea?" she said. Asked, but filled up the kettle anyway and put it on the stove.

Ollie the American wandered in, all Hawaiian shirt and baggy shorts.

"Howdy, lover boy," he said, blowing Dorritt a kiss across the room.

Dorritt felt himself blushing, heating up further despite the heat, sweating as much as Ollie who always seemed to be sweating.

Ollie sat at the table and rummaged around.

"Time for the pipe of peace," he said.

He produced a packet of rolling tobacco from one shirt pocket and a bag of dope from the other.

"And what brings you up here?"

"I thought I'd drop by," said Dorritt.

"On the way to wherever."

Dorritt nodded.

"And where would that be?"

"Where would what be?"

"Wherever."

Dorritt shrugged.

"Here," he said. "I've still got some questions to ask."

"I bet," said Ollie.

"Just to complete the—"

Huxter came in silently and joined them at the table. His arrival threw Dorritt, leaving him lost in mid sentence. Maybe he was looking for signs of lovemaking: sweat, the fresh smell of a shower, a smirk, anything. But Huxter neither smirked nor smiled. Nor spoke.

"The files?" said Ollie.

"The entry, yes," said Dorritt.

"Shoot," said Ollie. "Let's do it now, then you can go on your way."

Dorritt floundered, flustered.

"Maybe he doesn't have a way to go," said Rose.

"Is that so?" said Ollie. "Have you lost your way, is that it?"

"Well," said Dorritt.

"Well?" said Ollie.

"I thought I might stay here a couple of days or so," said Dorritt. "If that's all right, of course."

"We're full," said Huxter, in his Middle-Eastern innkeeper's voice.

"Every room occupied," Ollie elaborated.

"Oh, I don't need a room," said Dorritt.

"You wanna share?" said Ollie. Smiling.

"No spare beds," said Huxter.

"You wanna share my bed?" said Ollie.

"I've got a sleeping bag," said Dorritt. "I can sleep on the veranda."

"A sleeping bag?" said Ollie. "You are well prepared. Quite the boy scout."

Dorritt smiled. Until he realized that no one else did. Not Huxter or Ollie, anyway. He couldn't tell about Rose. She had her back to him, making the tea.

"So I slept out on the veranda," Dorritt said. "The sky was so clear. You could see the satellites tracking by. At first I thought they were shooting stars and I made wishes."

"What sort of wishes?"

"They don't come true if you tell them to people," said Dorritt.

"But they weren't shooting stars anyway."

"Later they were. Later there were lots of them."

He woke early, out on the veranda, scratching his midge bites. The first rays of the sun touched the tops of the trees.

"Gilding them," Dorritt said. "It sounds poetic but it was literal. The tops were touched with gold. It's something you never see in the city, somehow. Not that there aren't trees."

No one was moving inside the house. He walked down the steps, onto the grass, fending off the fresh strands of cobwebs that had been spun between the house and the trees in the night. Amidst the long, uncut grass the bees hummed with a high, firm note, a high-energy early morning work hum, gathering pollen from the meadow flowers that were blooming, blue and white and yellow. It was as if all nature were integrated in some spinning dynamo, generating the power to go on. And the finches and honeyeaters and tiny wrens twittered and chattered like little stabbing needles decorating the surface with needlework. And a few mosquitoes whined past, making the most of the memory of the half-light. He rolled down his sleeves and pulled his socks up. But the mosquitoes vanished as the sun touched more of the earth. And the cicadas started up like an outdoor factory of massed sewing machines.

It was an hour or more before anyone stirred, an hour and a half, maybe two hours. He went in eagerly to join them at the breakfast table. Rose in a diaphanous nightdress, Angela in an exotic dressing gown, all birds and snakes from some Oriental bestiary. Ollie waddled out in short pajamas. There was some visitor clad in a towel. Huxter alone was fully dressed. And Dorritt, of course.

"We were going to make an early start," said Huxter.

Angela lit a cigarette and groaned.

Rose busied herself making coffee.

"I'm ready," said the visitor.

Huxter glowered. At the visitor. At Angela. At Dorritt. At Ollie.

"Welcome to the prison farm," said Ollie, yawning, standing in the doorway, gazing with satisfaction at the world of nature. "Just listen to them whip-birds. Music on the ears."

"There's no hurry," said Angela.

"Yes there is," said Huxter. "I want to get moving on the next issue."

"I can help," said Dorritt.

All eyes turned to him.

"Can you, now?" said Ollie.

"Proofreading," he volunteered.

"You need something typeset before you can proofread," said Huxter.

"Or typesetting," Dorritt offered. "I can type."

"And before typesetting," said Huxter, "you need something written."

"I can—" Dorritt began.

"And before you get something written you need to know what the editorial collective has decided is to be written about."

"A fine analysis of the problem," said Ollie.

"There is no problem," said Huxter.

"You could've fooled me," said Angela.

"That's never hard," said Ollie.

"Anyway," said Dorritt, "anything. Odd jobs. I'd be happy to do anything."

"You can cut the grass," said Huxter.

"Cut the grass?" said Dorritt. "I thought Rose said she'd run out."

"Mow the lawns, smartarse," said Huxter.

It was not what he had had in mind. Not what he had hoped for. Not what he had expected. He tittered nervously.

"Show him where the mower is, someone," said Huxter. "Get him out of the fucking house and let's get started."

So Dorritt sweated his way through the early morning, the grass long and neglected, the motor cutting out whenever the grass was too high or too thick. He would tug start it again, wiping the sweat from his brow, sweat really did form on the brow, it wasn't just an expression, he was fascinated to find, and the insect repellent Rose had kindly found for him dissolved with the sweat and ran down into his eyes, so they smarted and burned and he could no longer see. He was drenched with sweat, his hair, his neck, his chest, his back, his armpits, his groin, even the socks on his feet. He pushed the mower past the house and back, from end to end of the rough lawns, the sun now high and beating straight down, and the trees providing no protection. He tried to glance inside, through the windows, to the cool room, the table, the bowl of fruit, the editorial conference, the mysteries of creation, the mystique of media, and he could make out nothing. Nothing but sweat and smarting eyes and the sense of exclusion, of being eternally outside the inner sanctum, peering into the house like some sub-tropical Heathcliff or a slave on a southern plantation. The noise of the motor deafened him. The sweat and insect repellent blinded him. The dust and grass clippings flew up and choked him. And there was no relief.

Early next morning the pigeons pecked around in the mown grass, flying up with a great whistling, fluttering of wings when Dorritt moved closer to examine them. Whip-birds called out to each other in the distant undergrowth, the long high wheew, and the fierce concluding crack. Crows cawed and crowed from the treetops. A king parrot piped its single high, piping note. Up the mountain kookaburras laughed and cackled. A dove settled into its remorseless hooting. It was not a dawn chorus, it was long past dawn, and they were still at it. Dorritt sat out there on the veranda, scratching at his bites in quiet amazement.

And then Rose emerged, all white muslin and soft, golden suntan and smiles.

"Up you get," she said.

"Up? Where?" he asked.

"The secret valley," she said. "We're going mushrooming. Then you'll learn how to read the Book of Nature."

She led him along the track, across the paddock.

"This is the time to find them," she said. "With the morning dew still on them. Before the sun gets too hot."

"How do you know where to find them?" Dorritt asked.

"You tune in," said Rose. "They call to you."

He tittered. Disbelievingly, of course. But happily so.

"You'll see," she said.

"What do they sound like?" he asked.

"It's not a sound," she said. "They speak to you. Telepathically. Without words. They let you know where they are."

"What do they look like?"

"Golden," she said. "Nuggets of fairy gold, glowing in the grass."

"Golden?" he said. "I thought mushrooms were white."

"So you do know what they look like."

"Only from shops," he said. "Vegetable stalls."

"Those are field mushrooms," she said. "If we see any of them we'll get them too."

"What are we looking for, then?"

"Magic mushrooms, what did you think?"

"Magic mushrooms?"

"Gold tops," she said.

"I don't know them," he said.

"Look for cow pats," she said. "You need a field where cattle have been at some time. Or horses. Horses are even better. The spores need to go through the intestines of a cow or horse. That's how they germinate or something. So look for cow pats and little golden tops sticking through them."

They found them. Cow pats and all.

She broke one off.

"See. See how the stem goes purple."

He watched, and it did, slowly the broken stem of the mushroom turned purple.

"Psilocybin," she said. "If they don't do that, they're toadstools. If they don't do that you don't eat them. They make you sick."

She gathered them, held up her dress to hold them in, her legs golden brown in the sun.

"We'll need more than this," she said.

Dorritt spotted them. He felt proud, confident, competent.

"That's enough," she said. "Off you go."

He picked them, handed them to her.

"No, those are yours," she said. "They were calling to you."

He tittered.

"I didn't hear them," he said.

"But you found them."

He started to put them in his shirt pocket.

"What are you doing?" she asked. As if it was something terrible he was doing.

"Putting them in my pocket," he said.

"What for?"

"To carry them."

"Carry them where?" she asked. "You'll crush them."

"Back to the house."

"No," she said. "You have to eat them where you find them. To appreciate them properly."

"What, raw?"

She nodded.

"Here?"

She nodded again.

He looked at them doubtfully. The cow dung.

"Shouldn't they be washed?"

"Spit in your hand and wipe them if you're worried," she said.

He was doubtful, more than doubtful, almost horrified. He felt in his trouser pocket for a handkerchief, rubbed his haul with it, as if he were buffing up a magic lantern.

"So," she said, "here we go."

She raised the gold top to her lips, bit into it, chewed, swallowed.

"Now you," she said.

He did the same, cautiously, a small nibble. He called out in disgust and spat it out.

"It tastes awful," he said.

"It's not the taste," she said. "The taste you have to put up with."

She picked up the partly chewed bits he had spat out and handed them back to him.

"Eat," she said. "Trust me."

He looked at her. The white muslin dress, the golden glow of her skin, her peach-tinged cheeks, her red lips, suntanned face and arms and legs. All suffused with a golden glow.

He trusted her and ate.

The snake slithered away through the grass.

He couldn't sit at the table. It was too rectangular. Squared and hewn. And slaughtered. A felled tree. Like a carcass of meat. He could see the carcasses hanging there, the doors of the meat van open, men in bloodstained white overalls and Wellington boots and white surgeons' hats, lifting the carcasses off the great iron meat hooks that impaled them, carrying them across the pavements, into the butchers' shops, the huge steel doors swung open, the freezing cold stores, lined with carcasses, rows and rows of meat trucks driving up, streams of men in bloodstained white with marbled white and red and blue carcasses on their backs.

He tried one of the old armchairs, its arms furry, furry moquette, was this moquette? What was moquette? Why was it called that? Because it was mock? Because it mocked? He examined the padded arms of the chair to see if it was mocking him, it gazed back imperturbably, its mocking potential enfolding him.

"So what's this survey really about?"

He heard the voice. But he wasn't sure where it came from. No, he knew where it came from, it came from the room, it came from a mocking armchair, but he wasn't sure whose voice it was. He tried to look at them but they kept dissolving. He looked at Huxter, where Huxter had been, but he had turned into a fish, a pallid, white fish, maybe a shark, predatory and menacing and sick, diseased, white fungus creeping over its face in striations, whatever striations were. And Ollie, Ollie dissolved into treacle pudding, the soft, crumbly face

194 MICHAEL WILDING

topped with golden syrup, dripping down over his eyes, reaching down his shoulders and arms like a lava of ants, lava carrying larva, or larva carrying lava. And some other ghostly figure who had been there had gone and an ectoplasm held its place, wafting this way and that way in the breeze, but there was no breeze, nothing to dispel the heat that filled the room, climbed up his legs from the floor, into his back from the mocking chair, now he knew why it mocked, it was an electric chair and its electric heat was spreading all through him, rising into the underside of his thighs and pressing into his back and shoulders and rising up into his head which would burst unless he could dispel the heat into the room and melt all the hanging carcasses, soften their frozen forms till they went soft and viscid and rotted there, putrefying around him.

The electric chair began buzzing. A short, sharp, imperious, high-pitched drilling, it was an electric dentist's chair, and the electric dentist was drilling into his teeth, up through his wisdom teeth and into his brain, and at each buzz of the drill, at each touch, his brain exploded into blue, violet, crimson. And it was familiar, a familiar light, a familiar pain, a familiar sound. And now the electric dentist went away and it was the water-pump, switched on whenever anyone turned on a tap, buzzing and buzzing, the water running and running, through the core of his brain, behind his eyes, and then he realized it was the shower, someone was taking a shower, why else did the pump keep straining, and it was Rose, he knew it, he could see her standing there naked, he could see through the solid walls, they were transparent, the water pouring over her rose red body, the pump singing its desperate song of penetration, drill, drill, drill, and the water ran over her breasts and belly and hair in translucent globules, beading there, glued jewels of morning dew. He smiled.

"Amanitas are even stronger," she said. "The berserkers used them. The bare shirts."

Sitting there before him with a towel round her waist but her breasts bare there, he could feel the berserker force rising in him, in his genitals, compelling, demanding, urgent.

"Reindeer love them," she said. "If you've taken amanitas you can't go out of the house to have a piss. You have to stay inside and piss in the soup. Otherwise the reindeer gallop at you to drink the piss and knock you over."

Rolling in the snow there, cooling the heat in his groin, wanting to piss now but unable to because of that sexual pressure.

"That's how they get to fly. With an amanita muscaria sitting on the sled. All red with white flecks."

And there she was, hot from the shower, steaming, her face and arms and breasts and back and belly flecked red and white, glowing there like an amanita in a birch forest.

"That's what Father Christmas is. A midwinter trip."

Men in white overalls flecked in red carrying slaughtered mushroom carcasses on their backs into the cold room.

While outside the cicadas trilled and drilled. His whole energy vibrated in rhythm with them, as if he was revving up higher and higher and about to ascend, burst through the crown of his skull, and soar up through the ceiling and the roof and the cloudless sky.

"It was like an assault," Dorritt said. "One minute I'd been outside with Rose, in the sun, in nature, it was like being in a Van Gogh painting, the sunflowers were vibrating with solar energy, the trees were swirls of life spiraling up to heaven, the birds were flying along the lines of the sky, you could see the different currents and densities of the air, the waves and swirls and vortexes. Vortices. You could hear it all pulsating along with the crickets and cicadas. Great waves of sound and then silence. The earth breathing. And then suddenly we were inside and everything was dark, the air was viscid, it was like being in an oil well, everything was moving slowly, trapped in this heavy fluid, and they were all shouting at me, all together, what was I doing, who was I working for, what was the survey for, what was I trying to find out?"

"You're sure of this?" Plant asked.

"That's what it seemed like," said Dorritt.

"All of them shouting at you?"

"That was my first impression," Dorritt said. "But that might have been subjective, of course. It had been so peaceful outside. Paradisal. So the contrast might have made it seem worse. And I might be projecting backwards. It was certainly like that later. I think. And I might be imagining it was like that from the beginning. It all merges into one, you see. One endless session. Endless interrogation."

"What did they want to know?"

"I told you. They kept asking what was I doing? Who was I working for? What was the survey about? I tried to answer. But it was so hard. It was hard even to talk. I just wanted to be within myself. Or within Rose."

He laughed.

"In consciousness, I mean," he said. "We'd been merging our consciousnesses outside. In the meadow. The mushrooms had allowed us to break down the usual barriers. And then suddenly this was happening. And all these other forces were trying to break in."

"And what did you tell them?"

"I didn't tell them anything," Dorritt said.

"Why not?"

"It was a secret project."

"And you'd been told not to reveal it?"

"It was a security matter."

"And you'd been trained to resist interrogation?"

"Had I?"

"I'm asking you."

"I don't know," said Dorritt. "I just didn't like the way they were bullying me. First one, then the other, then the next, it was a whole battery of questions and I couldn't handle them. Maybe if they'd just asked me one at a time, just one of them, more gently, it might have been different. But maybe not. They tried that later and it didn't work."

"Later in the day?"

"No, days later. When they'd locked me up."

"They locked you up?"

"Oh, yes," he said. He grinned. "They incarcerated me. It was quite dramatic. Horrific. Ollie even had handcuffs. 'I got handcuffs,' he said. 'You want to tie him up, I got the gear.'"

"He threatened you?"

"He was quite nice about it, actually. He was always smiling. He said some people would get off on it. Like his belt."

"His belt?"

"He had this studded leather belt. With a great brass buckle. When I was tripping I kept looking at it. It was extraordinary. Alive and brazen. 'I know it's cheap trash,' he said. 'I know it's very Western. As the cashier admitted when I opened my account. But divinely tasteless. Pure kitsch. The Wells Fargo Bank. They gave them out free with your checking account. Do you want me to take it off for you?' I kept seeing all these TV Westerns. Wells Fargo, you know. Cowboys and all that. 'You have an account with Wells Fargo?' I asked him. 'I opened one when I went to college,' he said. 'And you still keep it?' I said. 'Inquisitive little fucker, aren't you,' he said."

"So you were out of your brain on mushrooms and they asked you questions."

"They interrogated me," said Dorritt. "They didn't just ask me questions, this was an interrogation."

He sucked at the strands of his moustache with a heavy self-satisfaction.

"So who specifically asked the questions?"

"It was a team."

"A team?"

"An interrogation team."

"What, they borrowed one from the Stasi and flew it in?"

"It was never just one person asking, it was always a team of them."

"Consisting of who?"

"Huxter and Ollie and Angie and Rose," he said.

"All of them?"

"No," said Dorritt, "not altogether. But always two or three."

"And just random, or were some of them always there?"

"Huxter was usually there."

"And asking questions?"

Dorritt chewed on his moustache.

"Interrogating?"

"Yes."

"So it was mainly Huxter."

"I think there might have been other people, I can't remember who was there once or twice. I can't remember. Everyone took part."

"And Huxter always took part."

"Probably," said Dorritt. "And Ollie."

"And what did they want to know?"

"Who I was working for, basically."

"Just that."

"That's what it always came down to. Who sent me? Who paid me? Who did I report to? Who was the survey for?"

"You want me to tell you about the torture?" said Dorritt. "The incarceration. That was probably the worst part. Being locked up. That was torture in itself. That old shed. Timber and iron. I didn't know where I was. I'd never even seen it. It must have been some way from the house. There were trees around it. I know that because branches would crash down on the roof in the middle of the night. It was terrifying. Absolutely terrifying."

He looked at the ice cream beside his hot cakes reflectively. Like he knew it was made from slaughtered pigs. He bit into it, coating the fringe of his moustache and beard.

"They frog-marched me there. Literally. It's an interesting word, don't you think? I wonder why frog. I must look it up. But that's what they did. One on each side of me. They opened the door and threw in my sleeping bag and my rucksack. We didn't call them backpacks in those days. I wonder why that's changed. Americanization, I expect. Then they pushed me in and padlocked the door. There was no light. The windows were covered with corrugated iron. No glass. The floor was just dirt, no boards or anything. I was terrified of spiders and things. But that wasn't the worst."

In the end Plant took the cue.

"What was the worst?"

Dorritt held it for a while, his mouth fractionally open, delaying.

"Snakes," he said.

Plant felt himself shuddering. Give Dorritt his due, he could do it well. The timing. The sibilance.

"Snakes," he repeated.

He picked up his cappuccino, adding to the scum around his whiskers.

"Later I discovered farmers deliberately kept them in their sheds. To eat the rats."

"But they didn't eat you," said Plant.

"The rats or the snakes?" asked Dorritt.

"Either."

"They're not dangerous," said Dorritt. "Not carpet snakes. But I didn't know that at the time, did I?"

"Didn't you?"

"No, I didn't."

He went back to his breakfast.

"It was terrifying. Hearing this thing slithering in the roof. Seeing it move. Inching along. I thought I was going to be crushed to death. My breath squeezed out of me. My ribs caved in. I stayed right in the middle of the floor. I thought that way I might be safe. I knew they had to have their tail anchored round something before they could constrict their muscles enough to crush you."

"That's boa constrictors," said Plant.

"I know," said Dorritt. "But I didn't know what this was. Not till Rose came in. She comforted me. But it was still terrifying. I was terrified to go to sleep. With the rats as well."

"Wouldn't the snake have eaten the rats?" asked Plant.

"Eventually, probably," said Dorritt. "But the rats could still gnaw your toes when you were asleep. I kept my shoes on. And tried to stay awake."

"With Rose?"

He didn't answer.

"I have this recurrent dream. Still. A nightmare. It's terrible."

Plant groaned. Inwardly, but it was still a groan. The one thing he could do without was being told people's dreams. Over breakfast. Especially terrible dreams. If he'd wanted to be an analyst he would have been born a Viennese. Or gotten Americanized.

"I dream this snake is in my bed with me. Wrapped round me. Squeezing out my breath. Choking me."

A couple of bush-turkeys came out of the scrub and pecked around the tables, their bald-looking heads and bright red and yellow wattles bobbing up and down as they scavenged for crumbs and scraps. Dorritt seemed not to see them. He was back in the shed, struggling awake from his dream.

"Then they came and interrogated me."

"When was that?"

"I lost all track of time."

"Straight away? Or the next day?"

"Day after day," said Dorritt. "Day after day they'd come in, Huxter and Ollie and Angela and Rose."

"What, all of them?"

"All of them. I think there were other people too."

"All at the same time?"

"Yes," said Dorritt. "Well sometimes maybe one or two of them were off doing something else. Washing. Cooking. Cleaning. I don't know. But it was most of them."

"And they all asked questions?"

"I think so. Huxter asked the most. But the others did too. Huxter was quite aggressive. But Rose was friendly. Considerate. She'd bring me things. But Huxter never did."

"What sort of things?"

"Oh, mangoes, peaches, a joint."

"Gifts of love."

"That too," he said.

"And Angela?"

"Cigarettes mainly."

"And gifts of love?"

"Sometimes."

"You said you were drugged," said Plant.

"Did I?"

"Were you?"

"I suppose so," said Dorritt. "They're quite amazing, those mushrooms. They can be horrific. But they can be marvelous. Cosmic. You see the divine in everything."

"In everything?"

"Yes."

"Even in Huxter?"

"He has his place in the scheme of things," said Dorritt. "Everyone does. We all have out place in the grand design."

"That's reassuring," said Plant.

"It is," said Dorritt. "They are. Mushrooms are very reassuring. Ultimately."

"So you asked for more."

"I don't know that I asked for them. But Rose brought me some. She said the mushroom season was really very brief. It was nearly over. We should take them while we could."

"So you did."

"I suppose so," he said. "It's very hard to remember. You get flashbacks, you know. Suddenly you're in this mushroom state even though you haven't taken any that day. And sometimes they have no effect. If you've taken them one day they don't have much effect the next day. So it's hard to tell."

"And Rose gave them to you. Not Huxter."

"Huxter never gave me anything," said Dorritt. "He was very mean. You could see that when you'd taken mushrooms."

"You can see it without mushrooms," said Plant.

"Can you?"

"With him, yes."

"You must be quite perceptive," said Dorritt. "Looks can be deceiving."

"Thank you," said Plant.

"I was thinking particularly of Huxter. I wouldn't have realized unless I'd taken mushrooms."

"And they asked you questions while you were tripping?"

"Any time," said Dorritt. "Much like you."

He smiled.

"What sort of questions?"

"That must be the ultimate question," said Dorritt. "The question to end all questions. The question about questions themselves."

"So give me the ultimate answer," said Plant.

"Of course," said Dorritt.

He did some business with the coffee and the spoon and the packets of paper-wrapped sugar.

"I'm sure I've already told you. They wanted to know what I was doing. Was the survey my own idea? Or did someone hire me to do it? Did I apply for funding or was it given me? Who funded it? Who was I working for?"

"Did you tell them?"

"I imagine so," said Dorritt. "In the end. Psilocybin is like LSD. The security agencies use it with amytal as a truth drug."

"Did they give you amytal?"

"Oh yes," said Dorritt. "Angela gave me some of her sleeping pills when I couldn't sleep. They were amytal sodium."

"So you spilled it all."

"I expect so. I know when I saw Professor Oates afterwards, he said the project was finished. So they must have shut it down."

"Because you'd talked."

"I imagine anyone would talk in those circumstances and with those drugs," said Dorritt. "I don't feel bad about it. Not now. I did at the time. When I had my breakdown. I felt quite guilty then. Sometimes. But I felt all sorts of things then. I went quite mad. So I don't put much credence on what I felt then. And anyway, there wasn't much to feel guilty about. I'd got to the end of the project. There might have been one or two loose ends. But basically it was all done. I'd written it all up except for the rest of the *Rites* details before I went up there. It was going to be a holiday, going up to Byron Bay. A free holiday. You know, on expenses."

He looked at Plant, knowingly.

"But I guess there's no such thing as a free holiday, is there?"

"Tell me about the sex slavery," said Plant.

NICHOLAS JOSE

Born in 1950, Nicholas Jose is the author of fiction and essays, including the novels *The Rose Crossing* (1994), *The Red Thread* (2001), and *Original Face* (2005). He has written widely on contemporary Asian and Australian culture. He currently holds the Chair of Creative Writing at the University of Adelaide. Jose, as author, critic, and cultural ambassador, has been the single most visible link between Australian and Asian culture; his novels have engaged Asia not just in a topical but also in a formal sense. Adept at playing with and commingling genres such as the detective story, the historical novel, and the war story, Jose is also the author of a remarkable nonfiction narrative, *Black Sheep: Journey to Booroloola,* in which an investigation into the life of an eccentric relative in a remote northern territory town becomes a vehicle for investigating the ghosts in Australia's collective past, as well as measuring the degree to which the written word, whether in fiction or nonfiction, reveals the truth.

George

I can hear the lions roar and the monkeys gibber at feeding time across the park. Those animals are my neighbors, separated by a line of trees, a pea-green meander of water and a barbed-wire fence that angles inward out of sight. Each day, as I walk from home to work, I pass the grand Victorian gates of their enclosure. I never go in. It's a small zoo for a small city. The bigger animals—elephants, giraffes, rhinoceros—have mostly gone. The zoo advertises a sunbear, a Tasmanian devil, a cast of meerkats and some other attractions, and there are always people waiting by the turnstile to go in: kids, carers, young couples; babies in papooses against their parents' bodies.

I'm not sure about zoos. I know that a young man was impaled on the fence here one night as he attempted to climb in. He was intoxicated and bled to death. Animals have died in mysterious circumstances too. A zoo need not be a nice place. Still, it's a place where children like to go. With its kaleido-scope of environments, hidden behind high barriers in the heart of the city, it's a secret home of the wild. This one's old, with a history of caravanserai, jungle expeditions and circus-style entertainment in its memory. Yet I don't think about going inside until one day, quite unexpectedly, I feel my feet dragging as I approach on my regular route.

Since I came to this town some months ago, I have worked diligently, seven days a week, morning and night, putting one foot in front of the other. I should say since I returned to take a job in this place where I grew up. Until this moment I have kept my focus on the task in hand and now my feet turn decisively toward the entrance to the zoo. I let them go. What does it matter if the screen in my office stays dark for a day? Let the door go unanswered and the phone bleat in vain! I step up to the counter and ask for a single adult visitor's ticket.

As a child I came to this zoo often. That was the last time, and immediately, as I go in, I feel out of scale. The place seems to be shrunken and overtaken by the vegetation. The zoo's philosophy has changed too, of course. The animals are here for themselves now, a sign tells me, not for us. As I follow the path without knowing where I'm going, spying creatures in their compounds, I wonder how I'm supposed to behave. I look at them and they look at me. Or do they? It's hard to know. I gasp, frown, smile, rubbing and scratching as they do, in helpless imitation.

"Wait for me means you wait for me!" scolds an alarmed mother as her toddler careers down a walkway. A sunken-eyed father warns his runaway son, "Listen, mate, when I say 'Stop' . . ."

I stare at each new animal, having no one to vocalize with. What am I—what are they—supposed to do? Be ourselves? The citrine-eyed flamingo doesn't blink. We are surely close enough to sense each other's body heat in this hall of mirrors.

.

Blue macaws shriek from on high as sooty gibbons trapeze through the leaves. The zoo's pathways, curving and looping back, disorient and deflect. A tapir, half black, half white, stands side-on in columns of light and shade. There are multiple sights, strange smells, constant chatter. At the periphery I find myself at what used to be the elephant house, an Indian-style pleasure dome in orange and green that has an educational display to document the last of the children's rides. This is where my footsteps have taken me. Instead of elephants, however, there's a skeleton in a box. It has been meticulously prepared and reassembled and stands there erect. It's far too small for an elephant. Light, clean and fine-boned, it stretches a right arm back balletically, gripping a support as if to swing. The Latin name is *Pongo pygmaeus*.

It's George.

I remember you, suddenly, overwhelmingly, but not like this. You were big as King Kong, heavy, dark, fleshy, and losing your hair. Your concrete home had the thickest bars in the zoo and very little shade. You had that old sack as a comforter, draping it over your head like a shawl, putting it through the bars with your long arm to sweep things in from outside. We used to make you reach as far as possible for peanuts and cigarettes. I wondered if you ever grabbed children and pulled them in too. I could have squeezed through the bars myself. Were you happy, George? Your massive solitary sadness drew us all in; you were so strong and exposed in that bare cage, performing your antics, as far as imaginable from the rainforest canopy world where you would have been king.

George the orangutan arrived at the zoo as a juvenile in 1950, gift of the Government of Sarawak. His companion Martha traveled with him on the ship but died in her first year. The climate in Adelaide was so much cooler and drier than equatorial Borneo that it was hard to survive. Earlier females hadn't lasted either. They fractured the fence wire and pulled up the floorboards in their bid to escape. But George lived on for another twenty-five years. He was considered a "widower" by the public, a model of docility and domestication. In later years he would sit for hours on end with his sack over his head like a cowl, watching what was outside, living whatever was inside. After his death in 1976, people spontaneously gave money for a bust in George's memory: a grim shaggy bronze that is parked in the foliage in another corner of the zoo. Visitors loved George. Parents and grandparents, uncles and aunties, and children like me. Did he have a good life, alone in his cage for all those years? He was ours, tamed, here for us. Perhaps animals should not have human names. It brings them too close.

I remember the agitation of standing by the bars looking at him, smelling his strong odor, giggling at his private parts, his bare backside, his tough nipples and rippling chest. George was four years older than me. What was he doing here, delivering some sort of message that we couldn't understand?

.

You were Threatened Species before your time, George, destined to leave no offspring. Nowadays there'd be a planned breeding program and a mate would be traded for you from another zoo. The destruction of your habitat continues apace. Only 20% remains. Less than ten thousand of your kind are left in the wild. You could never have gone back, anyway, George. You could have lashed out, of course, with vengeful violence, as your human cousins do, jaws jutting, scratching their scalps and reaching for far more dreadful tools than a hessian sack. You could have joined the hundreds of thousands of victims of the unconsidered, all-too-considered destructive acts of greater apes of your name, George. Maybe you got past all that in your monastic situation, your simian way of non-violence, your Buddhist emptiness.

What's George to me or me to George that I should grin tearfully as I identify the imagined likeness, the intense remembered imprint, the evolutionary and individual fate?

Behind me comes the lightest sound of footprints. A child enters the shady space. I hear an adult stamping in pursuit.

"Stop or I'll belt you," the grown-up voice growls.

Our eyes meet. The little boy stops in his tracks, straining forward to George's skeleton but not quite daring to take the next step. The parent, angry and embarrassed, sticks out an arm. The child refuses to look back over his shoulder for permission.

I smile across the years. My breath is quietly excited as I behold your big-boned skull. You have found me in the labyrinth and pulled me in. Who has seen more in the long descents of time, you or I? Are we one memory now?

The father grabs the child by the hand and pulls him away. Left alone, I bend closer to the glass that protects your re-articulated form. You look like you could throw something. My lips start to move, up against the glass.

"Hello George," I whisper. "Nice to see you again."

GUEST EDITOR

Nicholas Birns lives in New York City where he teaches literature at Eugene Lang College, The New School. His teaching specialties include Victorian and modern fiction and literary theory. His book *Theory After Theory*, a survey of the current state of literary criticism, is under contract to Broadview Press. He is the author of *Understanding Anthony Powell* (2004) and *A Companion to Australian Literature since 1900* (2007; co-edited with Rebecca McNeer). He has written for journals such as *The Hollins Critic, Studies in Romanticism*, and *Arizona Quarterly*. He is the editor of *Antipodes: A North American Journal of Australian Literature* and has held visiting fellowships in Australia and Sweden.

BOOK REVIEWS

RAYMOND QUENEAU. *LETTERS, NUMBERS, FORMS: ESSAYS 1928-70.*
TRANS. JORDAN STUMP. URBANA AND CHICAGO: UNIVERSITY OF IL-
LINOIS PRESS, 2007. 251 PP. PAPER: $45.00.

"Few if any twentieth-century writers are as present in the twenty-first-cen-
tury French novel as Queneau," argues Jordan Stump in the introduction to
this volume. Raymond Queneau (1903-1976) was a writer's writer, a figure
who influenced at least two generations of French writers during his lifetime,
and whose vision of literature and its potential continues to shape progressive
literature in key ways, more than thirty years after his death, both in France
and beyond. Many of his novels have been rendered into English, but only a
few of his essays have been translated. This volume collects thirty-three pieces
from a variety of sources, arranging them in chronological order. It provides
a deeply compelling narrative of an encyclopedic, infinitely inquisitive, rigorous mind at work, right in the thick of things, over a period of four decades.
The pieces have been chosen very judiciously indeed: all of Queneau's most
important critical statements are present here, from his early days in Surreal-
ism to his foundational gestures in the Oulipo group. While most of the essays
deal with literature, either in practical or more theoretical terms, some focus
more closely on language itself, in particular on language as daily practice.
Others, like the piece on Joan Miró, deal more broadly with aesthetics; and
there is even a meditation on the role of mathematics in the classification of
sciences.

The translations are luminous ones, rigorously faithful to both the letter and the spirit of the original. They shine most brightly in those instances where Queneau's French presents the thorniest problems, displaying a depth of resource and creativity that Queneau himself would undoubtedly applaud. One has come to expect no less from Jordan Stump, who has brought a wide diversity of French writers into superb English translations in recent years, from Balzac and Verne to Claude Simon, Marie Redonnet, Eric Chevillard, Christian Oster, and Antoine Volodine. He is moreover a distinguished scholar of Queneau, with a book-length study of the latter's novels, *Naming and Unnaming: On Raymond Queneau* (1998), to his credit. The introduction that Stump provides in this volume is both useful and invigorating: it situates Queneau with regard to the intellectual history of the period and discusses the evolution of his thought with a great deal of insight. The notes to the individual essays are always informative, never obtrusive. In short, this is an "important" book, one that is long overdue, a book that will be welcomed by serious readers of any stripe, whether amateur or professional. — WARREN MOTTE

LYDIE SALVAYRE. *PORTRAIT DE L'ÉCRIVAIN EN ANIMAL DOMESTIQUE.* SEUIL, 2007. 240 PP. €18.00.

In her latest novel, Lydie Salvayre offers a "portrait of the writer as a household pet," an animal that has learned how to please its master, capering and fawning in order to ingratiate itself. That beast is the narrator herself, an anonymous writer who negotiates a Faustian bargain with Jim Tobold, the self-styled "King of Hamburgers," whose fast-food empire has consumed the entire world, just as the entire world consumes his burgers. Her task is to write his life: not a mere biography, but rather a testament, a Gospel-according-to-Tobold wherein the principle of unfettered capitalism will finally be elevated to the divine status that it surely deserves, thanks to the efforts of its one true prophet. More than an amanuensis, the narrator serves as the mirror in which Tobold admires his own person, sitting at the feet of the man as he explains to her who he was, who he is, and who he will become. Tobold breathes the rarified air of a person whose wealth mocks the very notion of wealth. A citizen of the world now, well removed from his humble beginnings in France, he is constantly in motion, flitting from continent to continent, summoning one of his innumerable Gulfstreams as a lesser being might hail a cab. Despite herself, the narrator finds that such a lifestyle—as crudely philistine as it might have seemed to her before she abandoned her principles—is not without its rewards. She rubs elbows (and other body parts) with the glitterati: Clooney, Melanie Griffith, Brad Pitt (sans Angelina), Leonardo DiCaprio, Sophie Marceau, Bill Clinton, and a disturbingly priapic Bill Gates. In terms of sheer charm, she feels "Bob" De Niro is without equal. Like the rest of Salvayre's work, this book is smart and pungent, simultaneously amusing and sobering. Swiftian in its conception, her *Portrait* puts satire to a variety of uses. Chief among them is a reflection upon art and power, and more precisely the ways in which the latter may tame the former, inveigling it to lie on its back in order to have its belly scratched. — WARREN MOTTE

LYDIA DAVIS. *VARIETIES OF DISTURBANCE*. FARRAR, STRAUS AND GIROUX, 2007. 240 PP. PAPER: $13.00.

With singular grace and audacious understatement, Lydia Davis structures a vision of contemporary experience that is as much *Seinfeld* as it is *the real world,* that is to say as much Beckett as Proust: the relentless scrutiny of the minutia of lives about nothing, hip tales, often flinty and spare, centering on serio-comic characters confident of their own consequence yet living, we see, in expectation of event, never quite finding a way to matter, a reading experience that is at once compassionate and analytical, playful and disturbing. In "The Caterpillar," for instance, the narrator frets over her heroic efforts to save a caterpillar she finds in her bed, eventually becoming a prisoner of her own compassion, when she loses the thing on the way to freeing it out the front door. Again and again, with a Carver-esque touch for finding the gently persuasive symbols scattered about unnoticed, Davis creates the quiet anxieties inevitably involved in negotiating the emotional terrorisms of friendship, marriage, and family. Yet she refuses the surrender to absurdity threatened whenever we look too closely at our lives. In the wonderful "What You Learn about the Baby," the narrator catalogues with generous humanity the marvelous insights newborns can bring to those of us ossified into wonderless non-lives. At times, Davis challenges, extends her range (she is most effective in the brief stories, snapshot insights that disturb with tsunamic effect). In "Helen and Vi: A Study in Health and Vitality," the longest selection, the narrator excavates the extraordinarily ordinary lives of two elderly women, juxtaposing their routines with generous detailing until we realize that analysis has its drawbacks, that the tedium of life is best evidenced when artists record it. Given such demands on the reader, the stories intrigue with rereading, the language so careful, so clean, so precise (Davis is an accomplished translator of Proust) that it reveals its devastating irony with an unassuming nonchalance. — JOSEPH DEWEY

RICHARD BURGIN. *THE CONFERENCE ON BEAUTIFUL MOMENTS*. JOHNS HOPKINS UNIVERSITY PRESS, 2006. 192 PP. PAPER: $18.95.

Earth, air, fire and water: nothing new there, but how important they remain. In a similar way, despite the complexities, impact, and limits of history, human knowledge, and transformative technology, and their varied influences on our expectations of culture, it is true that character, emotion, and human relationship, especially in literature, remain fundamental. Richard Burgin's achievement in this collection of ten short stories is to remember, reveal, and renew that significance. His are stories of ambition and failure; loneliness, desperation, and transgression; love taken for granted and rediscovered; friendship, competition, and cruelty between men; moral instruction through seduction and intimidation; the resources of family; confession as power play; the destruction of childhood innocence; money as determinate; and the devolution of contemporary public culture into a sharing of one's narcissism. Beginning with "Jonathan and Lillian," a story focused on a famous actress, her biographer, her butler, and one of the actress's celebrated parties, we are given insight into the actress's confidence and insecurity, the writer's mundane desperation, and the butler's resentments, all creating a compelling texture for a story in which more than one crime is committed. The homeless young woman in the "The Second Floor" is saved by a rare compassion, and finds perversity at the root of it, while late life doubts produce a romantic separation that is inevitable and intolerable for a Jewish professor and shiksa scholar in "Vivian and Sid Break Up." The reader shares the main character's terror at what may happen during a one-night stand in "Mayor Bat." Suspicion of others drives many of these stories, as does the mostly amoral quest to acquire money; and even the search for transcendence leads to something sinister in the last story "The Conference on Beautiful Moments." This is a work Chekhov could appreciate. — DANIEL GARRETT

ANTONIO MUÑOZ MOLINA. *IN HER ABSENCE*. TRANS. ESTHER ALLEN. OTHER PRESS, 2007. 126 PP. PAPER: $13.95.

Mario, a bureaucratically minded man from a provincial Spanish town, encounters Blanca, a highly cultured and highly troubled woman whose life is a fascinating snarl of drugs and destructive affairs. Desperately attracted to her, he offers her kindness and stability and their friendship blooms into love and marriage. After six years, his increasing insecurities about their relative intellectual stature and her apparent boredom precipitate a marital crisis that is both the climax and the beginning of *In Her Absence*. The novella is a continuous loop that opens with Mario confronted in his apartment by a nearly identical copy of his wife, then backtracks through the rise and fall of their relationship, and concludes with the entrance of "the woman he did not yet know was not Blanca." Whether she is a literal doppelganger, fantasy projection or something else is never made plain, which puts the entire narrative on shaky ontological ground and injects the story with a somewhat Hitchcockian suspense. It's an expert study of a couple's life together, worth reading for the quality of its characterization alone, especially on the subject of Mario contemplating his inadequacies: "How many times in his life had he tortured himself over a painting, a movie, a piece of chamber music, wondering whether he really liked it, whether he'd look stupid if he moved his head in time to the music or tapped his foot on the floor." On a deeper level it's also an open-ended rumination on perception and reality, a contemporary *Turn of the Screw.* Sadly, this is just the second of Molina's thirteen books to be made available in the U.S. After seeing what he can accomplish in just these few pages, readers should be inspired to seek out last year's much more broadly conceived *Sepharad,* and publishers should be motivated to put more of his titles on bookstore shelves. — JAMES CROSSLEY

ASSIA DJEBAR. *THE TONGUE'S BLOOD DOES NOT RUN DRY: ALGERIAN STORIES.* TRANS. BY TEGAN RALEIGH. SEVEN STORIES PRESS, 2006. 220 PP. PAPER: $13.95.

In this collection of stories, Assia Djebar, the gifted Algerian novelist, filmmaker, and translator attempts—like a modern Scheherazade—to tell tales to save her Algerian sisters. Remembering the terrible nights in the history of Algerian independence in 1962 and after, she writes between two places, Algeria and France, in the voices of women who have divided loyalties and who speak French, Arabic, and Berber. The tales begin with "Oran, Dead Language": Oran, an area in Algeria that had one of the highest concentrations of *pied-noirs,* Europeans who fled Algeria for France upon its independence. The female narrator recounts the mournful night when her parents were murdered, and how she left her city for Paris at the age of eighteen. She is drawn back to Algeria thirty-three years later—though she protests like many other Djebar characters that Algeria "is over" for her. In one of the most haunting stories in the collection, "The Woman in Pieces," Djebar traces the story of "the body of a woman cut into pieces" in Baghdad. Part Eastern fairy tale based on *A Thousand and One Nights,* grotesque and surrealist in effect, the tale describes the brutal entrance of armed soldiers into a gifted French teacher's classroom where she is condemned for her teaching. "They shot her in the heart, slit her throat," and though her head is severed, she continues the stories she began in class, a new storyteller, as "a woman in pieces." In another startling story, "Felicie's Body," a son narrates his French mother's life when she returns to France for hospitalization from Algeria. Reviewing her past—her marriage to and life with his dashing Arabic father in Algeria—he relates the complexities of this relationship for him and his brothers and sisters: "You see us divided, each with our two first names, our two first countries (which to disown, which to adopt?), our two religions absent in the background." And so, in story upon story, Djebar and her female characters, victims of political turmoil in Algeria, speaking French, Arabic, and Berber, go on: "in spite of everything, these words furiously level the bitter pain and capture the drop of light that is to be harvested from terror's ink." — PATRICIA LAURENCE

GEORGE KONRÁD. *A GUEST IN MY OWN COUNTRY: A HUNGAR-IAN LIFE.* TRANS. JIM TUCKLER. OTHER PRESS, 2007. 352 PP. PAPER: $15.95.

Konrád should have died, and after that, he should have left Hungary. He and his sister were able to escape their town in the great Hungarian *puszsta* for Budapest during the Second World War. All the other children died in the camps. Without exception. For the most part, his college classmates left to teach in American universities. "I wanted to know what was going on, in these streets," he writes in this memoir. "It was an unfinished story, and I refused to tear myself away from it." It is a story he is still writing, even though he acknowledges it is one that perhaps never can be told. "In place of a childhood," he writes, "there is an absence." In 1956, he looks out from a library at Russian tanks in the streets, submachine in hand. He becomes a well-known writer, critical of communism. "The living conscience of a deeply disturbed society," Istvan Deak calls him. But his books were not published in Hungary and circulated only in *samizdat*. He was, he notes, a non-person. The dislocations seem too great to overcome, bridge, or resolve and yet they are ones he needs to write, even if he says that his only "goal was internal emigration . . . I had no desire to win or lose, just hold out a while longer." Like Walter Benjamin, another Jew, who had difficulty leaving the hell Europe had become by the 1930s, Konrád had to live and write, "rung by rung," as Benjamin describes his life, "according as chance would offer a narrow foothold." He was, he says, a cautious young man, even if his socially conscious, highly critical (and more or less autobiographical) novels are not. When Robert Creeley was asked whether poetry was radical or conservative, he answered that it was conservative. Poetry conserved what was important to itself. Creeley did not add that in its conservatism poetry was radical. Konrád's conservatism only underlines how radical he is. Is this a Hungarian life? Yes and no. "For a man who no longer has a homeland, writing becomes a place to live," Theodor Adorno notes. Writing permitted Konrád to live in Hungary. But he never left the land he can no longer call home. — ROBERT BUCKEYE

DAVID MARKSON. *THE LAST NOVEL*. SHOEMAKER & HOARD, 2007. 190 PP. PAPER: $15.00.

Markson's latest novel—composed, as has his every work since *Reader's Block*, of fragments, quotations, and anecdotes from or about (mainly deceased) artists, writers, composers, philosophers, and critics—purports to be the last; not only of the series Markson's latest narrator/surrogate ("Novelist") is finally willing to acknowledge as such ("Novelist has lately appeared to be writing the same book over and over"—"Novelist's personal genre. . . . [O]bstinately cross-referential and of cryptic interconnected syntax"), but also, simply, the last novel ever from one of our great writers. May it not be so—but if *es muß sein,* it would be difficult to imagine a better sign-off. There is nothing portentous here. Gone is the mawkishness and moralizing of Author, in *Vanishing Point;* gone too the simple exhaustion of Writer, in *This Is Not a Novel;* indeed, not since the days of Reader himself—the first of these homunculi, and by comparison blithely egocentric and old-fashioned, the most resembling a "real" fictional character—has a Markson novel been so free of the weight of closure; free, paradoxically, of the need to end (and end breathtakingly!). Novelist is a marvelous companion with whom to await the end of the world, or just the end of a life (his). The usual suspects all make their appearances in *The Last Novel*'s litany of illnesses, deaths, and frustrations (Joyce, Wittgenstein, Malcolm Lowry, Dizzy Dean), accompanied by new and occasionally unexpected co-stars (Lillie Langtry, with whom Novelist has managed to fall in love despite her having died in 1929; Beatrix Potter, who had to pay to publish *The Tale of Peter Rabbit;* a snippet of dialogue from the heavenly Powell and Pressburger film *The Red Shoes*), but notwithstanding the general morbidity of the scraps Novelist shares with us—not least about his own grim and lonely day-to-day life in Greenwich Village (well, he can't be *that* bad off)—it's impossible to be anything but invigorated by them en masse, by the clarity and wit of their arrangement, by the magic of Markson's great trick: to assemble a work that gives us all the pleasure and poignancy of a novel without resorting to a single recognizable trope of novel-writing. If this really is Markson's last, it's a tremendous loss to American letters. Either way, however, his readers can only come out ahead. — JEREMY M. DAVIES

MICHAEL HAFFTKA. *CONSCIOUS/UNCONSCIOUS.* SIX GALLERY PRESS, 2007. 182 PP. PAPER: $18.00.

Midway through Michael Hafftka's weirdly alluring matrix of episodic narratives (I hesitate to call them short stories as they defy virtually every assumption of the genre with hip audacity and confident savvy), our narrator finds himself wrestling with a particularly nasty porcupine, its savage pelt of prickly quills ever threatening, until, in the logic appropriate to a dream, he understands that now he must strangle the porcupine, does so, and then slips gratefully into a heavy sleep. Across fifty-six such vignettes, which exist tenuously between memory and dream and move with a kind of associational logic, Hafftka, an accomplished neo-expressionist artist for the past thirty years, catapults us, with this collection, his first venture with narrative, into a fairytale world of Jungian imagery charged with Freudian implication, a symbolic landscape of winding staircases, stone towers, lush fields, quaint cottages, and forbidding forests. With Alice-like temerity, the narrator moves about the dreamscape, his journey recorded in flatline prose delivered without exclamation even as the narrator meets one after another mysterious, inexplicably threatening eccentrics who are distorted by carnal itches and/or by unspecified emotional woundings. We share these confrontations with the narrator/artist who comes to reveal an evolving complex

persona struggling with the unsettling implications of a series of irresolvable contemporary dilemmas: the relationship between sexuality and destruction; the appalling implications of the appeal of violence and the wellspring urges we share to do injury to others; the deception of appearances and the discomfortingly speedy process by which the familiar morphs into the strange; and above all the role—and challenge—of the artist whose inspiration and vision necessarily derive from shadowy and forbidding interior realms where we are ultimately most (in)human. Ably enhanced by twenty-seven original black and white drawings that are beautifully reproduced to reveal the Goyaesque dimensions of Hafftka's sensibility, these stories—part ironic parable, part fractured fairy tale, part skewed allegory—do not engage or entertain so much as haunt, lingering like the fragmentary recollection of a cryptic dream.
— JOSEPH DEWEY

YASUTAKA TSUTSUI. *SALMONELLA MEN ON PLANET PORNO*. TRANS. ANDREW DRIVER. ALMA BOOKS, 2006. 256 PP. PAPER: $17.95.

Comparisons with Haruki Murakami may be inevitable, but Yasutaka Tsutsui's *Salmonella Men on Planet Porno* brings more to mind the dystopian landscapes of George Saunders or the hybrid fantasies of Kelly Link. And while *Salmonella Men* may be familiar territory for readers of recent speculative fiction from the likes of Link, the fact that the original Japanese edition appeared in 1979 suggests the striking prescience of this eclectic collection. Tsutsui mingles suburban and magic realism in "The Dabba Dabba Tree," about a type of cedar that causes people to have erotic dreams. "Rumours about Me"—about a self-described nobody whose every embarrassing move is followed and broadcast by a secretive, aggressive media—could have been inspired by the latest spate of reality television: "I'd become *a nobody who was known by everybody*." The absurdist deadpan of "Commuter Army" follows the narrator's recruitment as a commuting soldier in a foreign war being fought a train ride away: "if anything, being out of a job scared me even more than going to war." Tsutsui is a shrewd satirist whose targets, at times, are toppled with a bit too much force, as in "Hello, Hello, Hello!" and "The

World Is Tilting," two fables of bureaucracy gone mad. More potent are those stories where the author eschews genre pyrotechnics and reveals the strangeness and horror of the ordinary, as in "The Very Edge of Happiness," which begins with the domestic realism of family life but concludes in surreal atrocity. Tsutsui reminds us of the fragile line separating the fantastic from the real, a line famously blurred in "The Metamorphosis" by Franz Kafka, who imagined the human in the insect while revealing the insect in the human. — PEDRO PONCE

MICHAEL JOYCE. *WAS*. FC2, 2007. 152 PP. PAPER: $17.95.

Like Joyce's earlier print novel *Liam's Going* (2002), *Was* extends several themes and techniques that have informed his celebrated hypertexts *afternoon, a story* (1987) and *Twilight, A Symphony* (1996). In this "nomadic annals," Joyce interweaves short fictional vignettes, passages resembling free verse, and non-narrative lists of words, things, and places. Never settling down, his hybrid prose makes random jumps and unexpected associations from one episode, character, or object to another. Through these deliberately baffling techniques, Joyce seems to be conveying the constant nomadicity and "global creolization" that characterize the experience of websurfing. In a recent essay on internet collaboration among artists, he described the network form in a way that could also describe this book—"a locale for accidental encounters." Many of the book's fragments and episodes follow people either in transit or traveling for its own sake, disoriented both physically and emotionally. A technique that amplifies their sense of disorientation is Joyce's frequent use of elaborate, multilingual puns (including some in the "Leetspeak" argot that has emerged from internet communication). In his nonfiction, Joyce has referred to the positive side of disorientation as "emergence," or the sense of new and surprising things and patterns arising from complex networked interactions. His own emergent style bears resemblances to Gertrude Stein's fictions, to A. R. Ammons's longer poems, and of course to the other Joyce's *Finnegans Wake*. Like its print and hypertext predecessors, *Was* challenges our basic assumptions about what forms narrative can and should take. Making even partial sense of it will require plenty of interpretive effort, and it will mostly appeal to readers who are already acquainted with hypertext fiction and criticism. But even for the ambitious novice reader, *Was* should prove to be a fascinating experiment in modeling what a "novel of internet" might look like. — THOMAS HOVE

MARTIN NAKELL. *SETTLEMENT.* SPUYTEN DUYVIL, 2007. 176 PP. PAPER: $14.00.

It's been some time since we've heard from Martin Nakell, who has established himself as a praiseworthy writer of both poetry and fiction. His last full-length work, the novel *Two Fields that Face & Mirror Each Other,* demonstrated the skills of a craftsman; Nakell created a narrative that is fascinating for its unassuming, self-reflexive qualities. *Settlement* comes six years after that fine effort, and proves to be just as well-wrought and perhaps even more engaging. *Settlement* is a dystopian novel, its title alluding to a desolate outpost created to deal with an unnamed emergency. Our narrator is the Settlement's governor, and his journal describes how he has become, at the time of his putting pen to paper, its sole inhabitant. He writes as a means of chronicling the plight of the Settlement, but also to keep the Settlement from completely disappearing from the face of the earth. Ultimately, it is an attempt to legitimize his own existence. He is, at times, painfully self-aware that the routine of writing provides him with a sense of meaning, and often waxes philosophical on his efforts to come to terms with living in absolute isolation. He is documenting his own freefall into relativity, and he knows it. His tale, then, is classically postmodern (if there can be such a thing). He is a man quite literally displaced, a situation he finds at once freeing and terrifying. What makes this novel so captivating are the nuances and details of the narrator's nostalgic reflections. His reminiscences of the bonds he shared with individuals within the Settlement's community are conveyed in so genuine a manner that it's hard to believe the whole thing is the work of Nakell's imagination. It seems Nakell cannot help but to appeal to the reader intellectually. However, it's the endearing manner by which he does so that sets him apart as a writer. *Settlement* confirms Nakell's emerging style, one that manages to be both compelling and rigorous. — CHRIS PADDOCK

PAVEL BRYCZ. *I, CITY*. TRANS. JOSHUA COHEN AND MARKÉTA HOF-MEISTEROVÁ. TWISTED SPOON PRESS, 2006. 156 PP. PAPER: $14.50.

I, City is Brycz's third book, published in 1998, and his first to be translated into English. It is a collection of forty-one vignettes told from the viewpoint of the bleak mining town of Most, in the northeast of the Czech Republic. The city's voice is dreamy, even slight, in what amounts to a clever and calculated critique of the city's depressed socioeconomic condition (the photos included in the book depict a seeming ghost town of crumbling buildings, Soviet-era apartment blocks, and strip mines). The whimsical tone is weighed down nicely here and there by more substantial chapters within which resonates a theme of confused identity: a coffee drinker's encounter in a bus station with a beautiful young woman who doesn't know whether she is a Gypsy; a funeral where a young man summons and loses the courage to propose to his girlfriend while the officials cremate a stranger instead of the man's father; and, most memorably, an elaborate yarn regarding the fate of a young Jewish man asked to renounce his faith to serve in Tsar Nicholas I's army, and how this story won a gentile the love of a Jewish woman. Further gravitas is provided by a fitting translators' note at the end, which fills in crucial historical and cultural information. Brycz has written two novels and two story collections since *I, City*; this reviewer hopes that more of his work will appear in English soon. — A.D. JAMESON

DAVID MARKSON. *EPITAPH FOR A TRAMP & EPITAPH FOR A DEAD BEAT*. SHOEMAKER & HOARD, 2007. 377 PP. PAPER: $14.00. REPRINT.

Cecil Day Lewis as Nicholas Blake, Julian Barnes as Dan Kavanagh, John Banville as Benjamin Black: the list of literary luminaries who have written thrillers on the side could go on. The re-release of *Epitaph for a Tramp and Epitaph for a Dead Beat*, originally published almost fifty years ago, reminds us that David Markson (as David Markson) has done some slumming too, and that, like his fellow moonlighters, Markson was not, when writing pulp, attempting to produce literature. Markson's work divides so neatly into two stacks that no one could mistakenly place his Epitaphs in the literature pile, a separation Markson affirmed when asked whether there was "any sort of natural growth between writing genre fiction and writing [his first non-pulp novel] *Going Down*." There was, Markson answered, "no connection at all." "I was never," he explained, "a—quote—crime novelist. I was always the person who was going to write *Wittgenstein* and the others. . . ." The good news for fans of Markson's masterpieces, the line of books stretching from *Wittgenstein's Mistress* to *The Last Novel*, is that even as we enjoy the wisecracks, booze, floozies, and batterings essential to a hardboiled detective novel, the artist "who was going to write *Wittgenstein*" is grinning at us from the wings. In *Epitaph for a Tramp*, for example, Markson's gumshoe, Harry Fannin, finds typed on a piece of paper in a suspected murderer's apartment: "And it is my conclusion that *The Recognitions* is not merely the best American first novel. . . ." Markson is certainly correct that there is no essential connection between his genre work and the rest of his writing, but to *littérateurs* who can't find the fun in these early potboilers, one wants to say, with one of Markson's characters: "Chew nails, huh?" — DAVID COZY

DEB OLIN UNFERTH. *MINOR ROBBERIES.* FROM *ONE HUNDRED AND FORTY FIVE STORIES IN A SMALL BOX.* MCSWEENEY'S, 2007. 144 PP. CLOTH. $25.00

Deb Olin Unferth's first story collection comes in a boxset from McSweeney's, along with collections of very short pieces by Dave Eggers and Sarah Manguso. Unferth's is the most substantial of the three volumes and is the most eventful in the sense that it marks the book-debut of an already mature and deeply talented writer whose work has until now been available only in magazines. Most of these pieces follow narrative arcs, although some present

themselves as lists or collages. What ties them together is a kind of quotid-
ian existentialism, where events do not result in consequences so much as
in other events. Life—be it the lives of famous composers or of Frank Lloyd
Wright or the lives of numerous unnamed narrators—is portrayed here as an
accumulation of details, an experience that is more approximately narrative
than actually so. Also shared between the stories is a ludic sense of language
and syntax: despite their brevity, Unferth's stories have strong maximalist
tendencies, using repetition and digression toward both comic and obsessive ends. The title story is a good example, where the first line—"One of the
sisters says they were robbed three times in the first town"—introduces a
litany of robberies, or possible robberies, in all the various places the sisters
go. "When they left the hotel room someone robbed it, she says, and when
they left the hotel room again, someone robbed it again." A few paragraphs
later: "In the second town, twice, says the younger. Somebody stole her soap
when she left if for a moment by the *pila*." As the story proceeds, this act of
counting the accumulated robberies takes on lyric significance, the weight of
things lost and things counted. In the end, we arrive at: "It all counts somehow. Her soap. It's gone. She herself can no longer count it. But it's out there
somewhere, somehow being counted by someone else." The pun, the simplest
of devices, which allows a writer to slip by association from one meaning to
another, here retroactively alters the whole list-story, making it mean differently: the act of counting becomes a question of what "counts." Like other
contemporary writers whose work has been influenced by Beckett, Unferth
allows the slipperiness of language to take her stories in unexpected direc-
tions, so that what we end up with is less often a plot per se than an artful
mess of experiences. — MARTIN RIKER

ANDRE FURLANI. *GUY DAVENPORT: POSTMODERN AND AFTER.* NORTH-
WESTERN UNIVERSITY PRESS, 2007. 247 PP. PAPER: $27.95.

When Guy Davenport died, the Provost of the University of Kentucky, Davenport's employer for most of his career, lamented: "We didn't recognize him
locally as well as we should have." He's probably right, but the Kentuckians

needn't beat themselves up for their neglect. They merely demonstrated that they were no different from the legion of readers that doesn't buy Davenport's books and the band of academics that considers his work unworthy of classroom time or sustained study. Happily, one academic, Andre Furlani, has declined to join the uninterested throng, and has produced, instead, the first English-language monograph on Davenport's work. Concerned primarily with the fiction, *Guy Davenport: Postmodern and After* has as much to offer those who have yet to read Davenport as it does those who know his work well. In the book's opening section—among the best introductions to the fiction available—Furlani isolates and begins to explicate key elements such as utopia, sexuality, and the archaic to which Davenport returned again and again, not only in his fiction but in all of his work. Furlani's introduction could stand alone, and indeed those new to Davenport will probably be excited enough upon finishing it to set the monograph aside so they can proceed directly to the stories. This would be a wise move, not only for the pure pleasure the fiction affords, but also because familiarity with that fiction will enable readers to better appreciate Furlani's achievement in the chapters after the introduction where he unpacks the concepts earlier introduced and shows in detail how they form the warp and woof of Davenport's work. If you suspect, for example, that something other than prurience accounts for the boys in briefs who have troubled so many critics of Davenport's fiction then you will delight in Furlani's more sophisticated understanding. — DAVID COZY

HAROLD JAFFE. *BEYOND THE TECHNO-CAVE: A GUERRILLA WRITER'S GUIDE TO POST-MILLENNIAL CULTURE.* STARCHERONE BOOKS, 2007. 181 PP. PAPER: $16.00.

Harold Jaffe's earlier "docufictions" have blurred the boundary between fact and fiction, and this new collection of fourteen pieces continues the same strategy with the difference that now the major points of reference are 9/11 and the war against terrorism. "The Writer In Wartime" establishes Jaffe's theoretical position, opening with brief vignettes of a Midwest writer being involved in the abuses in Iraq and of a painter living under the Third Reich.

These situate cultural production within the political circumstances of the time and make an ironic preamble to Jaffe's discussion of the supposed opposition between engaged and autonomous art. The belief in the latter, he argues, is a uniquely American delusion and one reinforced by a conservative publishing establishment. His title suggests the shadows on Plato's cave updated to express the ubiquity of the media in our processes of perception (Jaffe has incorporated quotations from Paul Virilio bearing on this issue). *Beyond the Techno-Cave* includes fiction and essays without any sense of incongruity because each piece testifies to the urgencies of the present moment. The opening piece, "Potlach," describes the opening of a food facility for the homeless, then ties in with 9/11 by asking about the fate of the New York homeless. Explicitly engaging with socio-economic processes, it is typical of the collection. Jaffe's subtitle indicates his subversive stance, which is directed towards questioning the dominant, official narratives circulating on the war against terror and other issues. For that reason he assembles most pieces out of brief, often surreal segments which disorient the reader and which invite us to speculate about connections between his images, and above all to question the official version of these images. — DAVID SEED

LAURA MULLEN. *MURMUR.* FUTUREPOEM BOOKS, 2007. 176 PP. PAPER: $15.00.

"Just This" is the title of one chapter (or is it section, division, segment?) of Laura Mullen's *Murmur,* and if "Just This" is the resolution of any detective novel, the mystery of the murder, the aim, for that matter, of the writer, it is never, finally, "Just This." The book always escapes its resolution. The writer stops writing it because he cannot make it "Just This," if even, by the end of the book, he no longer attempts to do so anymore. The completed book is only the place where he stops. The reader reads it her way. Her story has also been written by her husband who interrupts her reading, by how tired she is, by her rush to finish before she goes to work or sleep. "What you have hold of," the reader thinks in *Murmur,* "is always, in short, a little less than complete." "Never again will a story be told as if it were the only one," John Berger argues, and nowhere is that more apparent than in the detective novel. In this one, there is the wife who reads detective novels and may be the woman she reads about who is murdered. There is the husband who asks her questions about the murder mystery she is reading and offers comments and suggestions. There is the detective who may also be the woman's lover. To help the reader, one section tells us how to read murder mysteries, which is of no help at all. "There's this woman," begins every chapter of Peter Esterhazy's novel *She Loves Me,* and it might be the beginning at any moment of the narrative in Mullen's *Murmur.* There's this woman. There's this reader. There's this corpse. There's this husband. There's this detective. There's this lover. There's this . . . The last sentences of this reflexive metafiction reads (without a period to end the sentence)—"a text which changed at every instant, which never ceased moving, held open as if." Maurice Blanchot gives Mullen's title its reading (and ours): "A traceless murmur that he follows wandering nowhere, residing everywhere." — ROBERT BUCKEYE

ROBERT LOPEZ. *PART OF THE WORLD.* CALAMARI PRESS, 2007. 182 PP. PAPER: $17.00.

The title of Robert Lopez's newest novel cannot be anything but ironic. While the narrator lives among people, he is not really engaged in society. He is a man apart from the world, a man alone. He refers to the people around him as Teardrops, in part a commentary on their shape, but also, seemingly, to highlight how interchangeable and fundamentally similar they are. One person is the same as another, but he is somehow different. Reading *Part of the World* is like viewing the world through a fly's eye: the images are recognizable, but so oddly alien that the limits to your understanding are limitless. The narrator's tone is flat and almost psychopathically detached while maintaining a remote curiosity. In a manner reminiscent of David Markson's *Wittgenstein's Mistress,* Lopez's unnamed narrator lives internally, preoccupied with minutia as he circles nervously around the truths about his life in favor of the most irrelevant facts. It is stark and beautiful, a sort of rambling investigation of memory and uncertainty that pushes onward, seemingly without ever going anywhere at all. The novel is structured as a single chapter; the stream of words is fugue-like, with haunting variations on themes like agoraphobia, textures, and furniture, while sexual acts are described as dryly as car upholstery. This book, however, is a great deal more sophisticated than it appears; the words themselves are simple, but their depth is marvelous. Every event is so misleadingly commonplace that it lulls the reader into a quiet complicity with the narrator. Throughout, there are recurring references to the narrator's medication, seemingly innocuous remarks that quickly become darkly subversive as the book drifts on. The narrator's neuroses are, at first, unremarkable, but they intensify and the result is a snowballing effect, an imperceptible building of madness and memory that takes on a distinctly sinister aspect that was only hinted at in earlier pages. When the truth finally comes into focus, it passes almost unnoticed back into the kaleidoscopic fractures of the narrator's clouded mind. — JEFF WAXMAN

CHRISTINE BROOKE-ROSE. *THE CHRISTINE BROOKE-ROSE OMNIBUS: FOUR NOVELS: OUT, SUCH, BETWEEN, THRU.* CARCANET PRESS (U.K.), 2007. 742 PP. PAPER: $35.95.

The Christine Brooke-Rose Omnibus, first issued in 1986, provides a crash course in this prolific author's too long neglected fiction, offering four of her early novels: *Out* (1964), *Such* (1966), *Between* (1968), and *Thru* (1975). All are representative of their proto-postmodernist moment, aligned with Beckett and the New Novelists—engaging with questions of identity, consciousness, discourse, and science—and share a concern for transgressing both territorial and textual boundaries. As Brooke-Rose states in *Out,* "knowledge certain or indubitable is unobtainable." *Out* is set in the near future after a "displacement" that inverts race relations, so that whites—"the colourless"—are in servitude to an African upper class. Brooke-Rose pits this reversal—one that foregrounds an unsteadiness and even complete breakdown in self-identification—against narrative representation itself. In *Such,* which opens with the speaker rising from his own coffin, Brooke-Rose uses the language of astrophysics to explore a physical death that offers a cognitive rebirth. *Between*—whose central figure is a female translator, a circulator of linguistic codes—is written without the verb "to be," suggesting an absence of fundamental self-hood. Finally, *Thru* takes place in a university classroom and directly engages literary and philosophical debates via its formal arrangement of narrative interpolated with calligrammes and mathematical formulas. Although the full *Omnibus* is difficult, Brooke-Rose, indebted to continental philosophy and French modernism, offers clues to its decoding: "The author has lost authority many times in the history of narrative," she writes in *Thru*. "When one type has consumed itself, the element of manipulation becoming too visible thus destroying the fictive illusion, and no-one has yet come along to renew it, usually, as here, reconstructing it by perpetual destruction, generating a text which in effect is a dialogue with all preceding texts, a death and a birth dialectically involved with one another." This statement might just describe the project underlying all four novels—a death of the fictive illusion and the birth of a new kind of text, one in conversation with all preceding texts and linguistic possibilities. — STEFANIE SOBELLE

JOANNA GUNDERSON. *NIGHT.* RED DUST, 2007. PAPER: $12.95.

The words, voices, images, and sounds of Joanna Gunderson's experimental plays ripple over mind and body like a fugue. In her recently published collection of four experimental plays, *Night,* the reader experiences Gunderson's continuity of subject and object. Words and voices from writers like De-Quincey and Beckett, or images from a painter like Turner, or an interview with poet Audre Lord, or snatches of conversation, or personal memories, or the sounds of bells or of nature—all of these merge and float across the page (or, in performance, the stage). These plays were written and performed between 1994-1997 at Dixon Place and La Mama, venues for Gunderson's experiments since the 1960s. Encased in a black cover, *Night* contains four plays: "Hieroglyphics of the Night" and "Night," both preoccupied with blackness, darkness, death, and night skies; "Bells," itself three plays that, according to Gunderson, "seemed to touch each other and to be like the ringing of a bell";

and "Fire," inspired by the sun on the golden domes of Russian Churches in winter and also by the lives and works of Anna Akhmatova, Osip Mandelstam, and Lillian Halegua. Some critics have used the word "collage" to describe the fragmentation one experiences in reading Gunderson's plays, but the word threatens to limit one's experience to the visual. As the character, Beckett, states in "Bells,"

It is the shape of
certain
ideas

        All
        sounds
        of words carry the
        meaning

Throughout Gunderson's texts, the words of the play are in bold, and the words in smaller typeface give source and context. So reading her plays is different than experiencing them in a theater—*manqué* in that the kinetic, sculptural, architectural, and aural aspects are missing, but perhaps enriched in other ways. Reading becomes a theater of the mind. — PATRICIA LAURENCE

Books Received

Adderson, Caroline. *Sitting Practice.* Trumpeter, 2007. $21.95.

Alemi, Massud. *Interruptions.* Ibex, 2008. $24.95.

Allen, Sarah Addison. *Garden Spells.* Bantam, 2007. $20.00.

Alonso, Nancy. *Closed For Repairs.* Curbstone Press, 2007. $13.95.

Amerika, Mark. *29 Inches.* Chiasmus Press, 2007. $14.95.

Antoon, Sinan. *I'jaam, an Iraki rhapsody.* City Lights, 2007. $11.95.

Arnoldi, Katherine. *All Things Are Labor.* University of Massachusetts Press, 2007. $19.95.

Badaracco, Claire Hoertz. *Prescribing Faith.* Baylor University Press, 2007. $29.95.

Baldwin, Christina. *Life's Companion.* Bantam, 2007. $17.00.

Balzac, Honore de. *The Vicar's Passion*, trans. by Ed Ford. Green Integer 150, 2006. $14.95.

Barkan, Leonard. *Satyr Square, A year, A life in Rome.* Farrar, Straus and Giroux, 2006. $24.00.

Barry, Rebecca. Later, *At the Bar.* Simon & Schuster, 2007. $22.00.

Berman, Marshall and Berger, Brian, eds. *New York Calling From Blackout to Bloomberg.* The University of Chicago Press, 2007. $25.00.

Bontempelli, Massimo. *The Faithful Lover.* Host Publications, 2007. $15.00

Boyko, Michael C. *The Hour Sets.* Calamari Press, 2007. $11.00.

Brenna, Duff. *The Law of Falling Bodies.* Hopewell Publications, 2007. $18.95.

Chasin, Alexandra. *Kissed By.* FC2, 2007. $17.95.

Chester, Alfred. *Jamie Is My Heart's Desire.* Black Sparrow Books, 2007. $18.95.

Chester, Alfred. *The Exquisite Corpse.* Black Sparrow Books, 2003. $16.95.

Coleman, Wanda. *Jazz & Twelve O'Clock Tales.* Black Sparrow Books, 2007. $23.95.

Courter, Justin. Skunk, A Love Story. Omnidawn Press, 2007. $14.95.

Cox, John D. *Seeming Knowledge.* Baylor University Press, 2007. $39.95.

Davis, Leslie. *Keeper's Child.* EDGE, 2007. $19.95.

Di Blasi, Debra. *The Jiri Chronicles and Other Fictions.* FC2, 2007. $19.95.

Di Robilant, Andrea. *Lucia.* Knopf, 2008. $25.95.

Djaout, Tahar. *The Last Summer of Reason.* University of Nebraska Press, 2007. $ 14.95.

Doctorow, Cory and Holly Phillips, eds. *Tesseracts Eleven.* EDGE, 2007. $19.95.

Eck, Matthew. *The Farther Shore.* Milkweed Editions, 2007. $22.00.

Edge, Arabella. *The God of Spring.* Simon & Schuster, 2005. $24.00.

Edwards, Geoffrey S. *Fire Bell in the Night.* Touchstone, 2007. $15.00.

Estrin, Marc. *The Lamentations of Julius Marantz.* Unbridled, 2007. $14.95.

Fesperman, Dan. *The Amateur Spy.* Knopf, 2008. $23.95.

Freese, Mathias B. *Down to a Sunless Sea.* Wheatmark, 2007. $13.95.

Freilicher, Mel. *The Unmaking of Americans: 7 Lives.* San Diego City Works Press, 2007. $12.95

Gerdes, Eckhard. *Przewalski's Horse.* Red Hen Press, 2007. $15.95.

Ghibellino, Ettore. *Goethe and Anna Amalia. A Forbidden Love?* Carysfort Press, 2007. $44.95.

Gilmour, David. *The Last Leopard.* Dufour Editions, 2007. $32.95.

Gonzalez, Veronica. *Twin Time: Or, How Death Befell Me.* Semiotext(e), 2007. $14.95.

Grandbois, Daniel. *Unlucky Lucky Days.* BOA Editions, 2008. $14.00.

Griffin, Nicholas. *Dizzy City.* Steer Forth Press, 2007. $24.95.

Grimbert, Philippe. *Memory,* trans. by Polly McLean. Simon & Schuster, 2008. $19.95.

Haldeman, Bonnie. *Memories of the Branch Davidians.* Baylor University Press, 2007. $24.95.

Hampl, Patricia. *Blue Arabesque.* Harcourt Press, 2006. $22.00.

Hart, William. *Operation Supergoose.* Timberline Press, 2007. $15.00.

Hartwig, Julia. *In Praise of the Unfinished,* trans. by John and Bogdana Carpenter. Knopf, 2008. $25.00.

Hayward, Amber. *Darkness of the God.* EDGE, 2007. $20.95.

Hazlett, Randy Doyle. *The Pilgrimage and Dark Spaces.* Christian Artist's Workshop, 2007. $16.99.

Hunter, Stephen. *The 47th Samurai.* Simon & Schuster, 2007. $26.00.

Irani, Anosh. *The Song of Kahunsha*. Milkweed Editions, 2007. $22.00.

Jeppesen, Travis. *Wolf At the Door*. Twisted Spoon Press, 2007. $15.00.

Johnson, Greg. *Women I've Known*. Ontario Review Press, 2006. $23.95.

Johnson, Jason. *Alina*. Dufour Editions, 2007. $17.95.

Jones, Cynan. *The Long Dry*. Dufour Editions, 2007. $16.95.

Katz, Steve. *Kissssss*. FC2, 2007. $22.50.

Kennedy, A. L. *Day*. Knopf, 2007. $24.00.

Khalifeh, Sahar. *The Image, the Icon, and the Covenant*, trans. by Aida Bamia. Interlink, 2007. $15.00.

Kinzie, Mary. *California Sorrow*. Knopf, 2007. $25.00.

Klim, Christopher. *Idiot!* Hopewell Publications, 2007. $15.95.

Kohler, Sheila. *Bluebird, or the Invention of Happiness*. Other Press, 2007. $24.95.

Kornreich, Joshua. *The Boy Who Killed Caterpillars*. Marick Press, 2007. $14.95.

Kramer, Frederick Mark. *Apostrophe/Parenthesis*. Depth Charge Publishing, 2007. $35.00.

Lababidi, Yahia. *Signposts to Elsewhere*. The Sun Rising Press, 2006. $18.00.

LaSalle, Peter. *Tell Borges If You See Him*. The University of Georgia Press, 2007. $25.95.

Lawson, Mary. *The Other Side of the Bridge*. Dial Trade, 2007. $14.00.

Leppin, Paul. *Blaugast*. Trans. by Cynthia A. Klima. Twisted Spoon Press, 2007. $15.00.

Link, Kelly and Gavin J. Grant, eds. *The Best of Lady Churchill's Rosebud Wristlet*. Ballantine, 2007. $14.95.

Luik, Viivi. *The Beauty of History*. Dufour Editions, 2008. $24.95.

Manguso, Sarah, Dave Eggers, and Deb Olin Unferth. *One Hundred and Forty-Five Stories in a Small Box*. McSweeney's, 2007. $25.00.

Mann, Reva. *The Rabbi's Daughter*. The Dial Press, 2007. $23.00.

Marbrook, Djelloul. *Saraceno*. Open Book Press, 2005. $25.95.

Martin, Stephen-Paul. *The Possibility of Music*. FC2, 2007. $16.95.

Masters, Alexander. *STUART: A Life Backwards*. Bantam, 2006. $20.00.

McCullough, Colleen. *Anthony and Cleopatra*. Simon & Schuster, 2007. $28.00.

McDermott, Alice. *After This*. The Dial Press, 2007. $14.00.

McSweeney, Joyelle. *Nylund, the Sarcographer*. Tarpaulkin Sky Press, 2007. $14.00.

Melbye, Eric. *Tru*. Flame Books, 2007. $17.99.

Melman, Peter Charles. *Landsman*. Counterpoint, 2007. $26.00.

Miller, Sue. *The Senator's Wife*. Knopf, 2008. $24.95.

Millhauser, Steven. *Dangerous Laughter*, Knopf, 2008. $24.00.

Moody, Rick. *Right Livelihood, Three Novellas*. Little, Brown, 2007. $23.99.

Moya, Ana Gloria. *Heaven of Drums*, trans. by W. Nick Hill. Curbstone Press, 2007. $15.00.

Mozina, Andy. *The Women Were Leaving the Men*. Wayne State University Press, 2007. $18.95.

Nakell, Martin. *Settlement*. Spuyten Duyvil, 2007. $14.00.

Nash, Andrew. *Kailyard and Scottish Literature*. Rodopi, 2007. $73.

Némirovsky, Irène. *David Golder, The Ball, Snow in Autumn, The Courilof Affair*. *trans*. by Sandra Smith. Everyman's Library, 2008. $25.00.

Nesset, Kirk. *Paradise Road*. University of Pittsburgh Press, 2007. $24.95.

O'Brien, Dorene. *Voices of the Lost and Found*. Wayne State University Press, 2007. $18.95.

Oster, Christian. *The Unforeseen*. Other Press, 2006. $13.95.

Pate, Stephen Shane, II. *Ishmael's Wrath*. RoseDog Books, 2007. $18.00.

Penney, Stef. *The Tenderness of Wolves*. Simon & Schuster, 2006. $25.00.

Ping, Wang. *The Last Communist Virgin*. Coffee House Press, 2007. $14.95.

Popa, D.R. *Lady V and Other Stories*. Spuyten Duyvil, 2007. $14.00.

Reznikoff, Charles. *Holocaust*. Black Sparrow Books, 2007. $15.95.

Richards, Alun. *Home to an Empty House*. Dufour Editions, 2007. $16.95.

Rodgers, Johannah. *Sentences*. Red Dust, 2007. $10.00.

Rose, Alex. *The Musical Illusionist*. Hotel St. George Press, 2007. $14.95.

Ruffin, Paul. *Jesus in the Mist*. The University of South Carolina Press, 2007. $24.95.

Rutkowski, Thaddeus. *Tetched*. Behler Publications, 2005. $13.95.

Saddler, Allen. *Bless 'Em All*. Dufour Editions, 2007. $29.95.

Schatz, Kate. *Rid of Me*. Continuum, 2007. $10.95.

Shukman, Henry. *The Lost City*. Knopf, 2008. $24.95.

Silvis, Randall. *In a Town Called Mundomuerto*. Omnidwan Publishing, 2007. $12.95.

Smith, April. *Judas Horse*. Knopf, 2008. $23.95.

Stegner, Lynn. *Because a Fire Was in My Head*. University of Nebraska Press, 2007. $24.95.

Tesdell, Diana Secker, ed. *Christmas Stories*. Everyman's Library, 2007. $15.00.

Thewlis, David. *The Late Hector Kipling*. Simon & Schuster, 2007. $25.00.

Thompson, Jean. *Throw Like a Girl*. Simon & Schuster, 2007. $13.00.

Thompson, Pamela. *Every Past Thing*. Unbridled Books, 2007. $24.95.

Tuglas, Friedebert. *The Poet and the Idiot and Other Stories*, trans. by Eric Dickens. CEU Press, 2007. $16.95.

Uri, Helene. *Honey Tongues*. Dufour Editions, 2008. $24.95.

VanderMeer, Jeff. *Shriek: An Afterword*. Tor, 2006. $14.95.

Viramontes, Helena María. *Their Dogs Came With Them*. Atria Books, 2007. $23.00.

Von Der Lippe, Angela. *The Truth About Lou*. Counterpoint, 2007. $24.00.

Washburn, Frances. *Elsie's Business*. Bison Books, 2006. $17.95.

Whalen, Tom. *An Exchange of Letters*. Parsifal Editions, 2007. $13.95.

Witchel, Alex. *The Spare Wife*. Knopf, 2008. $23.95.

Wolff, Tobias. *Our Story Begins*. Knopf, 2008. $26.95.

Zink, William. *Ohio River Dialogues*. Sugar Loaf Press, 2007. $16.00.

Annual Index

Contributors:

Markfield, Wallace. "Teitlebaum's Window," 1: 10-32
Mosley, Nicholas. "Impossible Object," 1: 96-116
Murnane, Gerald. "Barley Patch," 3: 87-101
Richards, Tim. "Isnis," 3: 110-125
Rudan, Vedrana."Night," 1: 132-135
Shapcott, Thomas. "The Waterfall Pool," 3: 127-145
Szewc, Piotr. "Annihilation," 1: 33-42
Tsiolkas, Christos. "Dead Europe," 3: 147-167
Unt, Mati. "Things in the Night," 1: 154-158
Walker, Brenda. "Vast Partings out in Space," 3: 169-176
Wilding, Michael. "The Prisoner of Mount Warning," 3: 178-204
Yu, Ouyang. "The English Class," 3: 103-108

Books Reviewed:

Applefeld, Aharon. *Katerina,* 1: 161 (Joseph Dewey)
Bachmann, Ingeborg. *Last Living Words,* 2: 138 (John Vincler)
Bamberger, W.C., ed. *Selected Letters: Guy Davenport and James Laughlin,* 2: 140-141 (David Seed)
Bernheimer, Kate. *The Complete Tales of Merry Gold,* 1: 165-166 (Pedro Ponce)
Breckenridge, Donald, ed. *The Brooklyn Rail Fiction Anthology,* 2: 139 (Stefanie Sobelle)
Brooke-Rose, Christine. *The Christine Brooke-Rose Omnibus: Four Novels: Out, Such, Between, Thru,* 3: 229-230 (Stefanie Sobelle)
Brycz, Pavel. *I, City.* 3: 223 (A. D. Jameson)
Burgin, Richard. *The Conference on Beautiful Moments,* 3: 214-215 (Daniel Garrett)
Chapman, James. *Stet,* 1: 163-164 (Eckhard Gerdes)
Cixous, Helene. *The Day I Wasn't There,* 1: 161-163 (Robert Buckeye)
Davis, Lydia. *Varieties of Disturbance,* 3: 213-214 (Joseph Dewey)
Djebar, Assia. *The Tongue's Blood Does Not Run Dry: Algerian Stories,* 3: 216-217 (Patricia Laurence)

Duras, Marguerite. *Yann Andrea Steiner*, 1: 164-165 (Robert Buckeye)

Dutton, Danielle. *Attempts at a Life*, 2: 140 (Kate Zambreno)

Elsie, Robert, ed. *Balkan Beauty, Balkan Blood: Modern Albanian Short Stories*, 2: 141-142 (Michael Pinker)

Evenson, Brian. *The Open Curtain*, 2: 142-143 (John Vincler)

Federman, Raymond. *Return to Manure*, 2: 144-145 (Eckhard Gerdes)

Field, Thalia. *Ululu (Clown Shrapnel)*, 2: 152-153 (James Crossley)

Fitzpatrick-O'Dinn, Dominique. *Table of Forms*, 2: 151 (Joseph Dewey)

Furliani, Andre. *Guy Davenport: Postmodern and After*, 3: 225-226 (David Cozy)

Furst, Joshua. *The Sabotage Café*, 2: 150 (Irving Malin)

Genazino, Wilhelm. *The Shoe Tester of Frankfurt*, 1: 171 (Dick Kalich)

Goldstein, Rebecca. *Betraying Spinoza: The Renegade Jew Who Gave Us Modernity*, 1: 167-168 (Steven G. Kellman)

Gracq, Julien. *Reading Writing*, 1: 159-160 (Tayt Harlin)

Gunderson, Joanna. *Night*, 3: 230-231 (Patricia Laurence)

Hafftka, Michael. *Conscious/Unconscious*, 3: 219-220 (Joseph Dewey)

Houellebecq, Michel. *The Possibility of an Island*, 1: 163 (Thomas Hove)

Hunt, Laird. *The Exquisite*, 2: 145-146 (Michael Squeo)

Huysmans, J.K.. *Downstream*, 1: 160-161 (Brooke Horvath)

Jaffe, Harold. *Beyond the Techno-Cave: A Guerrilla's Guide to Post-Millennial Culture*, 3: 236-237 (David Seed)

Johnson-Davies, Denys, ed. *The Anchor Book of Modern Arabic Fiction*, 2: 146-147 (Brooke Horvath)

Jouet, Jacques. *Une Mauvaise Maire*, 2: 135-136 (Warren Motte)

Joyce, Michael. *Was*, 3: 221-222 (Thomas Hove)

Kalfus, Ken. *A Disorder Peculiar to the Country*, 2: 143-144 (Martin Riker)

Konrád, George. *A Guest in My Own Country: A Hungarian Life*, 3: 217-218 (Robert Buckeye)

Krasnahorkai, Lazlo. *War and War*, 1: 159 (Jeremy M. Davies)

Lee, Rebecca. *The City Is a Rising Tide*, 1: 164 (James Crossley)

Lopez, Robert. *Part of the World*, 3: 228-229 (Jeff Waxman)

Lustig, Arnost. *Fire on Water: Porgess and the Abyss*, 2: 137-138 (Michael Pinker)

Markson, David. *Epitaph for a Tramp & Epitaph for a Dead Beat*, 3: 223-224
(David Cozy)

Markson, David. *The Last Novel*, 3: 218-219 (Jeremy M. Davies)

Mason, Fran. *Historical Dictionary of Postmodernist Literature and Theater*,
2: 147 (Neil Murphy)

Milletti, Christina. *The Religious and Other Fictions*, 2: 148 (Steve Tomasula)

Mullen, Laura. *Murmur*, 3: 227-228 (Robert Buckeye)

Muñoz Molina, Antonio. *In Her Absence*, 3: 215-216 (James Crossley)

Murakami, Haruki. *Blind Willow*, 1: 166 (Joseph Dewey)

Musil, Robert. *Posthumous Papers of a Living Author*, 1: 166-167 (Michael
Pinker)

Nakell, Martin. *Settlement*, 3: 222-223 (Chris Paddock)

Olson, Toby. *The Bitter Half*, 1: 169-170 (Chris Padock)

Petrovitch, Aaron. *The Session*, 2: 152 (Pedro Ponce)

Queneau, Raymond. *Letters, Numbers, Forms: Essays 1928-70*, 3: 211-212
(Warren Motte)

Rolin Olivier. *Paper Tiger*, 2: 136-137 (Jeremy M. Davies)

Roth, Gerhard. *The Will to Sickness*, 1: 168 (Robert Buckeye)

Russell, Karen. *St Lucy's Home for Girls Raised by Wolves*, 1: 171-172 (Irving
Malin)

Salvayre, Lydie. *Portrait de l'écrivain en animal domestique*, 3:212-213
(Warren Motte)

Smilevski, Goce. *Conversation with Spinoza: a Cobweb Novel*, 2: 149-150
(Jeffrey Twitchell-Waas)

Stosuy, Brandon, ed. *Up Is Up, But So Is Down: New York's Downtown
Literary Scene*, 2: 153-154 (Noah Eli Gordon)

Tabucchi, Antonio. *It's Getting Later All the Time*, 1: 169 (Irving Malin)

Tsutsui, Yasutaka. *Salmonella Men on Planet Porno*, 3: 220-221 (Pedro Ponce)

Unferth, Deb Olin. *Minor Roberries*, 3: 224-225 (Martin Riker)

Ungar, Hermann. *Boys and Murderers*, 1: 161-162 (Brian Evenson)

Washburn, Frances. *Elsie's Business*, 2: 154-155 (Peter Grandbois)

Xue, Can. *Blue Light in the Sky & Other Stories*, 1: 170-171 (Danielle Dutton)

DELILLO FIEDLER GASS PYNCHON
University of Delaware Press
Collections on Contemporary Masters

UNDERWORDS
Perspectives on Don
DeLillo's *Underworld*

Edited by Joseph Dewey, Steven
G. Kellman, and Irving Malin

Essays by Jackson R. Bryer,
David Cowart, Kathleen
Fitzpatrick, Joanne Gass, Paul
Gleason, Donald J. Greiner,
Robert McMinn, Thomas Myers,
Ira Nadel, Carl Ostrowski,
Timothy L. Parrish, Marc Singer,
and David Yetter

$39.50

LESLIE FIEDLER
AND AMERICAN
CULTURE

Edited by Steven G. Kellman
and Irving Malin

Essays by John Barth, Robert
Boyers, James M. Cox, Joseph
Dewey, R.H.W. Dillard, Geoffrey
Green, Irving Feldman, Leslie
Fiedler, Susan Gubar, Jay L.
Halio, Brooke Horvath, David
Ketterer, R.W.B. Lewis, Sanford
Pinsker, Harold Schechter, Daniel
Schwarz, David R. Slavitt, Daniel
Walden, and Mark Royden
Winchell

$36.50

INTO *THE TUNNEL*
Readings of Gass's
Novel

Edited by Steven G. Kellman
and Irving Malin

Essays by Rebecca Goldstein,
Donald J. Greiner, Brooke
Horvath, Marcus Klein, Jerome
Klinkowitz, Paul Maliszewski,
James McCourt, Arthur Saltzman,
Susan Stewart, and Heide Ziegler

$35.00

PYNCHON AND
MASON & DIXON

Edited by Brooke Horvath and
Irving Malin

Essays by Jeff Baker, Joseph
Dewey, Bernard Duyfhuizen,
David Foreman, Donald J.
Greiner, Brian McHale, Clifford
S. Mead, Arthur Saltzman,
Thomas H. Schaub, David Seed,
and Victor Strandberg

$39.50

ORDER FROM ASSOCIATED UNIVERSITY PRESSES
2010 Eastpark Blvd., Cranbury, New Jersey 08512
PH 609-655-4770   FAX 609-655-8366   E-mail AUP440@ aol.com

Distributed for **Other Voices Books**

O Street
CORRINA WYCOFF

"Shot through with a painful radiance and level intelligence that keeps you with it every step of the way."—*Seattle Times*

"Wycoff works over an idée fixe in her debut collection, 10 stories about a young woman's difficult transition to adulthood after an abusive childhood. . . . Over and over these degradations and disappointments are sounded like elements in therapy, and the result is a straightforward look at pain and renewal. —*Publishers Weekly*

Paper $17.95

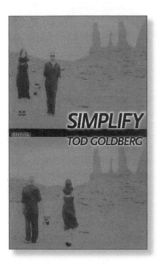

Simplify
TOD GOLDBERG

From the author of the acclaimed novel *Living Dead Girl,* a finalist for the Los Angeles Times Book Prize, come twelve haunting stories about people caught somewhere between love and madness.

"These stories are superlatively smart, friggin' hilarious, stab-in-the-chest painful, and overall super rad and awesome. Best of all, this is a book with some serious heart. . . . This is the kind of book I wait for." —Elizabeth Crane, author of *When the Messenger is Hot* and *All This Heavenly Glory*

Paper $14.99

Studies *in* American Fiction

A journal of articles and reviews on the prose fiction of the United States

Published semiannually by the Department of English, Northeastern University

Mary Loeffelholz, Editor

Recent numbers include

Deborah Clarke, *Domesticating the Car: Women's Road Trips*

Laura Korobkin, *Legal Narratives of Self-Defense and Self-Effacement in* Their Eyes Were Watching God

Caroline Levander, *Witness and Participant: Frederick Douglass's Child*

Annual subscriptions: $12.00 for individuals, $15.00 for individuals outside the United States; $18.00 for domestic institutions, $20.00 for institutions outside the United States. Send subscriptions and inquiries to Studies in American Fiction, Department of English, 406 Holmes Hall, Northeastern University, Boston MA 02115-5000. Phone: 617-373-3687; fax: 617-373-2509; e-mail: americanfiction@neu.edu

"These outrageous and ferociously strange stories test the limits of behavior, of manners, of language, and mark Diane Williams as a startlingly original writer worthy of our closest attention." —BEN MARCUS

IT WAS LIKE MY TRYING TO HAVE
A TENDER-HEARTED NATURE

A Novella and Stories

DIANE WILLIAMS

FC2
The University of Alabama Press
http://fc2.org

NOON

NOON

A LITERARY ANNUAL

1324 LEXINGTON AVENUE   PMB 298   NEW YORK   NEW YORK   10128

EDITION PRICE $12 DOMESTIC $17 FOREIGN

EDWARD DORN
LOUIS ZUKOFSKY
LISA ROBERTSON
KENNETH REXROTH
CHRISTOPHER MIDDLETON

CHICAGO REVIEW

5801 SOUTH KENWOOD AVENUE • CHICAGO ILLINOIS 60637
visit humanities.uchicago.edu/review to subscribe and order special issues

Dalkey Archive
Scholarly Series

Don't Ever Get Famous:
Essays on New York Writing
after the New York School
DANIEL KANE

Reading Games:
An Aesthetics of Play in
Flann O'Brien, Samuel Beckett, and Georges Perec
KIMBERLY BOHMAN-KALAJA

Rayner Heppenstall:
A Critical Study
G. J. BUCKELL

Fever Vision:
The Life and Works of
Coleman Dowell
EUGENE HAYWORTH

The Paradox of Freedom:
A Study of the Life and Writings
of Nicholas Mosley
SHIVA RAHBARAN

Energy of Delusion:
A Book on Plot
VIKTOR SHKLOVSKY

The Walk:
Notes on a Romantic Image
JEFFREY C. ROBINSON

I am Otherwise:
The Romance between Poetry and
Theory after the Death of the Subject
ALEX E. BLAZER

The essays in this book focus attention on the vibrant New York poetry scene of the 1960s and 70s, on the poets who came after what is now known as the New York School. Amiri Baraka, Bernadette Mayer, Hannah Weiner, Clark Coolidge, Anne Waldman, and Ron Padgett are just some of the poets who extended the line that John Ashberry, Frank O'Hara, Kenneth Koch, and James Schuyler started. In *Don't Ever Get Famous*, a range of writers and scholars examine the cultural, sociological, and historical contexts of this wildly diverse group of writers. These poets, many of whom are still writing today, changed American poetry forever, and this book provides the first large-scale consideration of their work.

Don't Ever Get Famous:
Essays on New York Writing
after the New York School

DANIEL KANE

Dalkey Archive Scholarly Series
Literary Criticism
$34.95 / paper
ISBN-13: 978-1-56478-460-5

"Kane's volume is the first to tackle the period in New York's downtown literary history most closely tied to the group of poets known as the 'Second Generation New York School.' . . . [It] is a must-have for historians of American poetry in the 20th century."
—*Publishers Weekly*

"It was the historian Johan Huizinga who first elaborated a theory of play. Martin Heidegger, Ludwig Wittgenstein, Roger Caillot and other luminaries have also been drawn to the subject. Now, Kimberly Bohman-Kalaja has applied play-theory to the works of three authors—Flann O'Brien, Samuel Beckett and Georges Perec, with illuminating, sometimes startling results. I was in turn bemused, enlightened and exhilarated by the realization of what adept game-players these authors were."

—Anthony Cronin, author of *Samuel Beckett:*
The Last Modernist and *No Laughing Matter:*
The Life and Times of Flann O'Brien

Reading Games:
An Aesthetics of Play in
Flann O'Brien, Samuel Beckett,
and Georges Perec

KIMBERLY BOHMAN-KALAJA

Dalkey Archive Scholarly Series
Literary Criticism
$34.95 / paper
ISBN-13: 978-1-56478-473-5

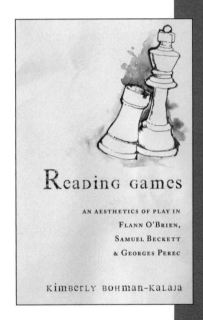

"We all know that there's more to games than fun. Bohman-Kalaja's remarkable study of O'Brien, Beckett and Perec is the first to get to grips with the deeper issues involved in the ludic practices of these post-modern masters. It also teaches us a great deal about what kind of games can be played with and through words. Learned, illuminating, original and profound, this is a study that should transform the teaching of modern literature—and bring back some of the fun!"

—David Bellos

This book examines the first five novels of Rayner Heppenstall (1911-1981). During his lifetime, many critics cited Heppenstall as the founder of the nouveau roman, believing his debut novel *The Blaze of Noon* (1939) anticipated the postwar innovations of French writers such as Alain Robbe-Grillet and Nathalie Sarraute. Since his death, however, Heppenstall's reputation has faded, and his fiction is out of print. His final novels were structurally simplistic and politically unpalatable, and their disastrous critical reception clouded critical judgment of his previous novels. G. J. Buckell examines the importance of technical experimentation, rather than the ideological content, within Heppenstall's earlier works, and seeks a more favorable standing for him within our critical and cultural memory.

Rayner Heppenstall:
A Critical Study

G. J. BUCKELL

Rayner
Heppenstall
A Critical Study

G. J. Buckell

Dalkey Archive Scholarly Series
Literary Criticism
$29.95 / paper
ISBN: 978-1-56478-471-1

"Heppenstall's novels were poetic, considered, and intelligently realised engagements with literary form, and, regardless of the sub-discourses of Modernist writing they can justifiably be situated within, they deserve a far better reputation."
—G. J. Buckell

From his birth in rural Kentucky during the Great Depression to his suicide in Manhattan in 1985, Coleman Dowell played many roles. He was a songwriter and lyricist for television. He was a model. He was a Broadway playwright. He served in the U.S. Army, both abroad and at home. And most notably, he was the author of novels that Edmund White, among others, has called "masterpieces." But Dowell was deeply troubled by a deperssion that hung over him his entire life. Pegged as both a Southern writer and a gay writer, he loathed such categorization, preferring to be judged only by his work. *Fever Vision* describes one of the most tormented, talented, and inventive writers of recent American literature, and shows how his eventful life contributed to the making of his incredible art.

Fever Vision:
The Life and Works of
Coleman Dowell

EUGENE HAYWORTH

Dalkey Archive Scholarly Series
A Biography
$24.95 / paper
ISBN: 978-1-56478-457-5

Photo credit: Christopher Cox

"Gene Hayworth has done his homework by interviewing surviving family members and friends and by reading early drafts and letters and everything unpublished that the estate has made available. . . . This is a cautionary tale, perhaps—though what it mainly seems to be cautioning us against is a sentiment that overtakes most people with time: disappointment."
—Edmund White,
from the Introduction

As the first book-length study of Nicholas Mosley, *The Paradox of Freedom* combines a discussion of the author's incredible biography with an investigation of his writing. The son of Oswald Mosley, a British Lord, a Christian convert, a war veteran, a voracious reader, and an important thinker, Nicholas Mosley has employed all of these experiences and ideas in novels and memoirs that seek to describe the paradoxical nature of freedom: how can man be free when limiting structures are necessary? The answer lies in the ways telling and retelling stories allow one to escape the seemingly logical boundaries of life and discover new meanings and possibilities. This is a much-needed companion to the work of one of Britain's most important postwar writers.

The Paradox of Freedom:
A Study of the Life and Writings of Nicholas Mosley

SHIVA RAHBARAN

Dalkey Archive Scholarly Series
Literary Criticism
$29.95 / paper
ISBN: 978-1-56478-488-9

"Nicholas Mosley is one of the most intellectually stimulating, imaginative and occasionally perplexing of contemporary novelists. We have long needed a critical study of his work in all its range and variety, and Shiva Rahbaran has now supplied this. Her study of Mosley's fiction is distinguished by the intelligence of her appreciation and the sympathy of her approach. It will be of great value to students and the common reader alike."

—Allan Massie

One of the greatest literary minds of the twentieth century, Viktor Shklovsky writes the critical equivalent of what Ross Chambers calls "loiterature"—writing that roams, playfully digresses, moving freely between the literary work and the world. In *Energy of Delusion,* a masterpiece that Shklovsky worked on over thirty years, he turns his unique critical sensibility to Tolstoy's life and novels, applying the famous "formalist method" he invented in the 1920s to Tolstoy's massive body of work, and at the same time taking Tolstoy (as well as Boccaccio, Pushkin, Chekhov, Dostoevsky, and Turgenev) as a springboard to consider the devices of literature—how novels work and what they do.

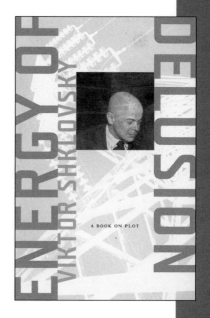

Energy of Delusion:
A Book on Plot

VIKTOR SHKLOVSKY
TRANSLATION BY
SHUSHAN AVAGYAN

Dalkey Archive Scholarly Series
Literary Criticism
$14.95 / paper
ISBN: 978-1-56478-426-1

"A rambling, digressive stylist, Shklovsky throws off brilliant aperçus on every page . . . Like an architect's blueprint, [he] lays bare the joists and studs that hold up the house of fiction."
—Michael Dirda, *Washington Post*

"Perhaps because he is such an unlikely Tolstoyan, Viktor Shklovsky's writing on Tolstoy is always absorbing and often brilliant."
—*Russian Review*

The Walk, a meditation on walking and on the literature of walking, ruminates on this pervasive, even commonplace, modern image. It is not so much an argument as a journey along the path of literature, noting the occasions and settings, the pleasures and possibilities of different types of walking, and the many literatures walking has produced. Jeffrey C. Robinson's discussion is less criticism than appreciation. With an autobiographical bent, he leads the reader through Romantic, modern, and contemporary literature to show us the shared pleasures of reading, writing, and walking.

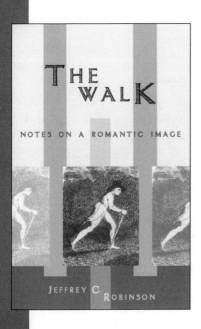

The Walk:
Notes on a Romantic Image

JEFFREY C. ROBINSON
AFTERWORD BY ROGER GILBERT

Dalkey Archive Scholarly Series
Literary Criticism
$19.95 / paper
ISBN: 978-1-56478-459-9

"Jeffrey C. Robinson's *The Walk* is a lively and intelligent omnibus for thinkers as well as for walkers. His evident love of literature is a genuine enthusiasm for all that is best in life."
—Annie Dillard

"The Walk is a stunning, revealing, and thought-provoking revision of Romantic studies, one that forces us to reexamine the conditions of our own lives and minds."
—*Wordsworth Circle*

I Am Otherwise: The Romance between Poetry and Theory after the Death of the Subject examines the contemporary poet's relationship with language in the age of theory. As the book works through close readings and interpretations of Adrienne Rich and Harold Bloom, John Ashbery and Paul de Man, Jorie Graham and Maurice Blanchot, and Barrett Watten and Jacques Lacan, it shows how the main psychological modes of contemporary poetry and the postmodern poet are anxiety, irony, abjection, and destitution. The book ultimately concludes that the new theoretical poetry self-consciously renders the effect of critical theory in its own construction. Whereas poets of the past tarried with nature, self, or philosophy, poets of our time unite lyric feeling with literary theory itself.

I Am Otherwise:
The Romance between Poetry and Theory after the Death of the Subject

ALEX E. BLAZER

Dalkey Archive Scholarly Series
Literary Criticism
$34.95 / paper
ISBN: 978-1-56478-458-2

I AM OTHERWISE:
THE ROMANCE BETWEEN
POETRY AND THEORY
AFTER THE DEATH
OF THE SUBJECT

ALEX E. BLAZER

"Like Ashbery, I too am nostalgic for an understanding of subjectivity—replete with inner being, in control of the outer language—which current thinking does not afford."
—Alex E. Blazer

ORDER FORM

Individuals may use this form to subscribe to the *Review of Contemporary Fiction* or to order back issues of the *Review* and Dalkey Archive titles at a discount (see below for details).

Title	ISBN	Quantity	Price

Subtotal _____

Less Discount _____
(10% for one book, 20% for two or more books, and
25% for Scholarly titles advertised in this issue)

Subtotal _____

Plus Postage _____
(U.S. $3 + $1 per book; foreign $5 + $3 per book)

1 Year Individual Subscription to the **Review** _____
($17 U.S.; $22.60 Canada; $32.60 all other countries)

Total _____

Mailing Address _____

_____

_____

_____

xxvi/3

Credit card payment   ☐ Visa   ☐ Mastercard

Acct. # _____   Exp. Date _____

Name on card _____   Phone # _____

Please make checks (in U.S. dollars only) payable to *Dalkey Archive Press*

mail or fax this form to: Dalkey Archive Press, University of Illinois, 1805 S. Wright St., MC-011, Champaign, IL 61820
fax: 217.244.9142 *tel:* 217.244.5700